IMAGES
of America

HADDAM
1870–1930

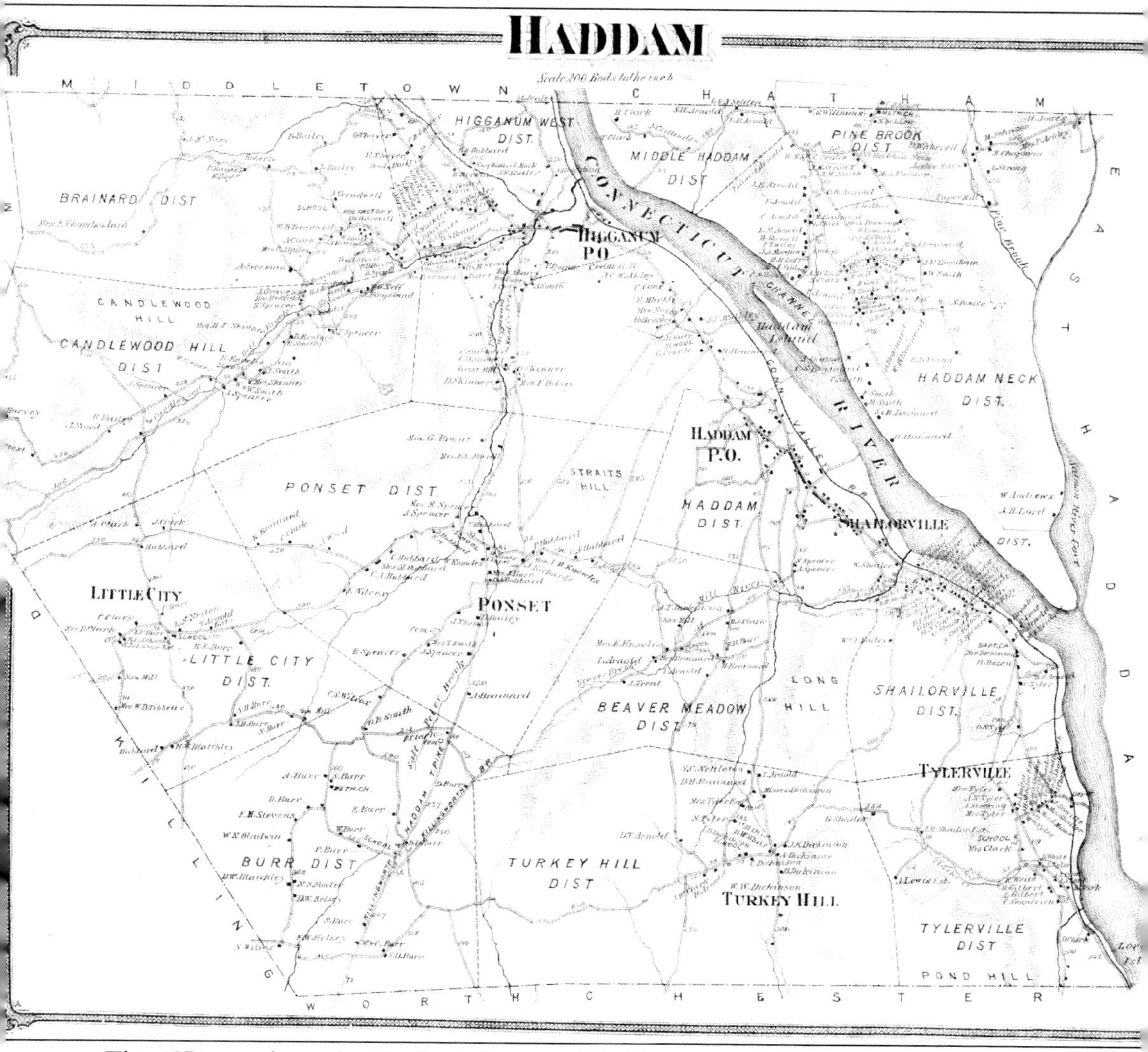

This 1874 map shows the 13 school districts of Haddam.

On the cover: The Haddam courthouse later became the town hall.

IMAGES
of America

HADDAM
1870–1930

Charlotte Gradie and Jan Sweet
for the Haddam Historical Society

ARCADIA
PUBLISHING

Copyright © 2005 by Charlotte Gradie and Jan Sweet for the Haddam Historical Society
ISBN 978-0-7385-3795-5

Published by Arcadia Publishing
Charleston, South Carolina

Printed in the United States of America

Library of Congress Catalog Card Number: 2005923924

For all general information contact Arcadia Publishing at:
Telephone 843-853-2070
Fax 843-853-0044
E-mail sales@arcadiapublishing.com
For customer service and orders:
Toll-free 1-888-313-2665

Visit us on the Internet at www.arcadiapublishing.com

This book is gratefully dedicated to all those who have made contributions to the Haddam Historical Society's photographic archives.

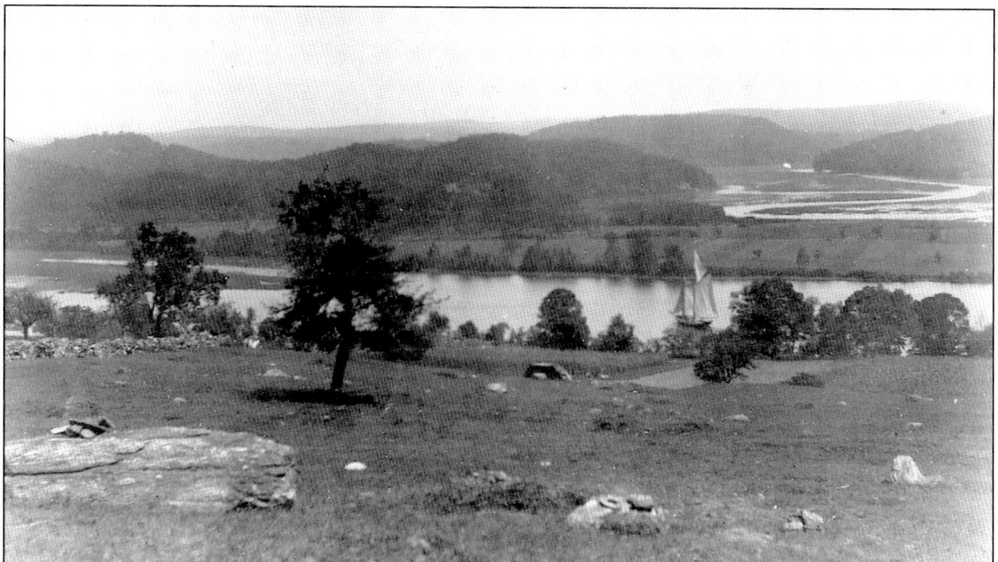

An elegant topsail schooner makes its way downriver, past Salmon Cove, in this early-20th-century picture taken by Charles "Charlie" Church, a local resident and amateur photographer. The dark hull with a white stripe indicates that this may have been a commercial trade ship.

Contents

ACKNOWLEDGMENTS

Thanks go to Rod Auclair, Bob Averill, Paul Bischoff, Nancy and Stanley Brittingham, Augusta Priest Chadsey, Bud Hall, Dave Lenzi, Lisa Malloy, Max Miller, Gladys and Leslie Peck, Don Sampson, Leslie Starr, Alan Webb, Richard Williamson Jr., Camp Bethel, and the Middle Haddam Library.

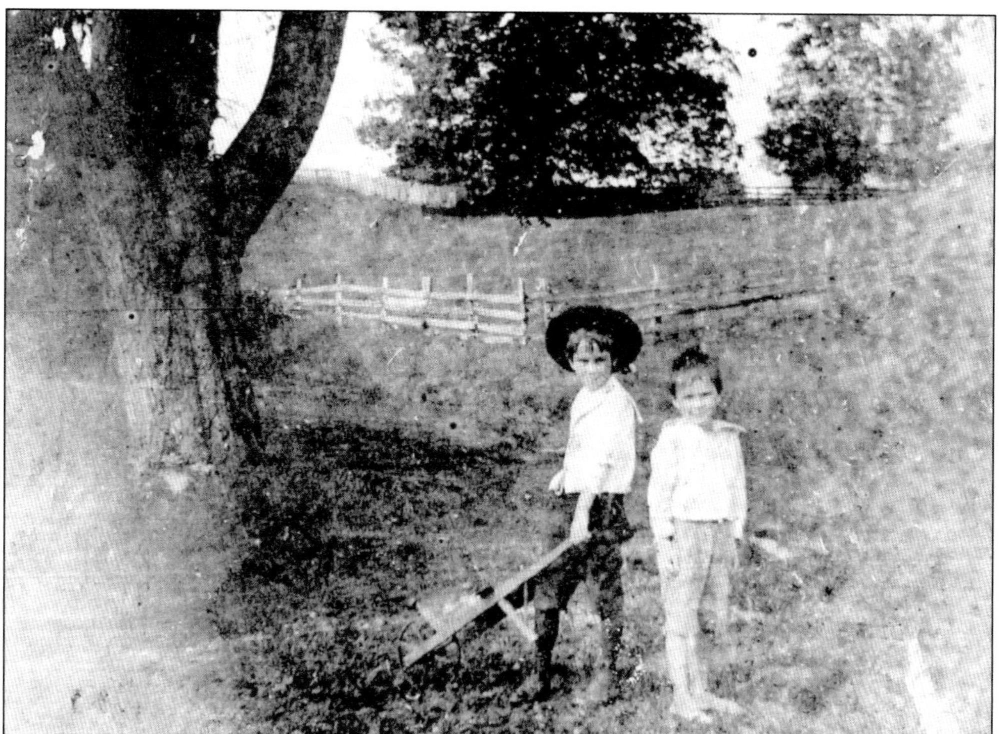

Theron and Charlie Parmelee are shown here in a family photograph. The Parmelee family has resided in Haddam since the 18th century. (Courtesy Parmelee family.)

INTRODUCTION

Three villages on the Connecticut River make up the town of Haddam. They are Haddam and Higganum, on the west bank of the river, and Haddam Neck on the east bank. The town was at one time divided into 13 school districts, such as Tylerville, Shailerville, and Ponsett, which residents continue to refer to today, well past the time of the one-room district schoolhouse. Haddam, originally known as Thirty Mile Island Plantation, was founded in 1662 by 28 men from Hartford and other river towns who paid 30 coats to the Wangunk Indians for use of the land. These men were mostly the younger sons of the first settlers of Hartford. The town's first name derives from the belief that Haddam Island lay 30 miles from Long Island Sound, and Haddam originally included what are today the town of East Haddam and a section of Durham known as the Haddam Quarter. The settlers first occupied what are now known as Haddam Center and Shailerville, laying out house lots perpendicular to the river along the Native American trail. This later became Main Street, which is also called Saybrook Road or Middlesex Turnpike.

From its early days, agriculture was the economic lifeblood of Haddam and remained the occupation of many of its residents. In her history of Haddam Neck, Lillian Kruger Brooks notes that as late as World War I, the majority of families here relied on subsistence agriculture: "The biggest means of support for the local people was small-scale farming and catering to the 'outsiders' selling them milk, cream, eggs, homemade butter, vegetables, and fruits from their gardens. The Haddam Neckers also exchanged their farm products for their groceries." Aside from some fertile Connecticut River bottomland, much of the land in Haddam is rocky ledge, which presented a challenge to the farmer. For example, when George Clark came into possession of the Bonfoey Farm in Haddam through his marriage to Clementine Bonfoey, in 1860, he removed 16,000 tons of rock from the property.

Because arable land was limited, many Haddam natives moved west or left the land altogether for city life. Town population statistics from 1870 to 1930 demonstrate this phenomenon. From 1870 to its nadir in 1920, the net population of Haddam declined from more than 2,000 residents to 1,736 persons, a drop of about 17 percent.

In this same period, however, immigrants moved in and manufacturing activity expanded, aided by Haddam's swift-running streams, such as Candlewood and Pine Brooks, and the town's Connecticut River location. The completion of the Connecticut Valley Railroad in 1871 also stimulated economic activity. For those who chose to stay, manufacturing offered an alternative means to agriculture for making a living.

With the turn of the century, the pace of change in Haddam quickened. By the 1920s, running water, indoor plumbing, electricity, radios, and telephones made their appearance in many homes. The automobile led to paved roads, a sidewalk in Haddam Center, and the appointment of a traffic officer in Higganum. The one-room schoolhouse became a memory when the town meeting voted in June 1921 to approve school consolidation so that "the quality of school service will be much improved and taxes lowered." The 18th amendment to the Constitution in 1919 prohibited the sale of liquor and ended the annual town meeting vote on whether to grant or prohibit businesses liquor licenses. Some of the most far-reaching changes concerned women, who began to participate in local politics when they received the vote in 1919. That year, Belle Russell was elected to the school committee. Throughout the following decade, a small number of women also served as justices of the peace, registrars of voters, and assistant town clerk. In 1929, Ethel M. Williams was elected Haddam's first female town clerk.

The following pages present a journey through Haddam between the years 1870 and 1930. This journey begins with a trip up unpaved Saybrook Road, then across the Connecticut River by ferry to Haddam Neck, before crossing back over the river to Tylerville. It continues with a look at Haddam agriculture, industry, and its historic houses. The journey ends with the changing times of the 1920s. Many of the historic photographs reproduced in this volume show landmarks familiar to Haddam residents today, while some of the images show sites that have since disappeared. The photographs were chosen with the goal of picturing for the reader Haddam as it once was.

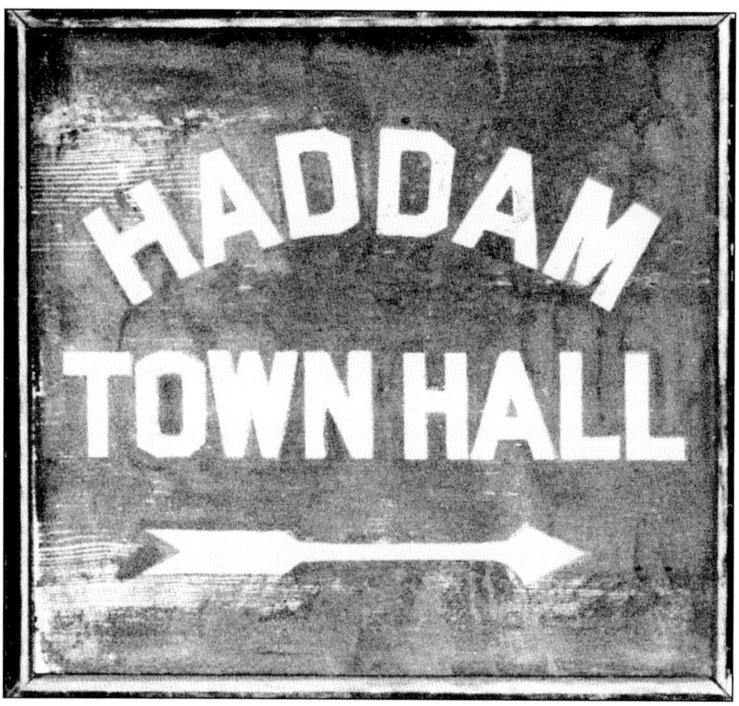

This sign hung outside the former Brainerd Academy until 1967.

One

Shailerville to Haddam Center

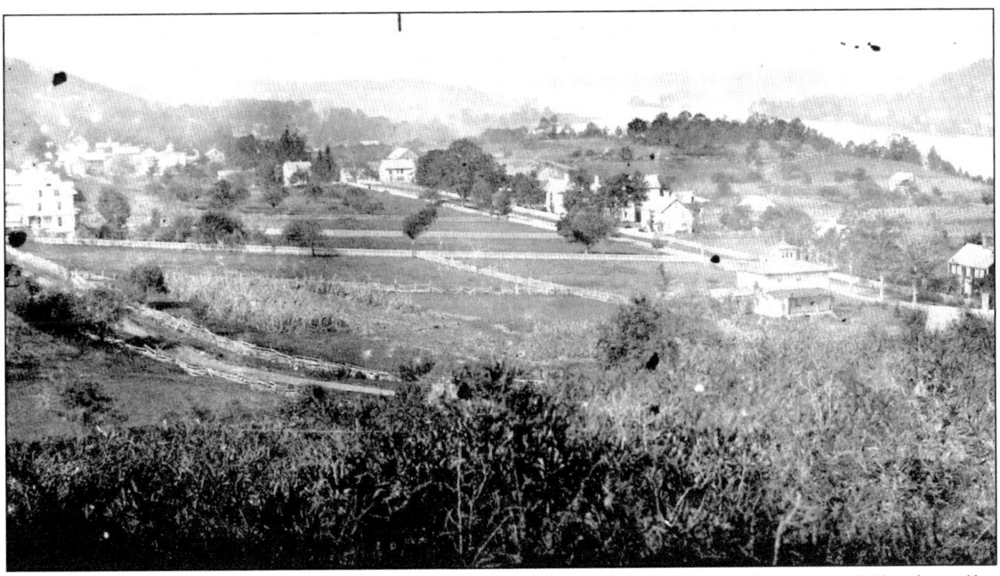

Travelers looking west from Cremation Hill could see the entire settlement of Shailerville. This 1877 photograph and others in this book were taken by Haddam Neck native George Bradford Brainerd, who was an active amateur photographer in the 1870s and 1880s. (Courtesy Brainerd Library.)

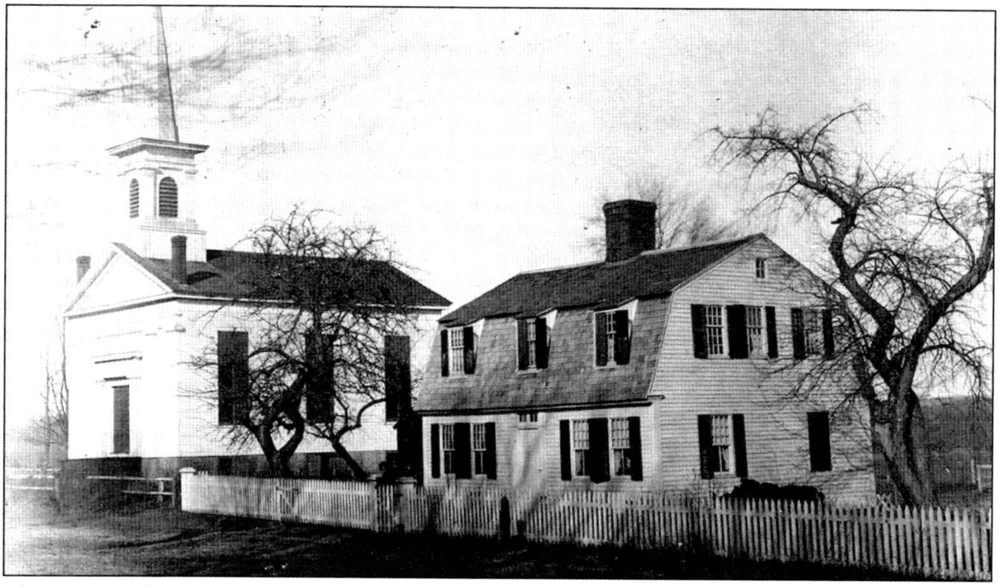

The Baptist church, located next to the George Bailey House, has stood on the east side of the road since the 1830s. It was built in the Greek Revival style. The Baptist congregation rejected what it felt was the worldliness of the Congregationalists. Many members of the congregation and several ministers were members of the Shailer family.

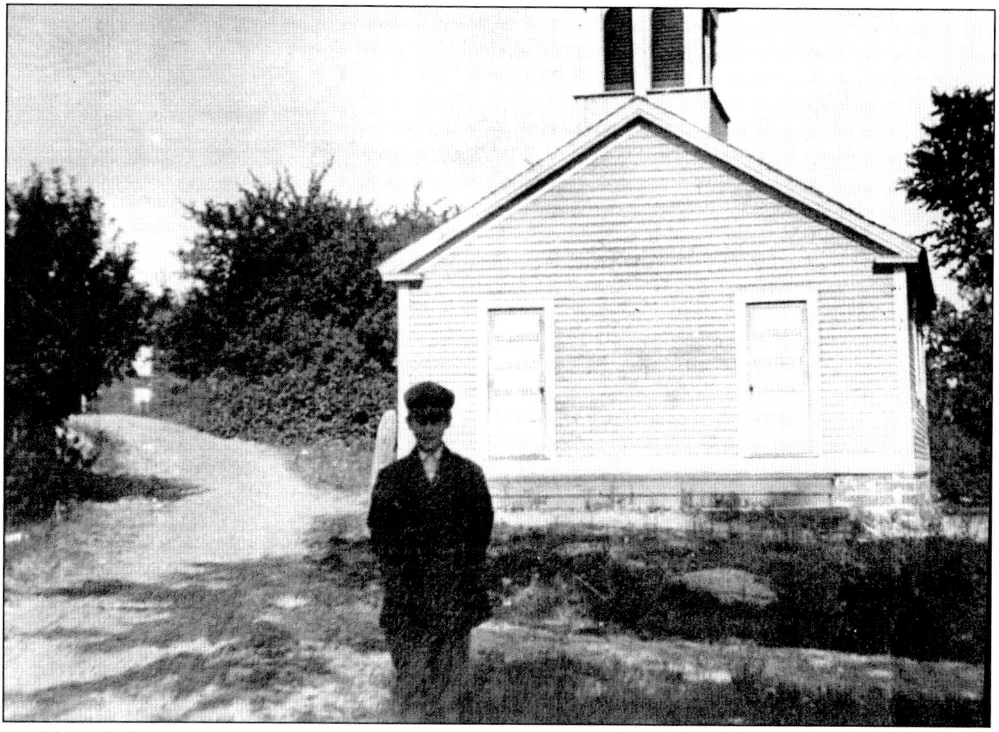

Haddam children attended one of 15 one-room schoolhouses. The schools were run by a single teacher, often a woman, and accommodated all grade levels below high school. The town paid for students to attend high school in Deep River; those students choosing to attend Middletown High paid additional tuition. The Shailerville school, shown here, is a residence today.

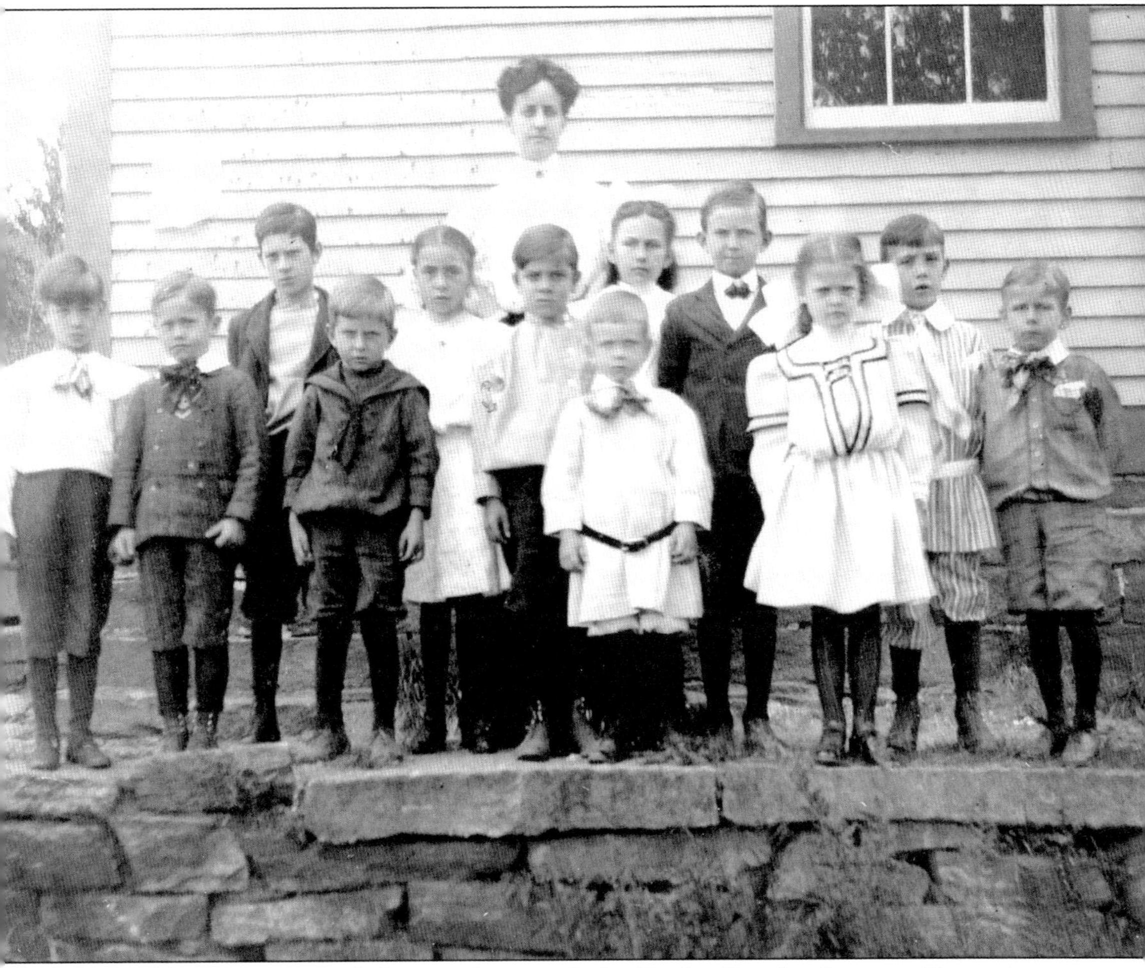

These children are posing with their teacher outside the Shailerville schoolhouse on Decoration Day, May 30, 1907.

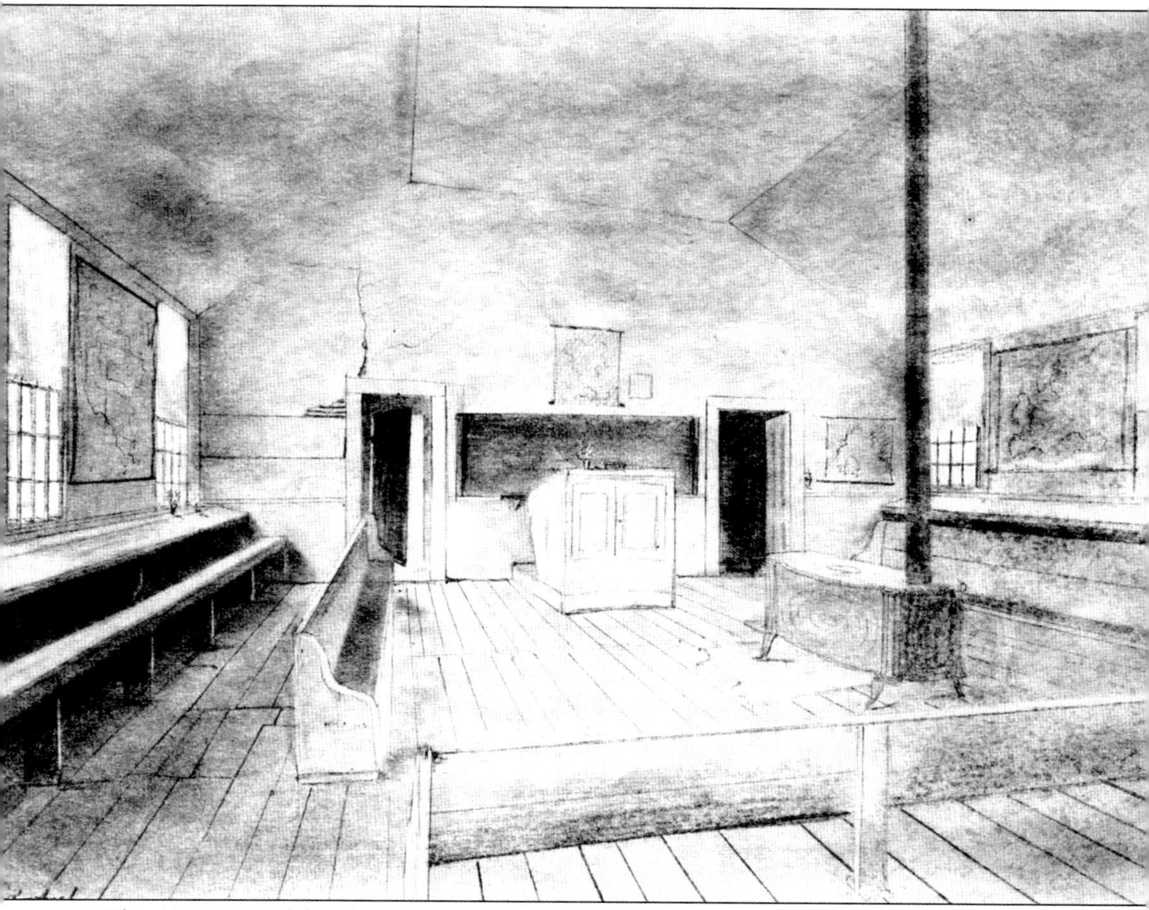

This 1894 view of the Shailerville schoolhouse reveals a plain interior. The taxpayers provided the desks, blackboard, and map. Parents provided the books, slates, and pencils until 1908, when it was voted at the town meeting to provide textbooks and supplies to comply with new state education laws. Instruction focused on rote learning and the three Rs.

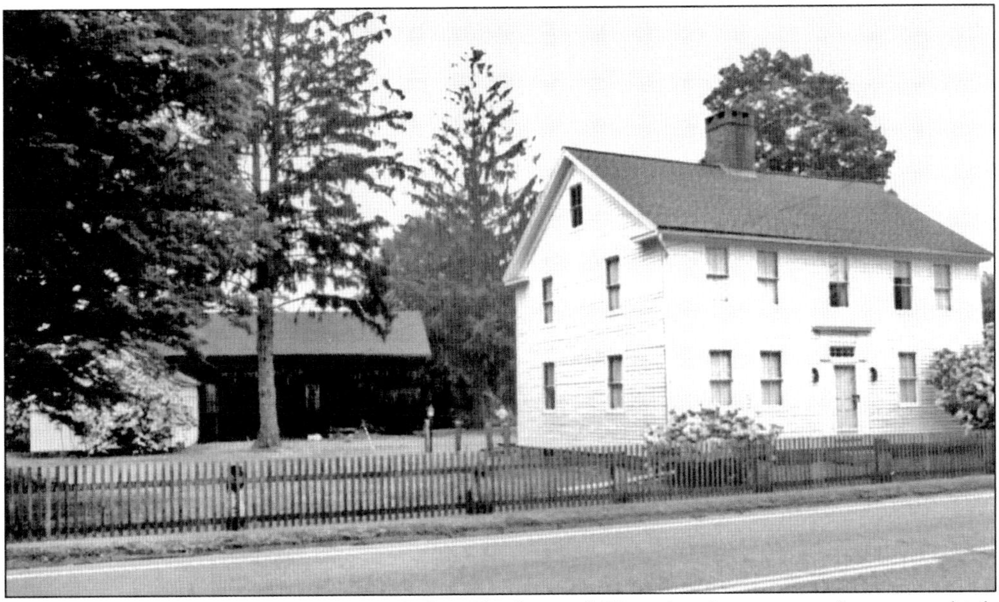

Farther up the road, travelers passed the Shailer and Knowles factory on the east, which manufactured stamped and pressed-metal products from the 1870s to 1914. The factory is the barnlike structure in the left background, behind the Russell Shailer House.

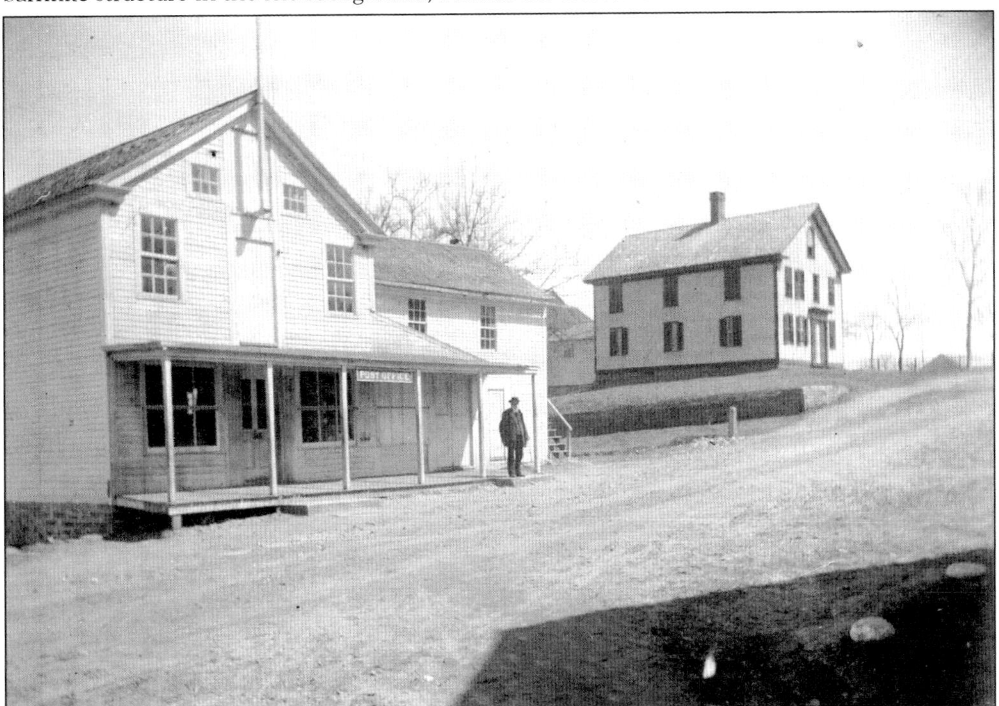

The post office, located on the east side of the road, next to a Shailer family house, was also a familiar landmark for many years. An Episcopal congregation regularly met on the second floor. After 1871, the mail stage was discontinued, and mail arrived by rail. The post office building was later converted to apartments. It was destroyed by fire in 1952, when a tenant left a pot of grease on the stove.

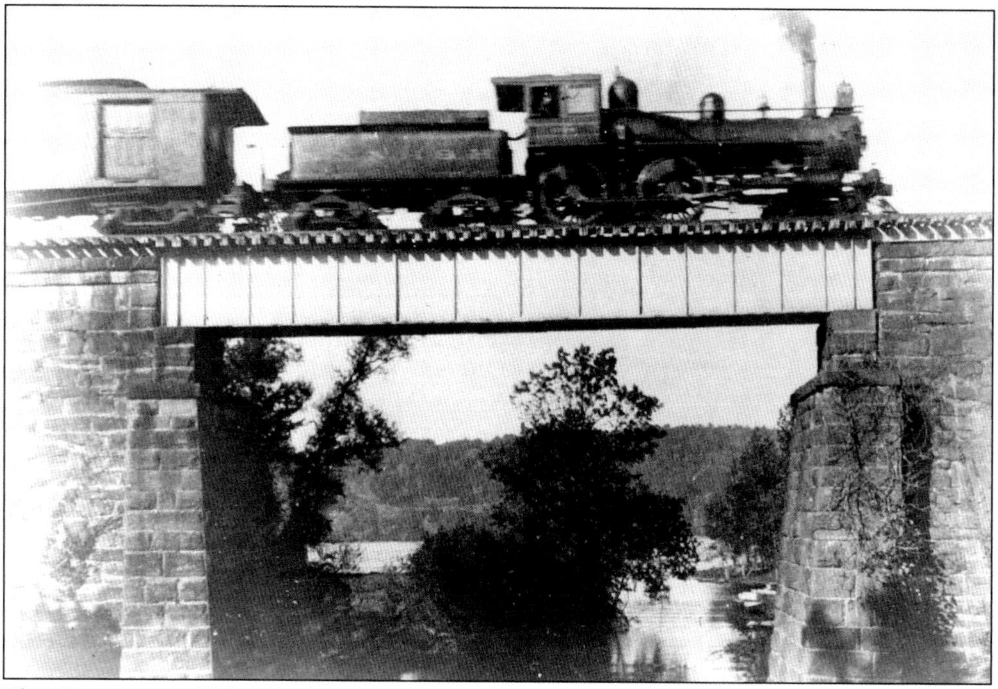

The Connecticut Valley Railroad passed over Mill Creek. Even today, passersby can see its foundation of huge, beautiful brownstone blocks. In 1871, a wooden covered bridge was built. In 1894, it was replaced by the iron-plate girder bridge seen in this photograph. The creek is the informal boundary between Shailerville and Haddam Center.

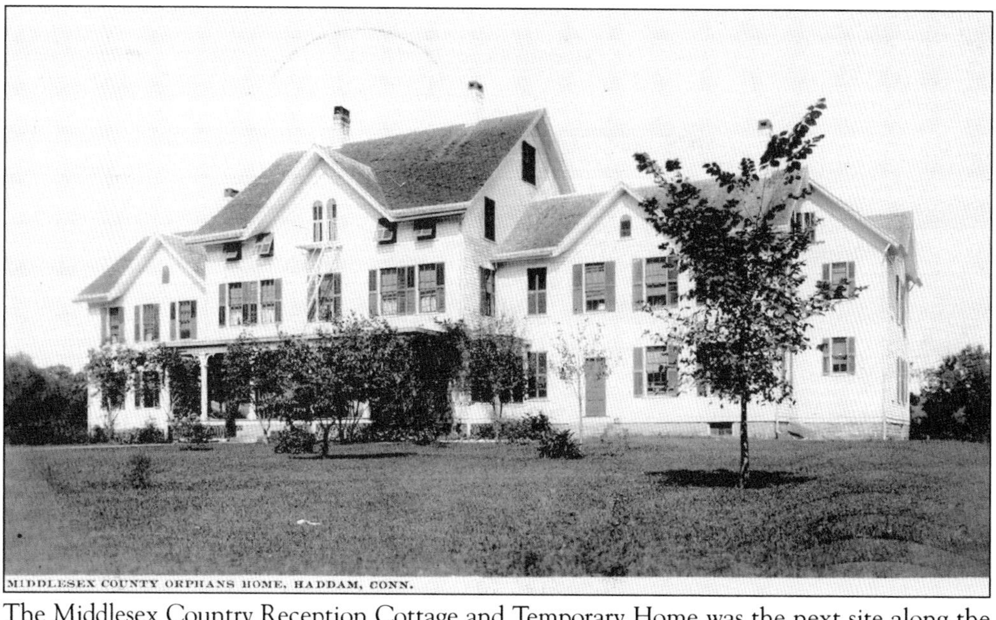

The Middlesex Country Reception Cottage and Temporary Home was the next site along the road. Shown here in 1913, it was built in 1887 to house 60 orphans. In 1891, it was established as a school district by the town. The younger grades had classes at the temporary home, and the older children attended local schools.

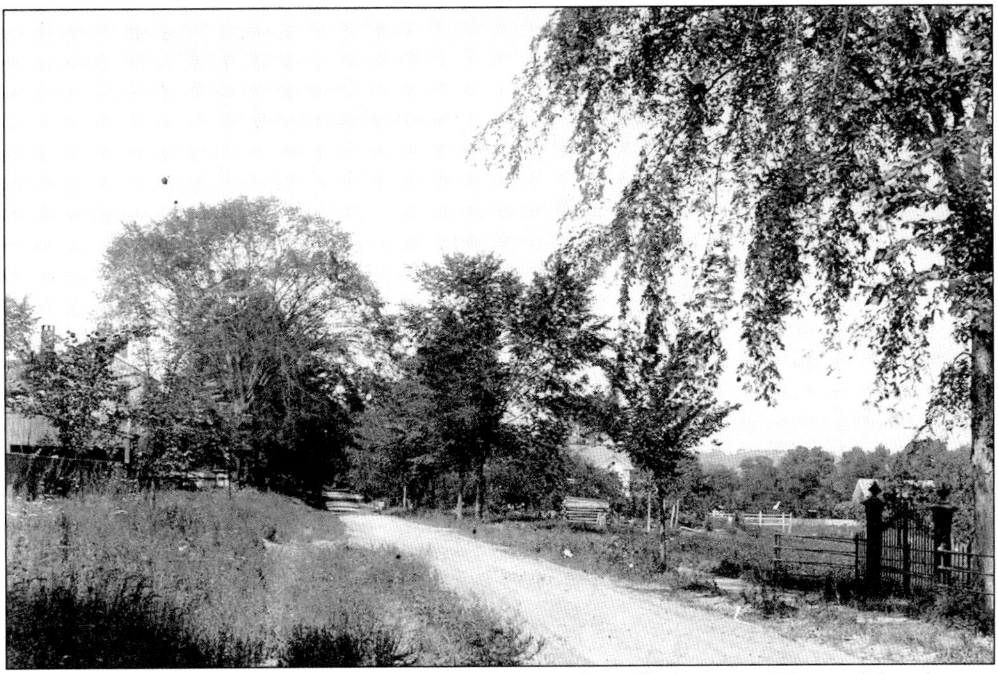

The road went past the Greenwood cemetery and under tall elm trees. Many of the elms on Saybrook Road were lost in the Hurricane of 1938; others succumbed to Dutch elm disease.

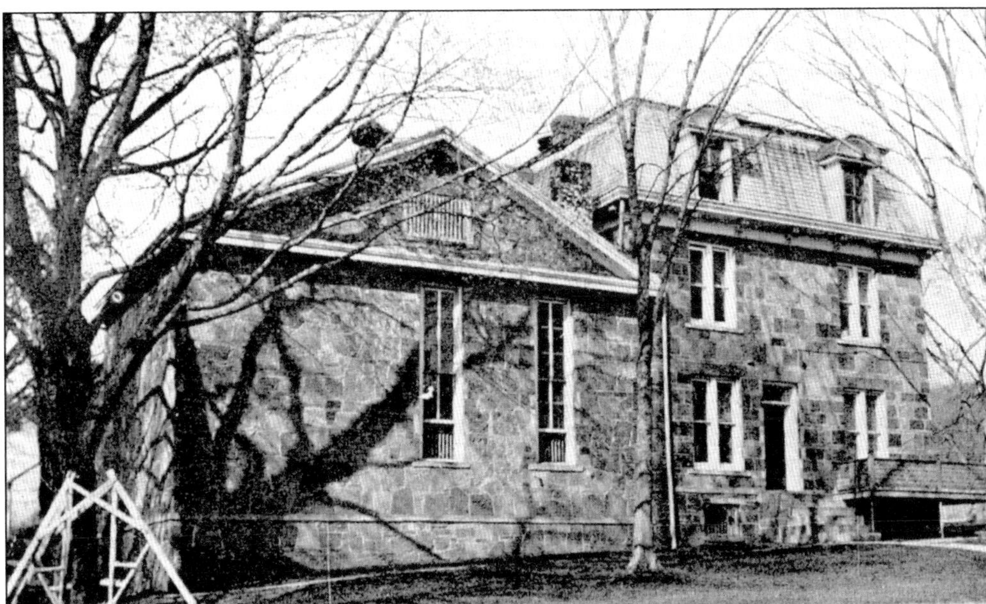

Haddam Jail.

Beyond the cemetery, on the west, was the Middlesex County jail, shown here in 1916. Built by inmates in 1845, the facility was expanded in 1855. In 1876, it acquired a Second Empire–style addition. Debtors, women inmates, and hardened criminals shared the building with the jailer and his family. Prisoners grew their own food. Some of the inmates worked in town as mill hands, in local quarries, and on town roads.

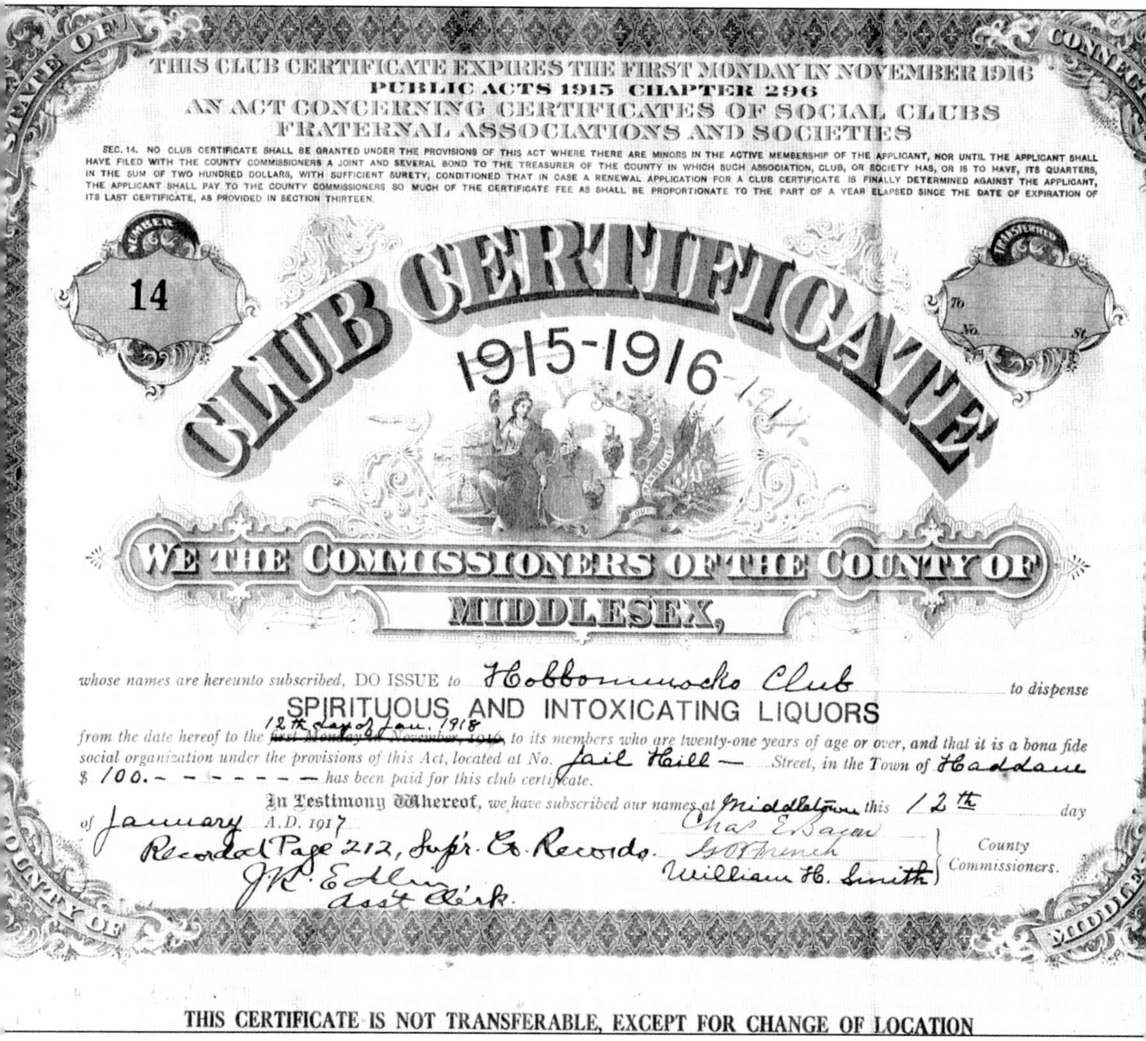
STATE OF CONNECTICUT

THIS CLUB CERTIFICATE EXPIRES THE FIRST MONDAY IN NOVEMBER 1916

PUBLIC ACTS 1915 CHAPTER 296

AN ACT CONCERNING CERTIFICATES OF SOCIAL CLUBS FRATERNAL ASSOCIATIONS AND SOCIETIES

SEC. 14. NO CLUB CERTIFICATE SHALL BE GRANTED UNDER THE PROVISIONS OF THIS ACT WHERE THERE ARE MINORS IN THE ACTIVE MEMBERSHIP OF THE APPLICANT, NOR UNTIL THE APPLICANT SHALL HAVE FILED WITH THE COUNTY COMMISSIONERS A JOINT AND SEVERAL BOND TO THE TREASURER OF THE COUNTY IN WHICH SUCH ASSOCIATION, CLUB, OR SOCIETY HAS, OR IS TO HAVE, ITS QUARTERS, IN THE SUM OF TWO HUNDRED DOLLARS, WITH SUFFICIENT SURETY, CONDITIONED THAT IN CASE A RENEWAL APPLICATION FOR A CLUB CERTIFICATE IS FINALLY DETERMINED AGAINST THE APPLICANT, THE APPLICANT SHALL PAY TO THE COUNTY COMMISSIONERS SO MUCH OF THE CERTIFICATE FEE AS SHALL BE PROPORTIONATE TO THE PART OF A YEAR ELAPSED SINCE THE DATE OF EXPIRATION OF ITS LAST CERTIFICATE, AS PROVIDED IN SECTION THIRTEEN.

NUMBER 14

TRANSFERRED To No. St.

CLUB CERTIFICATE

1915-1916-1917

WE THE COMMISSIONERS OF THE COUNTY OF MIDDLESEX,

whose names are hereunto subscribed, DO ISSUE *to* Hobbommocko Club *to dispense*

SPIRITUOUS AND INTOXICATING LIQUORS

from the date hereof to the 12th day of Jan. 1918 ~~first Monday in November, 1916~~ *to its members who are twenty-one years of age or over, and that it is a bona fide social organization under the provisions of this Act, located at No.* Jail Hill — *Street, in the Town of* Haddam

$ 100.— — — — — — — *has been paid for this club certificate.*

In Testimony Whereof, *we have subscribed our names at* Middletown *this* 12th *day of* January *A.D.* 1917

Chas E. Bacon
G.O. French
William H. Smith
County Commissioners.

Recorded Page 212, Sup'r. Co. Records.
J.K. Edler
Ass't Clerk.

COUNTY OF MIDDLESEX

THIS CERTIFICATE IS NOT TRANSFERABLE, EXCEPT FOR CHANGE OF LOCATION

The private Hobbammacko Club built a meeting place on Jail House Road in 1897 and applied for a liquor license to help achieve its objective to "promote harmony and good feeling among its members." Actor William Gillette was a member. (Courtesy Bob Averill.)

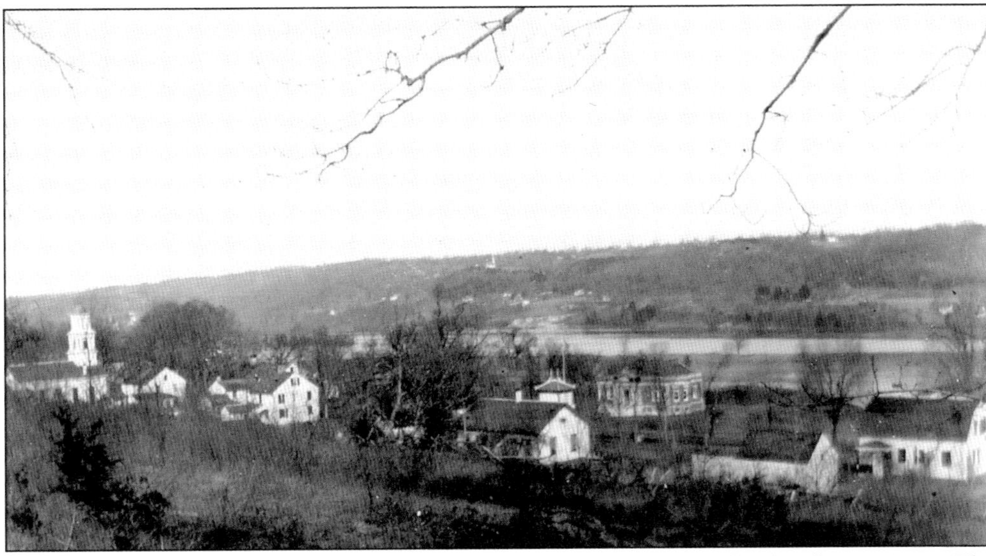

Travelers had a panoramic view of Haddam Center from the top of Schoolhouse Lane. The Congregational church and the Brainerd Library can be seen in the foreground; Haddam Neck is on the opposite side of the river.

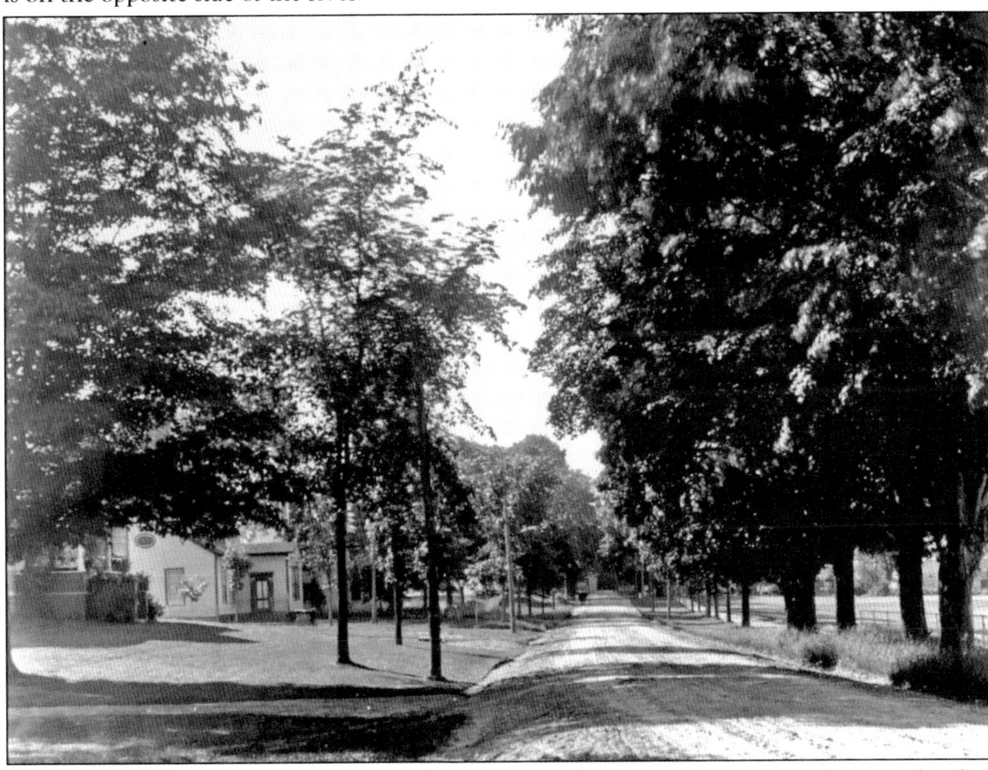

Saybrook Road continues past the First District schoolhouse, seen here in a photograph taken before the library was built (1906–1908). The first library associations in town date to 1791, but they had no permanent location. These associations included Higganum's Wide Awake Society and the Antislavery Society, which kept its books under the staircase of the Congregational church on Walkley Hill Road.

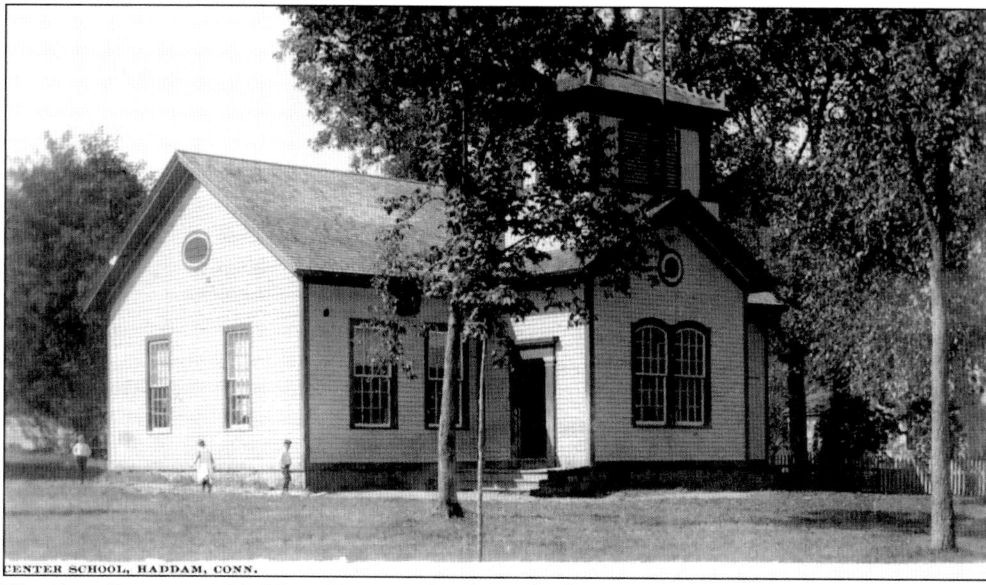

The First District, or Haddam Center, school was built in 1866. Today it is known as the Old Schoolhouse Meeting Place. The number of school districts was gradually reduced beginning in 1880—when the Beaver Meadow School District was combined with the Center School District—and continuing through 1893. School buildings were converted into residences, commercial buildings, or church halls.

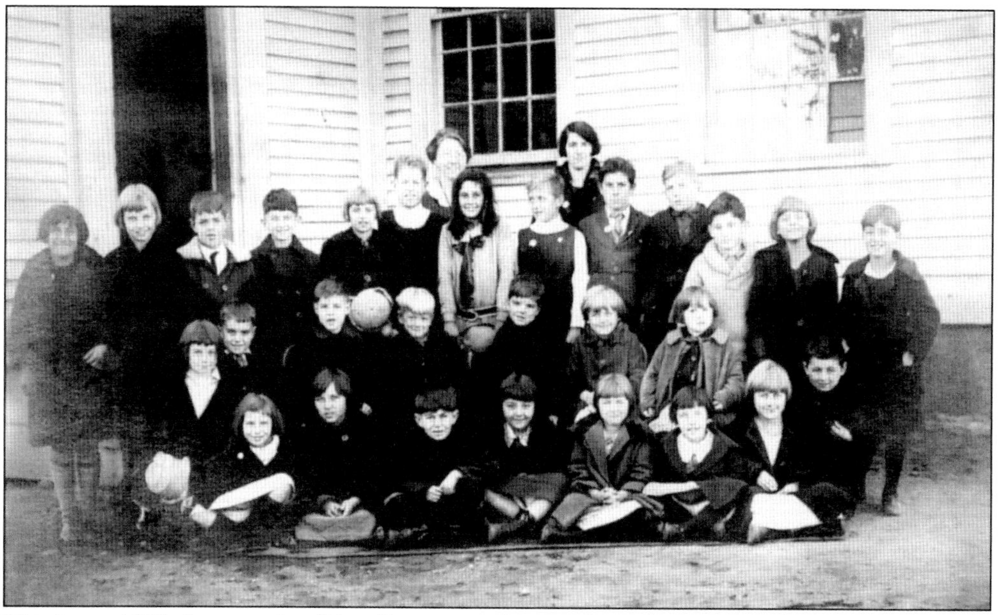

This is a *c.* 1926 photograph of First District grades one through seven. At the back are teachers Elizabeth Hutchinson Bedini and Betty Jones House. Students pictured are, from left to right, as follows: (first row) unidentified, Mary Supik, Berkley Zagoren, Margaret Caliendo, unidentified, ? Marica, and Francis Caliendo; (second row) Lucy Arnold, Robert Gisner, three unidentified students, ? Marica, and Annie Supik; (third row) Katie Beloisi, Ruth Peck, Ellsworth Beckwith, Charles Zagoren, Mae Bailey, William Pierce, Elizabeth Parmelee, Louis Gazo, Wilson Schutte, Joseph Muzik, Samuel Goodrich, ? Marica, and unidentified.

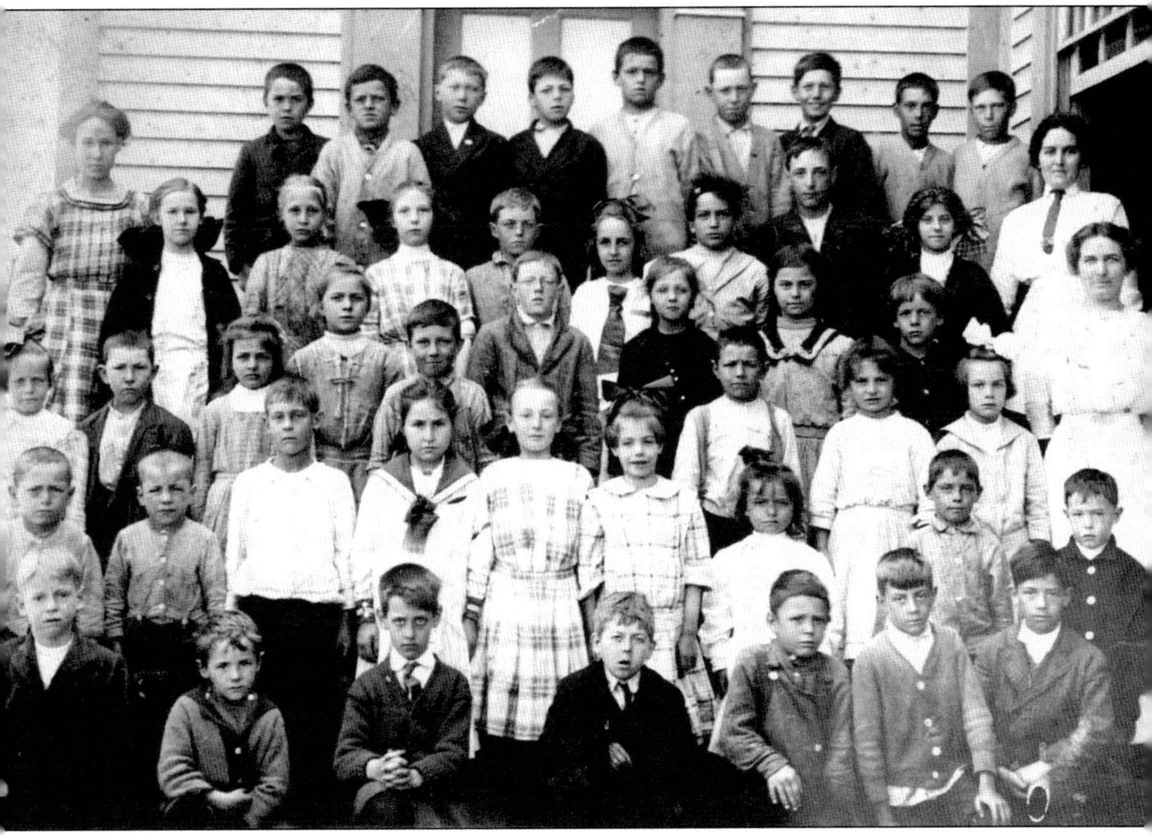

This 1913 photograph shows the students of the First District School. Included in the group are David Russell, Chester Brainerd, Annie Goggin, Elizabeth Shailer, Charles Negrelli, Loula Stephens, William Arnold, Lillian Meyer, James Williams, Waldo Parmelee, Aura Bow, Dorothy Hall, Calmers Lang, William Meyers, Tom Negrelli, John Goggin, John Ely, Ellis Parmelee, and Art Hall. The teachers are identified as Mrs. Allans and Miss Harris.

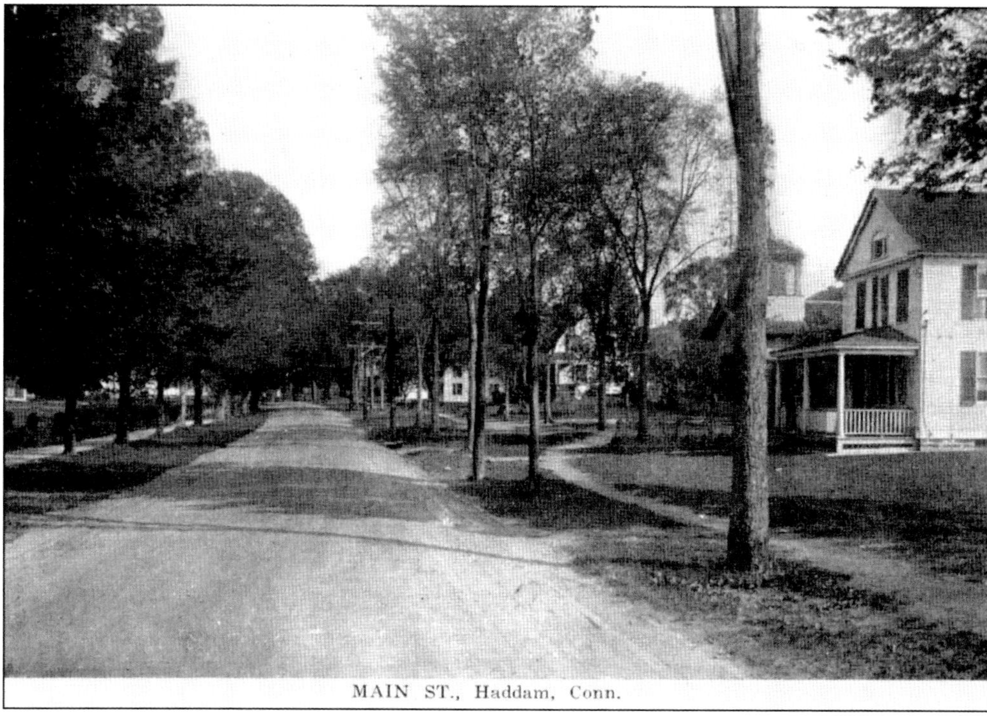

This view looks back at the Center Schoolhouse.

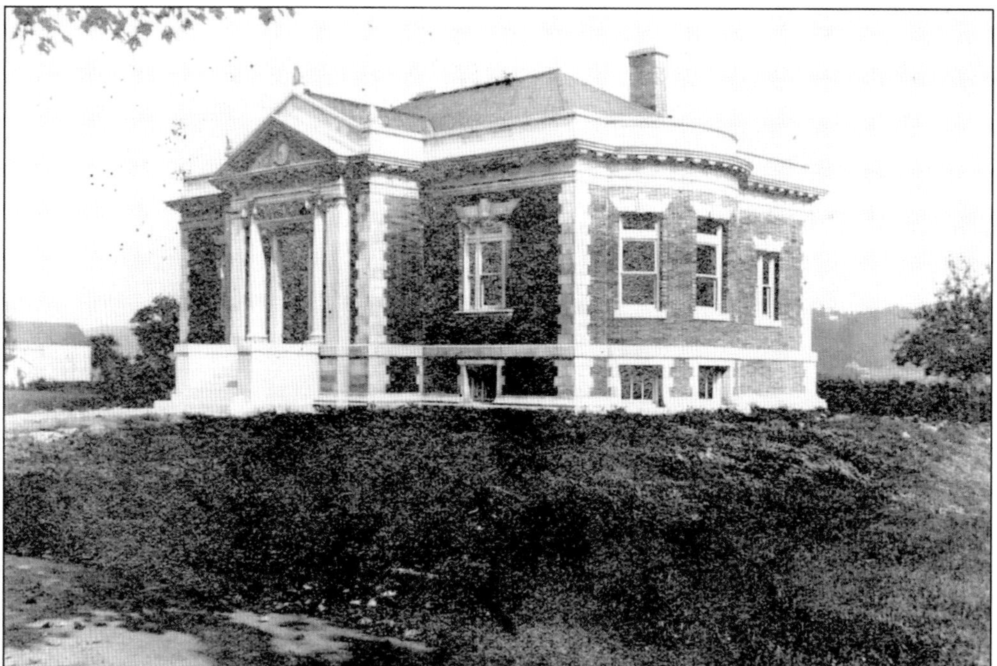

The Brainerd Library was built between 1906 and 1908 on land donated by Judge Ephraim P. Arnold. Its elegant Beaux-Arts architecture reflects the generosity of Cyprian Story Brainerd, the library's principal benefactor. The facility originally had gas lights and a gas generator, but its forward-looking builders also wired it for electricity.

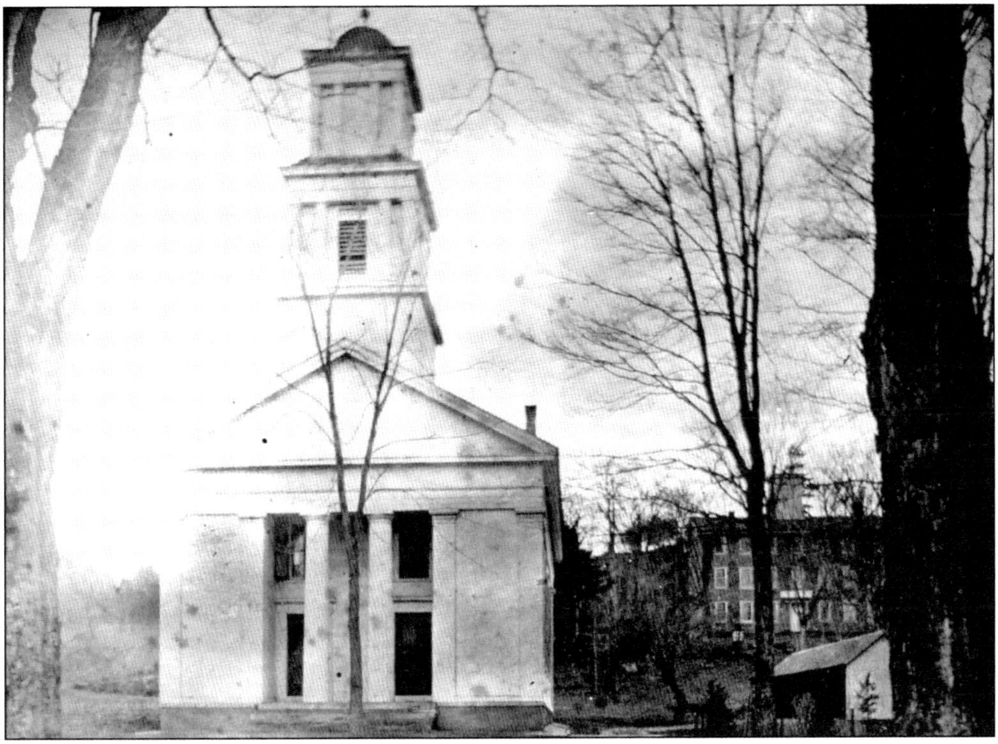

Haddam's fourth Congregational meetinghouse was constructed in Haddam Center in 1840. After the meetinghouse burned in 1979, it was reconstructed in the same Greek Revival style, using the original front columns and entablature, the only portions of the first building to survive the fire.

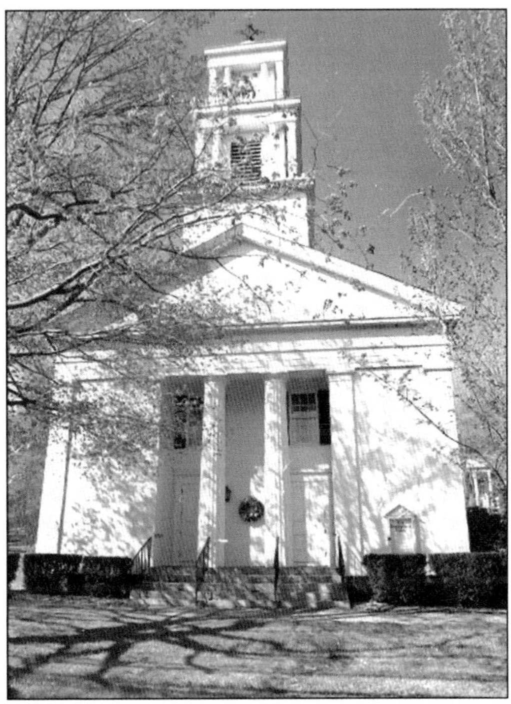

Shown as it looks today, this exact reproduction of the 1846 structure houses the 300-year-old pewter Communion service that was used by the first Congregational society, established soon after the founding of Haddam in 1662. The Communion service was one of the few items salvaged from the 1979 fire. (Courtesy Dave Lenzi.)

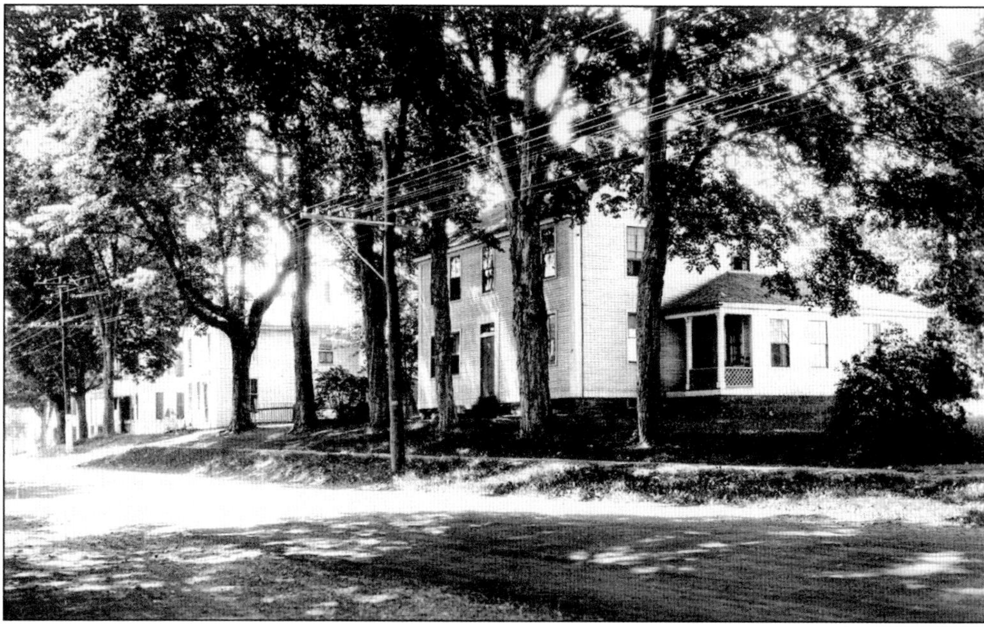

South of the church is the Smith-Brainerd House, built about 1805 by John and Mary Smith, who sold it to George Brainerd in 1817. A sixth-generation descendant of the original Haddam Brainerd, George was a prominent figure in Haddam politics. The residence remained in the Brainerd family until 1960, when it was donated to the Congregational church as a parish house.

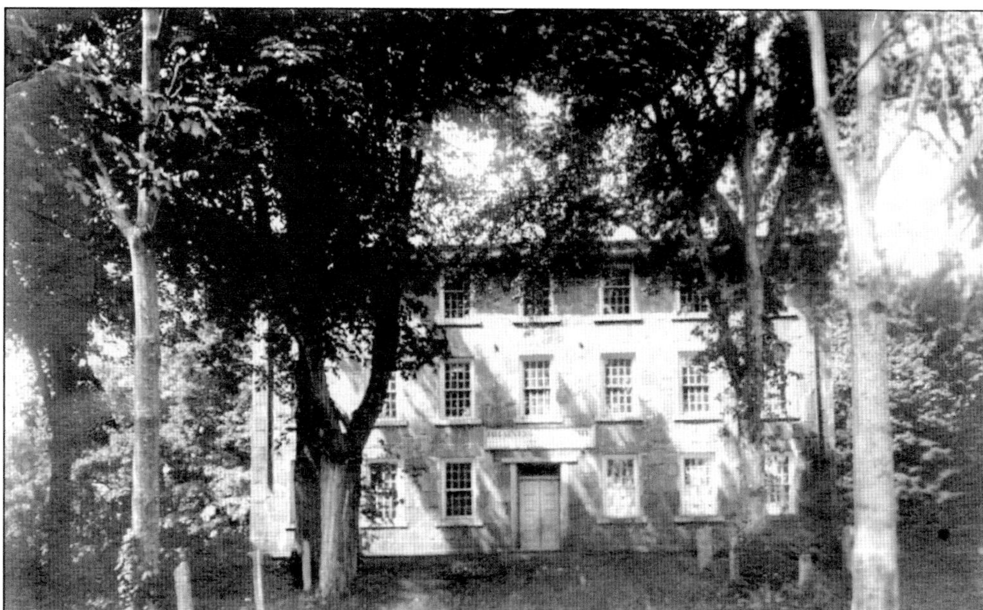

This building, which later became the town hall, is Brainerd Academy, established in 1839 by John and Nehemiah Brainerd. The academy accepted boys and girls from as far away as the Southern states and even Ceylon (Sri Lanka). Among the amenities offered were individual desks, an exercise room, and a library. Students boarded in town, and the school held public lectures. Brainerd Academy closed in the 1890s.

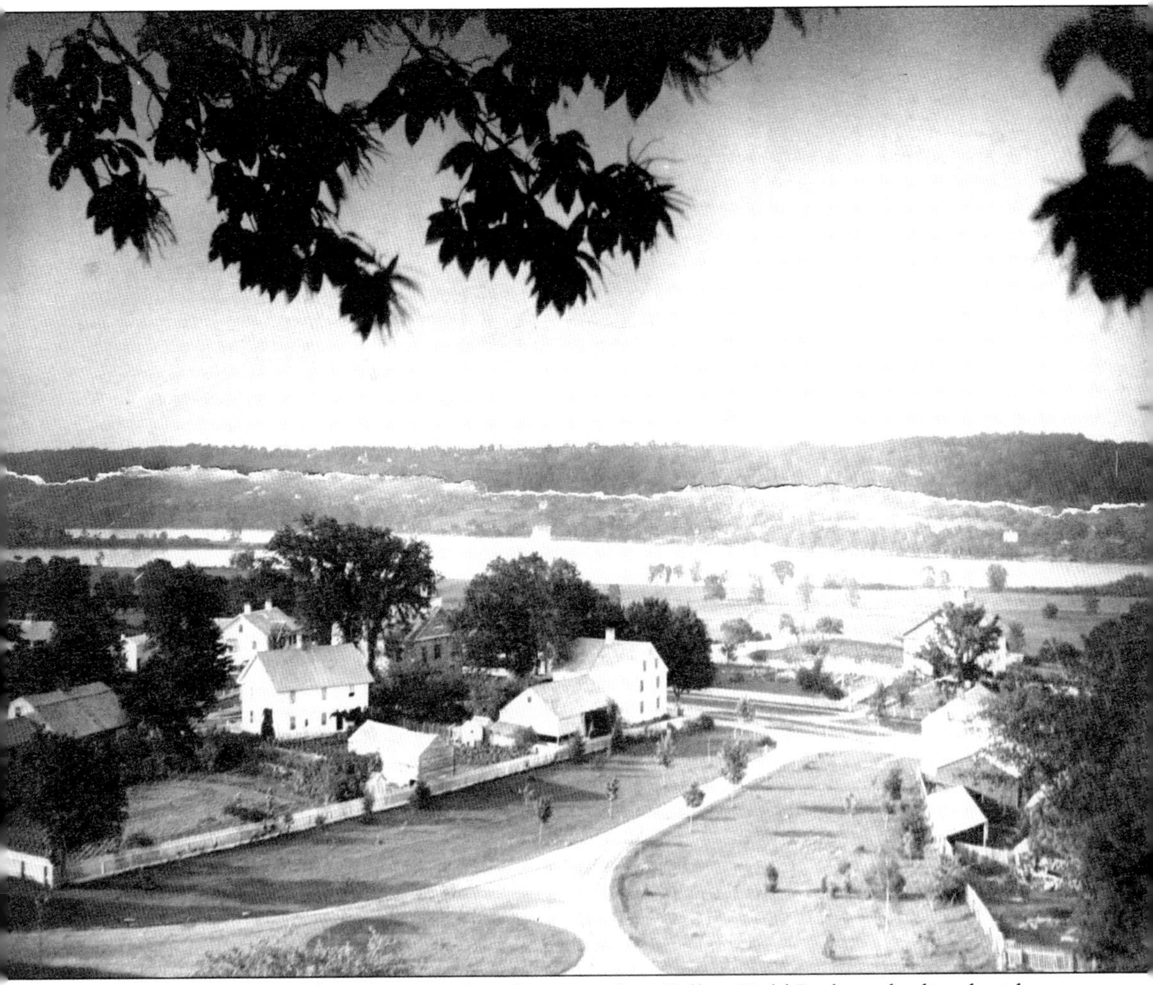

This photograph of Haddam Center, taken from Isinglass Hill in Field Park, embodies the idea of community and order integral to small-town life in New England. The park was designed by B. S. Olmsted of Rye, New York, not by Frederick Law Olmsted, as is sometimes noted. The courthouse at the center represents the town's position as a half-shire town until the 1880s. To its right sits Brainerd Hall, constructed in 1795 as a place for social gatherings. The houses on the extreme right and left belonged to the Arnold family. Both the Brainerd and Arnold families were prominent business, political, and social leaders in Haddam until the 20th century. In the background flows the ever present Connecticut River, linking Haddam Center to its sister villages. (Courtesy Parmelee family.)

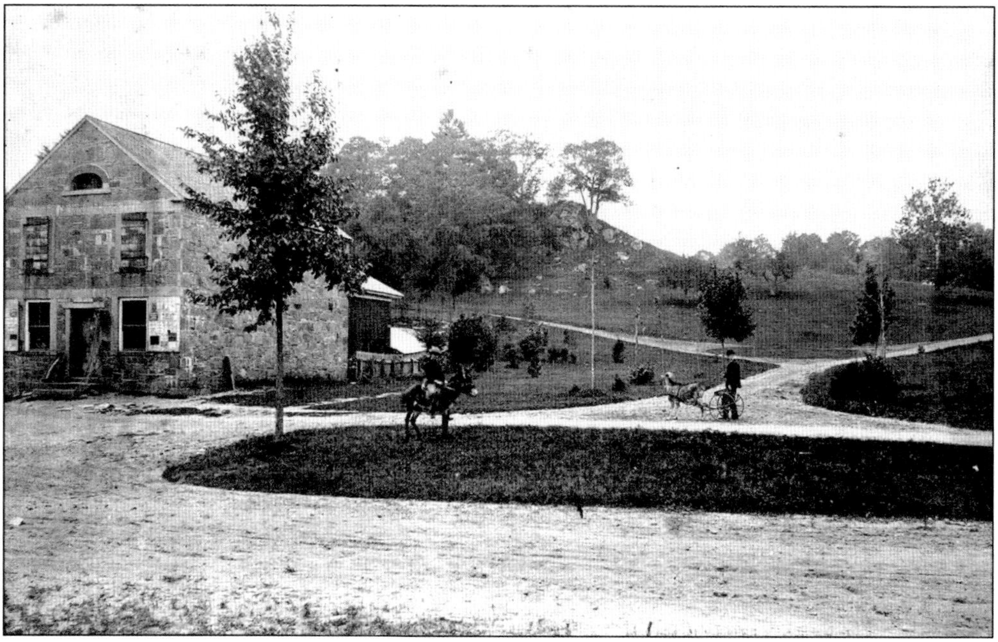

Isinglass Hill dominates this photograph of Field Park, which was dedicated in 1878 by the sons of David Dudley Field to commemorate their parents and "to be kept as pleasure ground for the people of Haddam in all time to come." Field was the minister of the Congregational church in the early 19th century. Many of the park's native and ornamental trees were destroyed in the Hurricane of 1938. The stone building is Dickenson's store and post office. (Courtesy Parmelee family.)

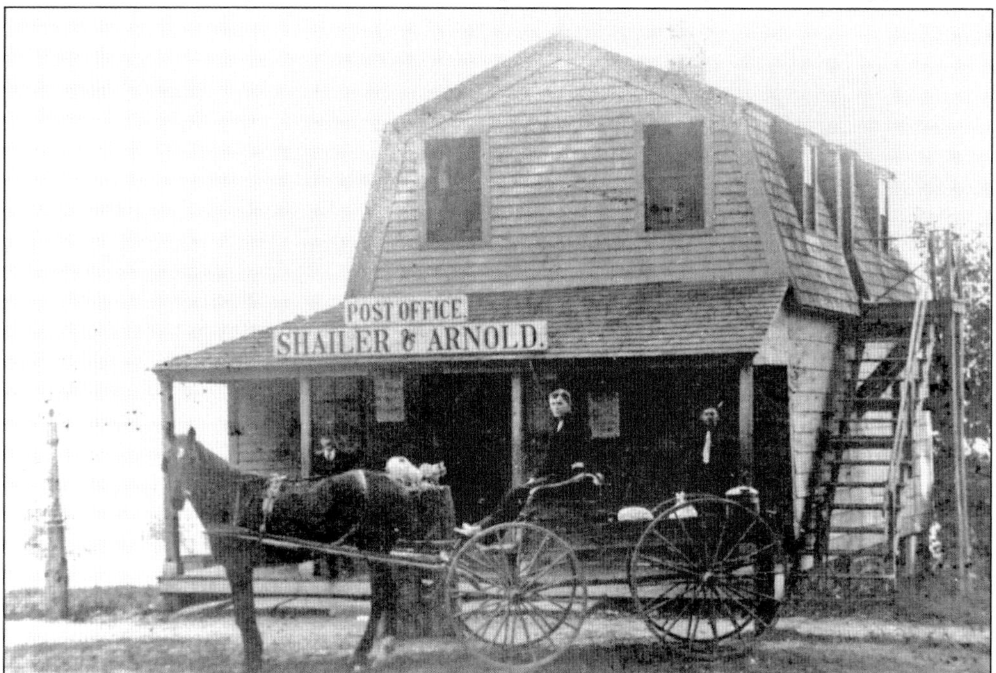

The Shailer and Arnold store stood across from Field Park on Saybrook Road. The building was constructed in 1791 on Station Hill Road and was moved several times.

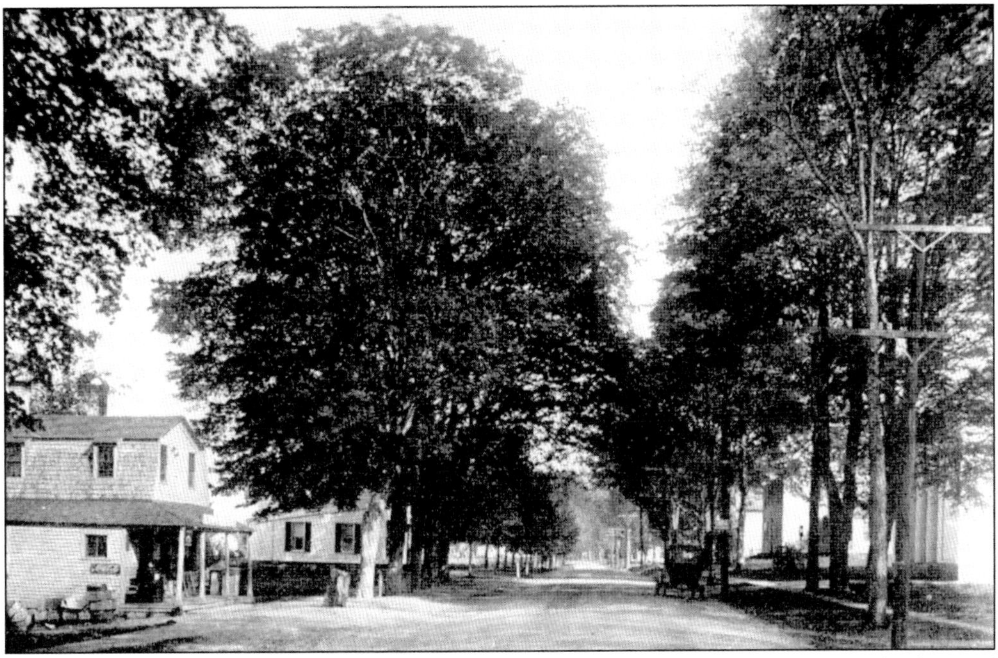

In this view to the south, the Congregational church is on the right. The Shailer and Arnold store (in the left foreground) and the house next to it have since been moved back from the road.

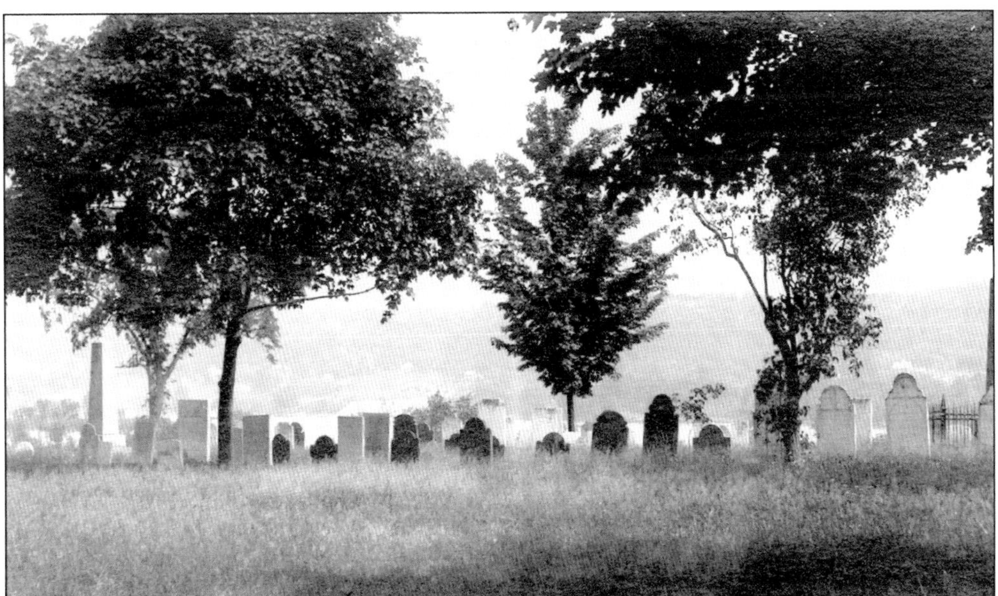

The oldest cemetery in Haddam is the Ancient Burial Yard of Thirty Mile Island Plantation, established in 1667.

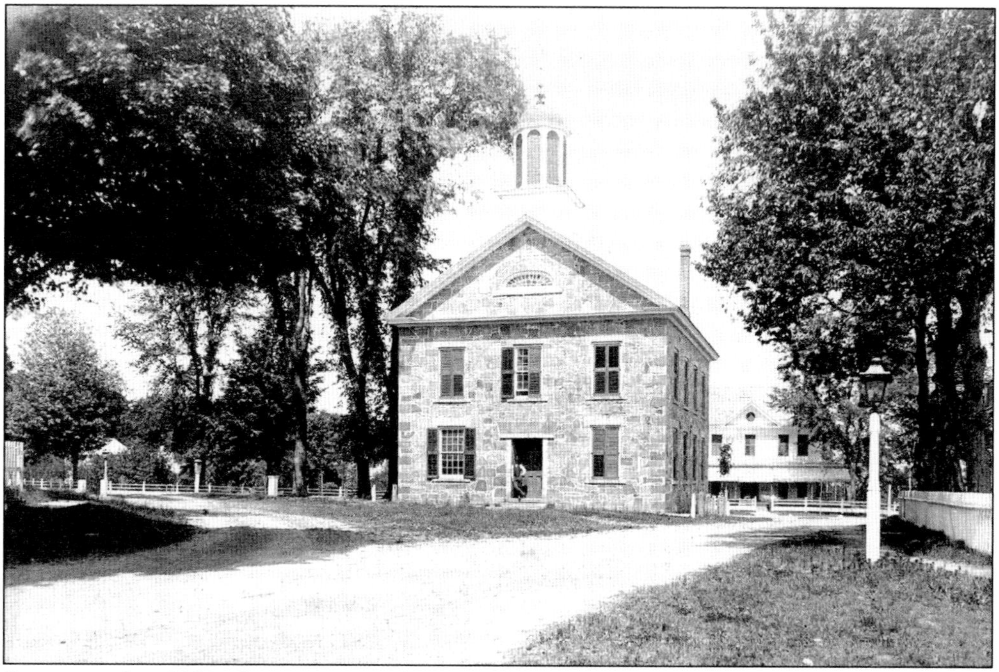

Constructed in 1829 of granite gneiss from Haddam quarries, this Federal-style courthouse was built in the 19th century, when Haddam shared the position of county seat with Middletown. Haddam later lost its position as a half-shire town when Middletown's economic and political power grew. (Courtesy Parmelee family.)

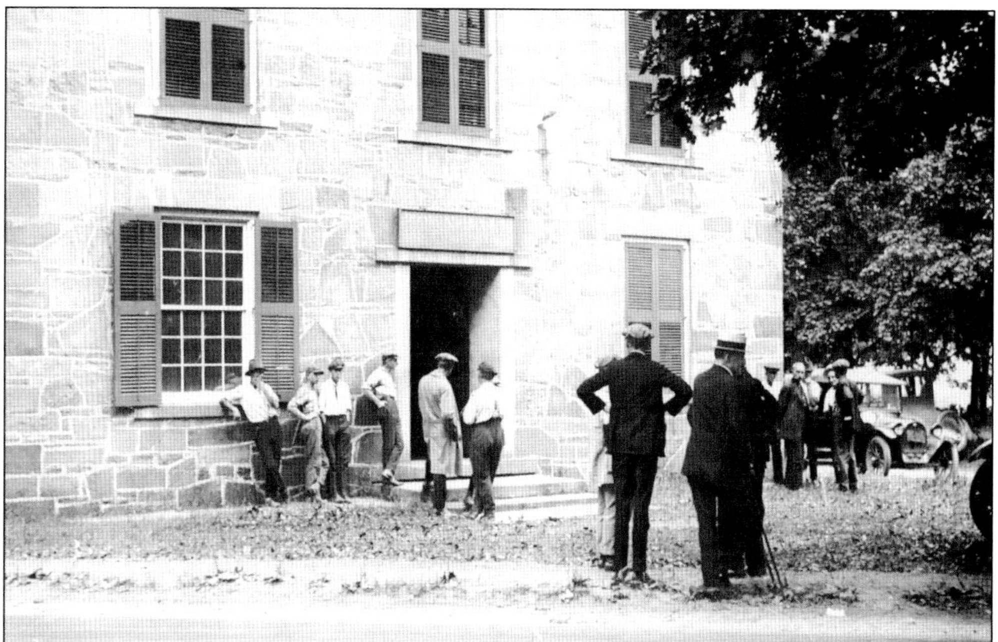

The courthouse had long ceased to serve its original purpose when these men gathered in the 1920s for a town meeting. The old courthouse served as the town hall from 1888 until it was destroyed by fire on February 12, 1929.

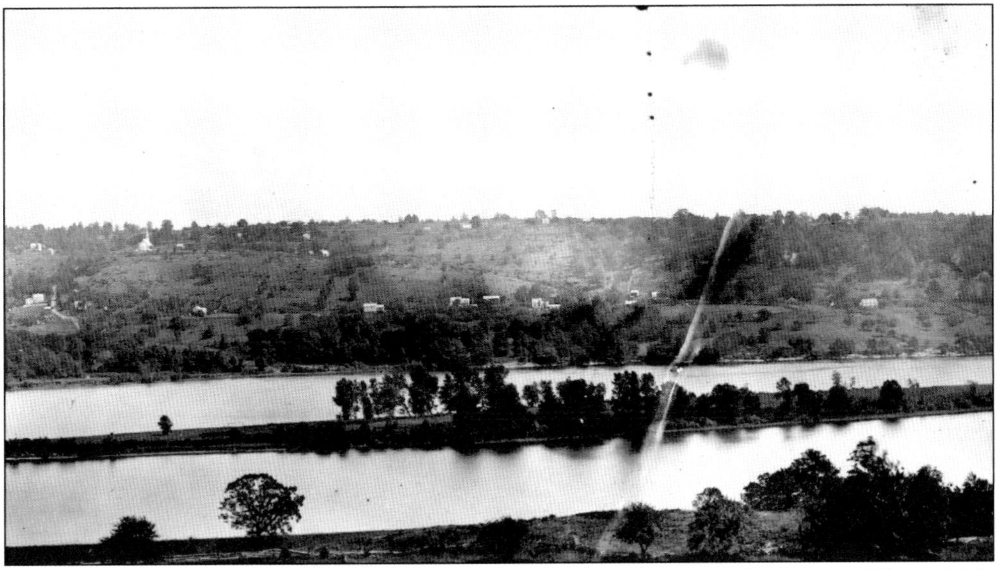

As seen in this 1877 photograph, travelers had a clear view across the river to Thirty Mile Island (now called Haddam Island) and Haddam Neck. (George Bradford Brainerd photograph, courtesy Brainerd Library.)

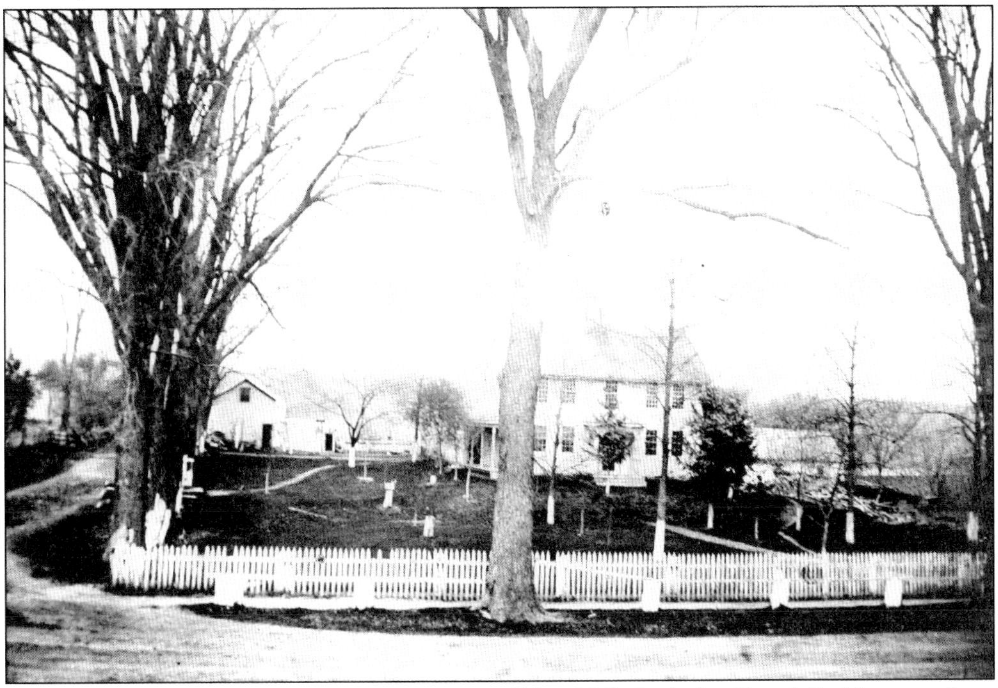

The Congregational church parsonage on Walkley Hill, built by David Field across from a Methodist church, was gone by 1890. Field was the minister of the First Congregational Church from 1804 to 1818 and from 1837 to 1844; he subsequently served as minister of the Higganum Congregational Church until 1851. Field's children became prominent citizens: David and Stephen were justices of the U.S. Supreme Court; Henry was a minister and editor of the *Evangelist*, a Presbyterian weekly; Cyrus led the effort to establish the first transatlantic telegraph cable; and daughter Rachel was an author.

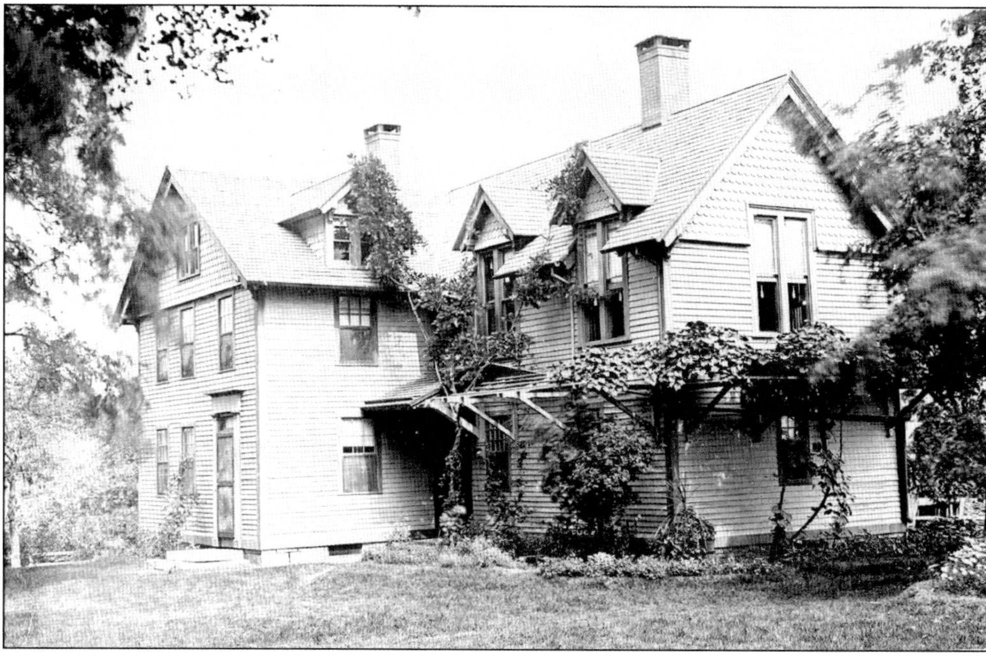

Continuing up Walkley Hill Road, travelers passed Eveline Brainerd's house, which she named Chrysoberyl Knoll after a mineral found in the area. Haddam is world renowned for its variety of minerals and semiprecious stones, which include sulfur, iron pyrite, thulite, beryl, chrysoberyl, tourmaline, kyanite, lepidolite, columbite, epidote, molybderite, spinel, zircon, rose and smoky quartz, garnet, copper, silver, gold, and even Haddamite, a mineral first identified here in 1870.

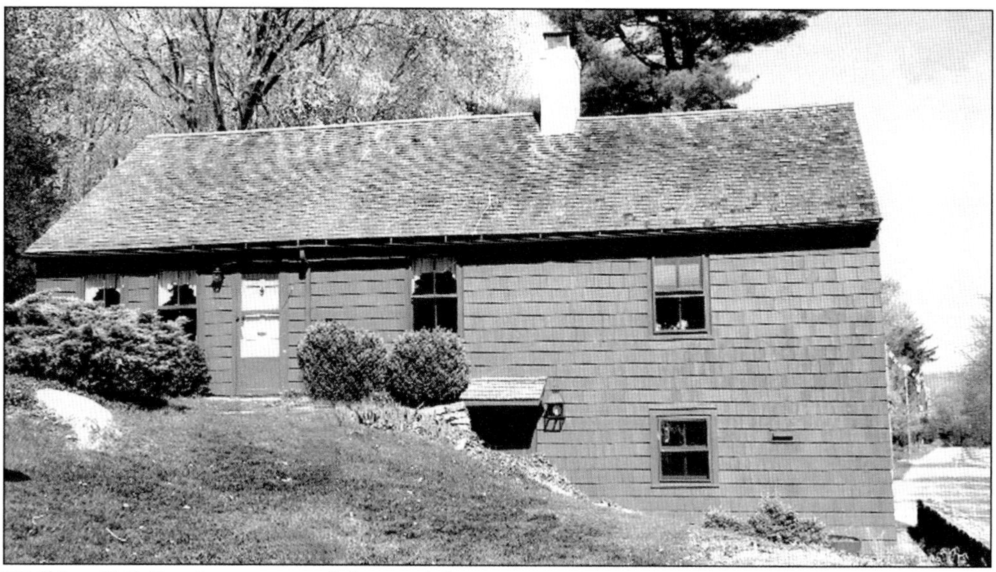

Walkley Hill Road was part of the Middlesex Turnpike, the major overland route between Saybrook and Hartford. Opened in 1804, the turnpike had four tollhouses. The third is shown here. Toll keepers received 10 percent of receipts but did not charge local traffic, travelers going to church, or those attending militia meetings. Tolls were discontinued by 1874, probably because of competition from the Connecticut Valley Railroad, which opened in 1871. (Courtesy Dave Lenzi.)

Two

HIGGANUM

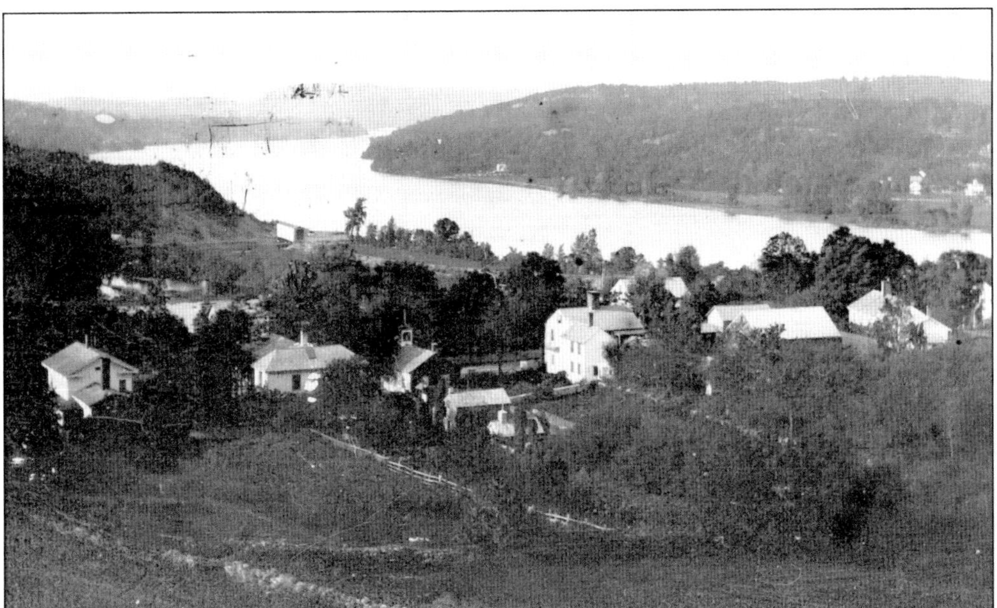

Upriver from Haddam Center, Higganum became the industrial and commercial district of the town in the 19th century. Its name derives from the Algonkian word *Higganompos*, meaning "at the axe rock." This 1877 photograph looks toward Swan Hill. (George Bradford Brainerd photograph, courtesy Brainerd Library.)

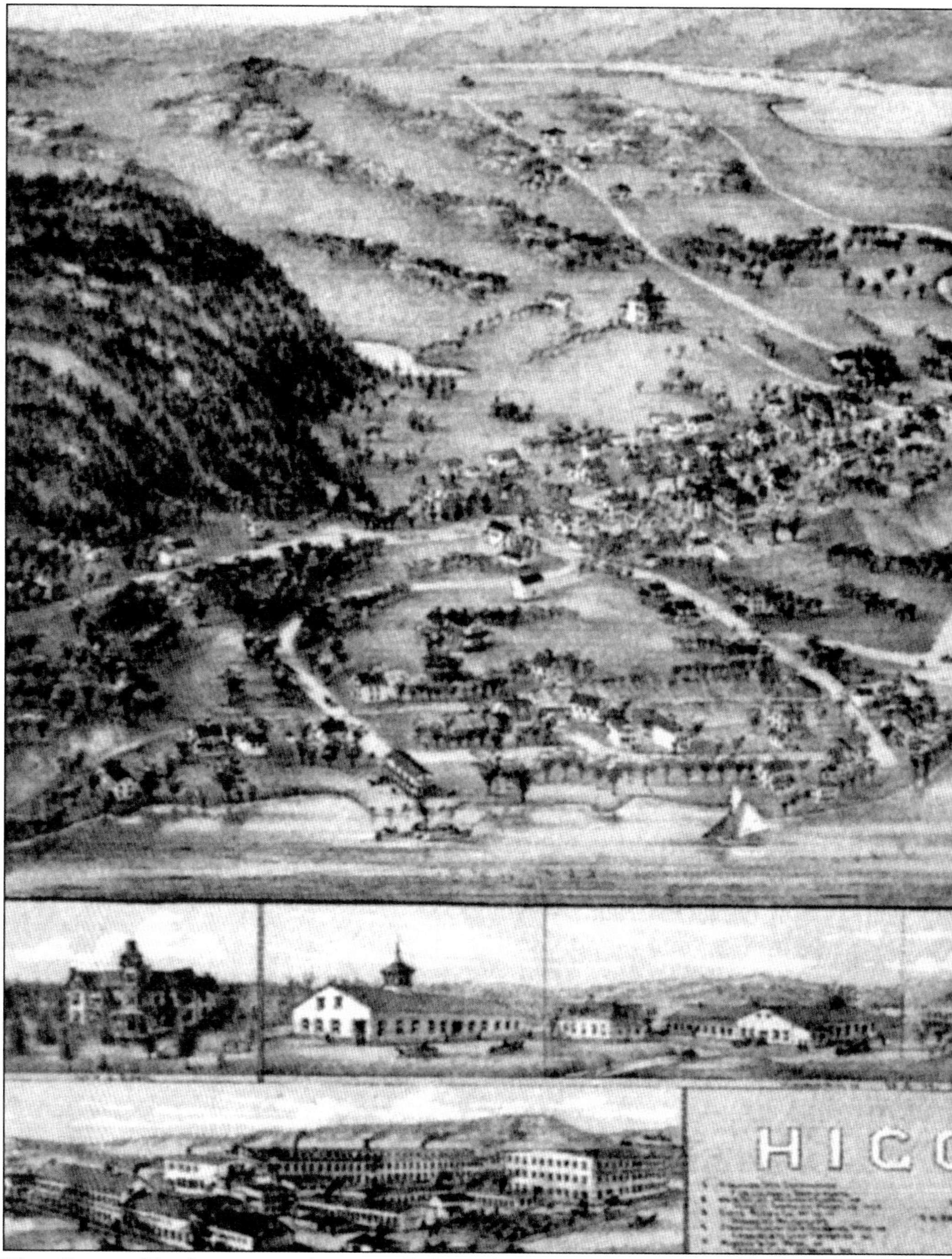

This illustrated bird's-eye view shows small shops that were established at Higganum Landing beginning in 1752. Shipbuilding was the principal industry here until 1840, after which factories dominated. Shown below this 1881 map of Higganum are, from left to right, the following: (top row) the residence of Hezekiah Scovil; four buildings of the D&H Scovil Hoe Company—the grinding shop, the Black Shop, the Bell Shop, and the Upper Shop (no longer standing); and the residence of Daniel Scovil; (bottom row) Higganum Manufacturing Company, producer

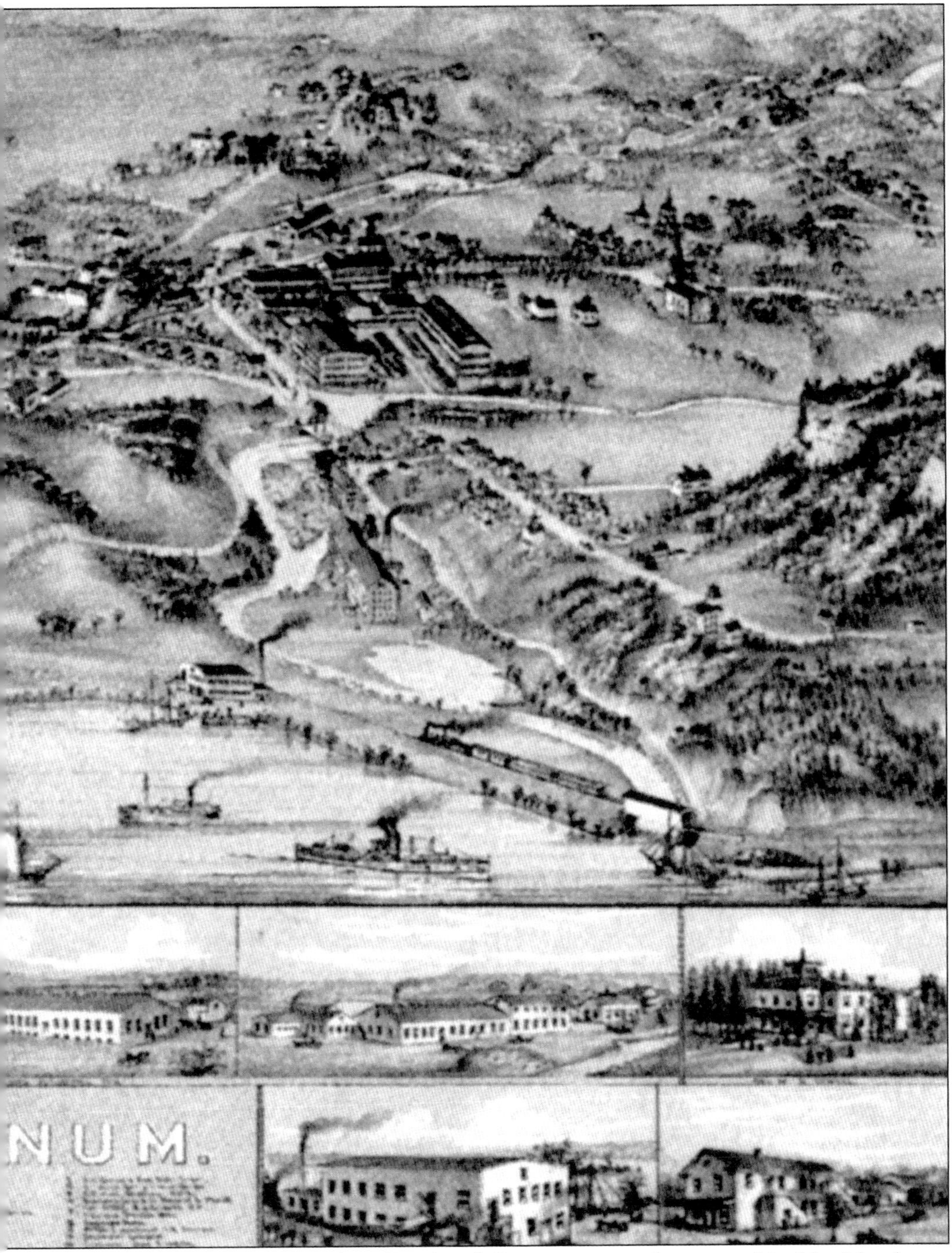

of agricultural implements; Chase Reed and Company, manufacturers of builders' hardware; and the L. C. and L. D. Barry Company, sellers of general merchandise. On the map itself, the buildings of the Higganum Manufacturing Company dominate the village. In the foreground is Higganum Landing, and at center is the railroad station. Note the covered railroad bridge over Higganum Creek, and the Higganum Manufacturing Company reservoir in the background.

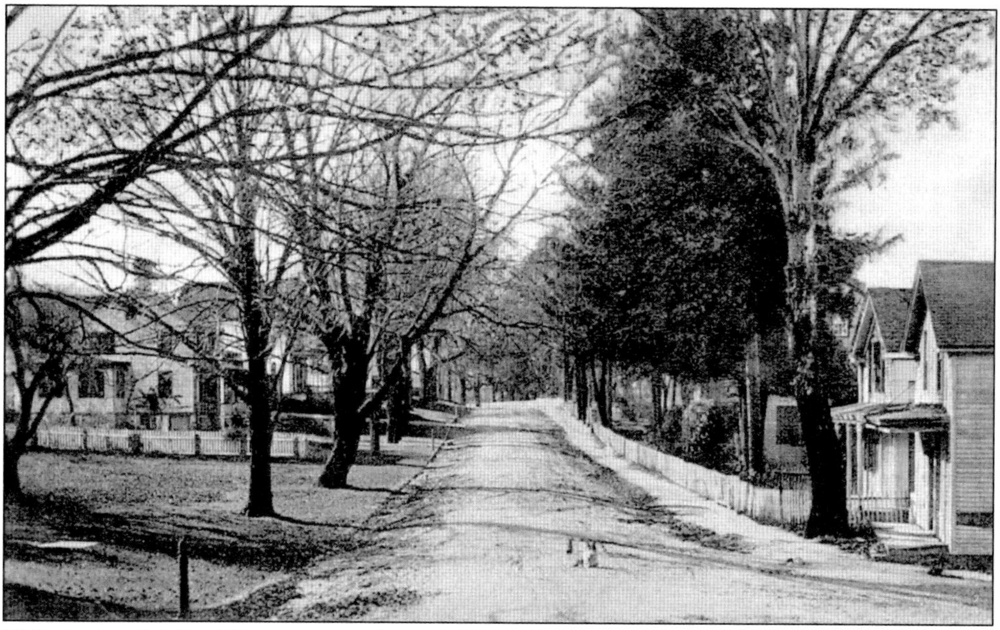

This scene, which might greet travelers coming into Higganum, reveals that the town was not far removed from its rural roots. The first house on the right was later moved farther north on Saybrook Road.

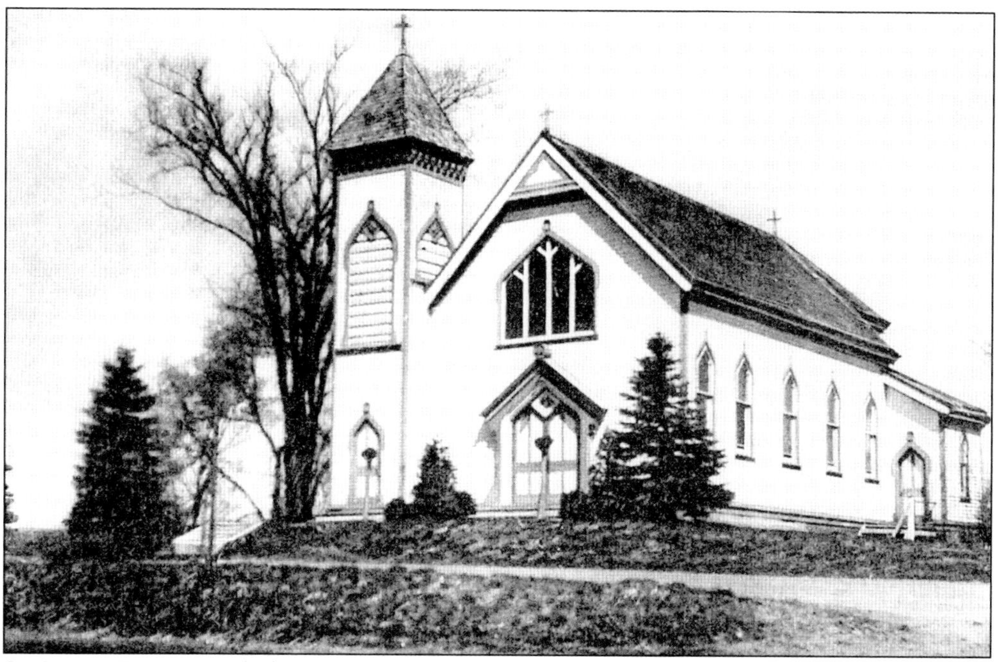

St. Peter's Roman Catholic Church was designed by Owen Brainerd, a local architect, and was erected on Saybrook Road in 1887. Its architectural style combines Carpenter Gothic and Islamic Revival elements. The church served communicants who had immigrated to Haddam to work in local factories. This photograph was taken from Cedar Hill.

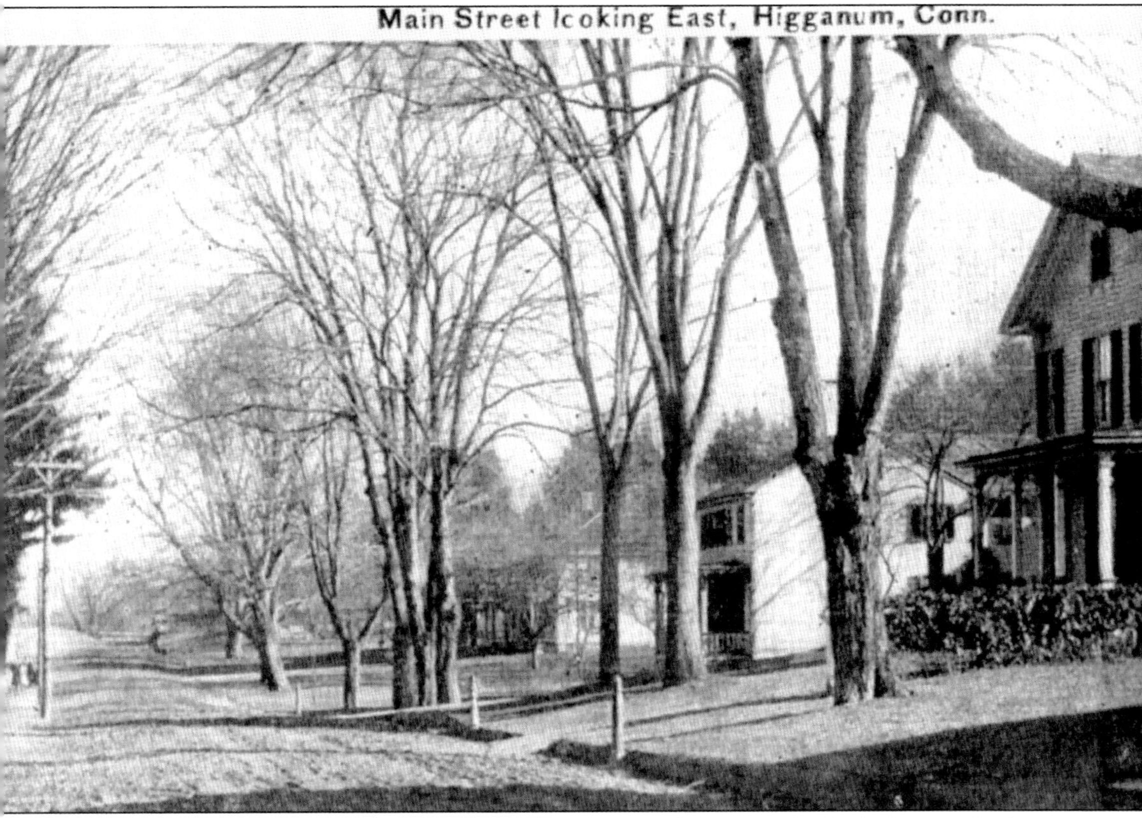

By 1910, when this scene was photographed, Main Street in Higganum had telephone poles but was still unpaved.

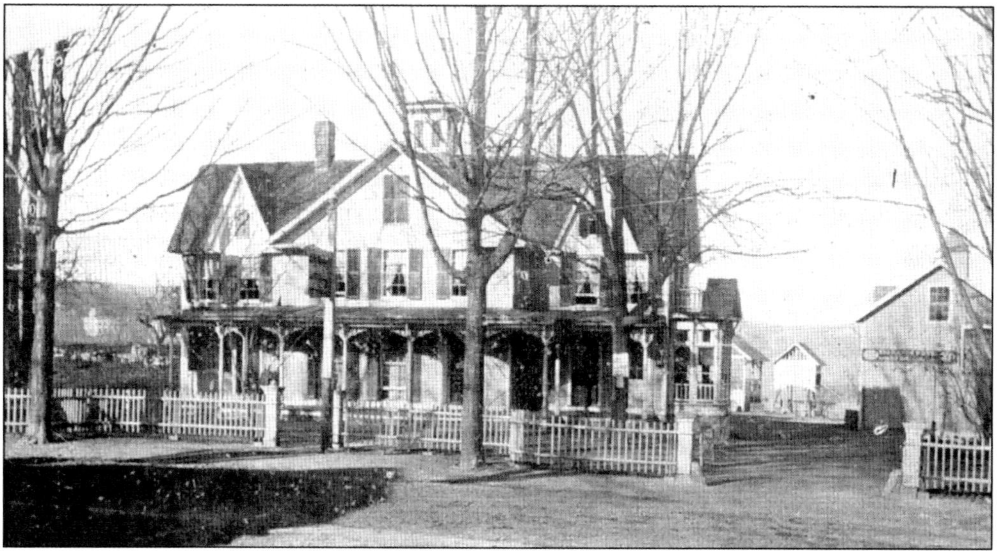

The Higganum Hotel was built in 1867 as the private residence of George L. Dickenson, a retired ship captain. The house was bought in 1875 by English immigrant Robert A. Brookes, who turned it into a hotel. It was a short walk from the steamboat landing and, after 1871, stood not far from the Higganum railroad station. The ell burned in the 1930s, ending the dwelling's career as a hotel. (Courtesy Brookes family.)

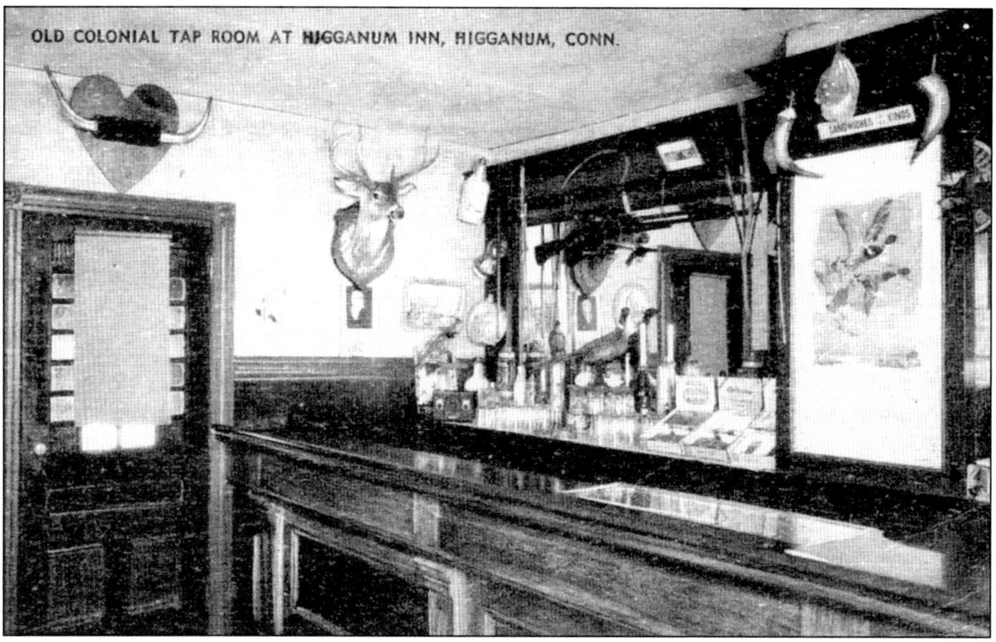

Between 1892 and 1919, the pre-eminent social controversy in Haddam concerned the granting of liquor licenses. The question appeared on the town meeting agenda almost every year, and the vote almost invariably alternated between those in favor and those opposed. The ratification of the 18th amendment to the Constitution in 1919, which prohibited the sale of liquor, ended the controversy, although Connecticut voted against the amendment.

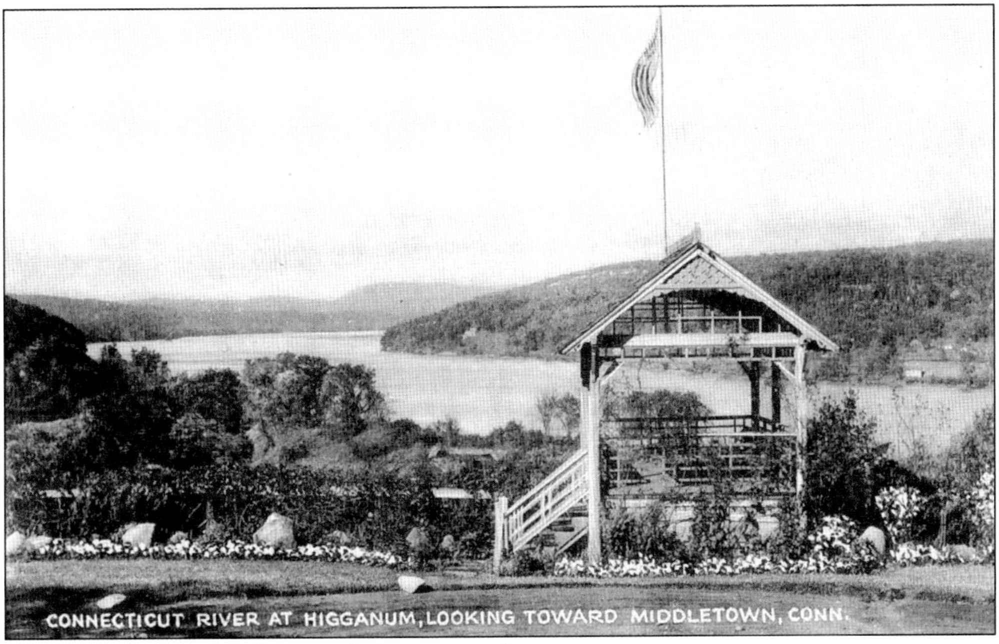

Behind the hotel, a gazebo provided a view up the river.

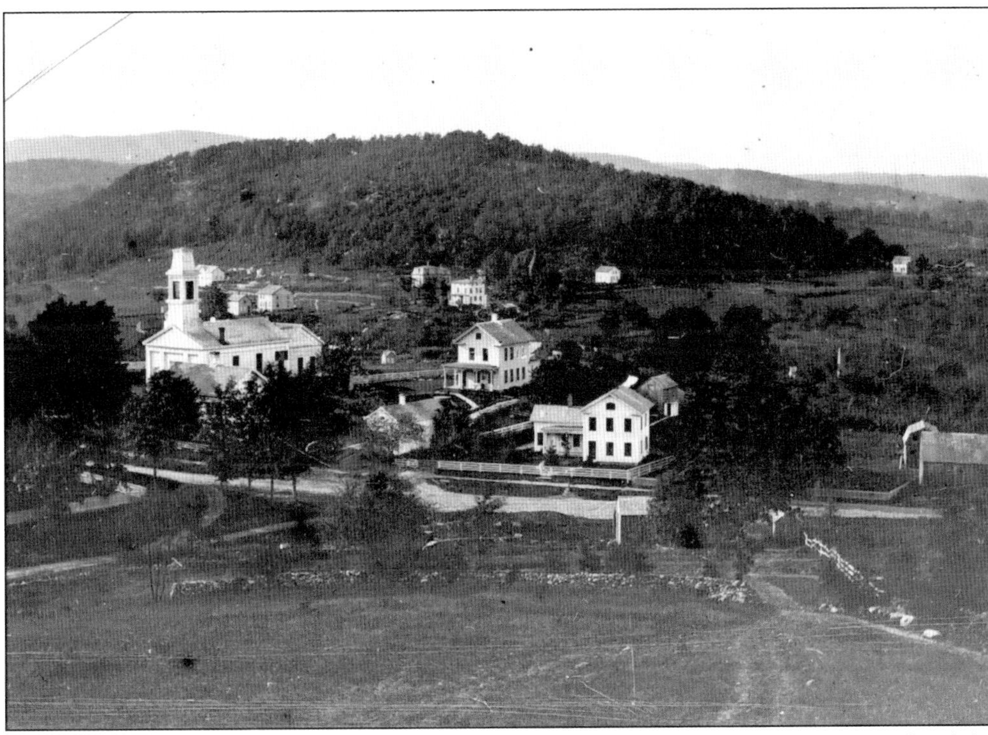

This 1877 photograph of Higganum shows the Congregational church in the foreground and the houses of Dublin Hill; Swan Hill is in the background. The Congregational church carries the distinction of having been struck by lightning twice. The building survived, but the steeple shown here is a replacement. (George Bradford Brainerd photograph, courtesy Brainerd Library.)

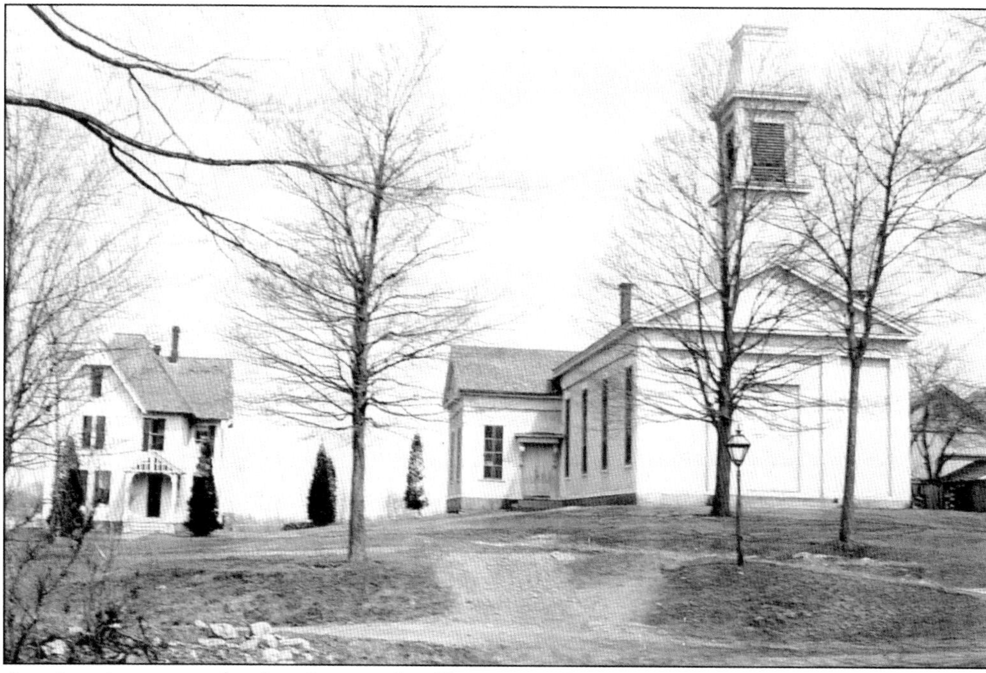

Another important landmark was the Higganum Congregational Church, built in 1845. Higganum residents petitioned for many years for their own meetinghouse. When they succeeded in 1844, 135 members left, taking the minister, David Dudley Field, with them. This was a watershed event in the history of the town. It gave Higganum its own identity and created a division between it and Haddam Center. The church parsonage is at the left.

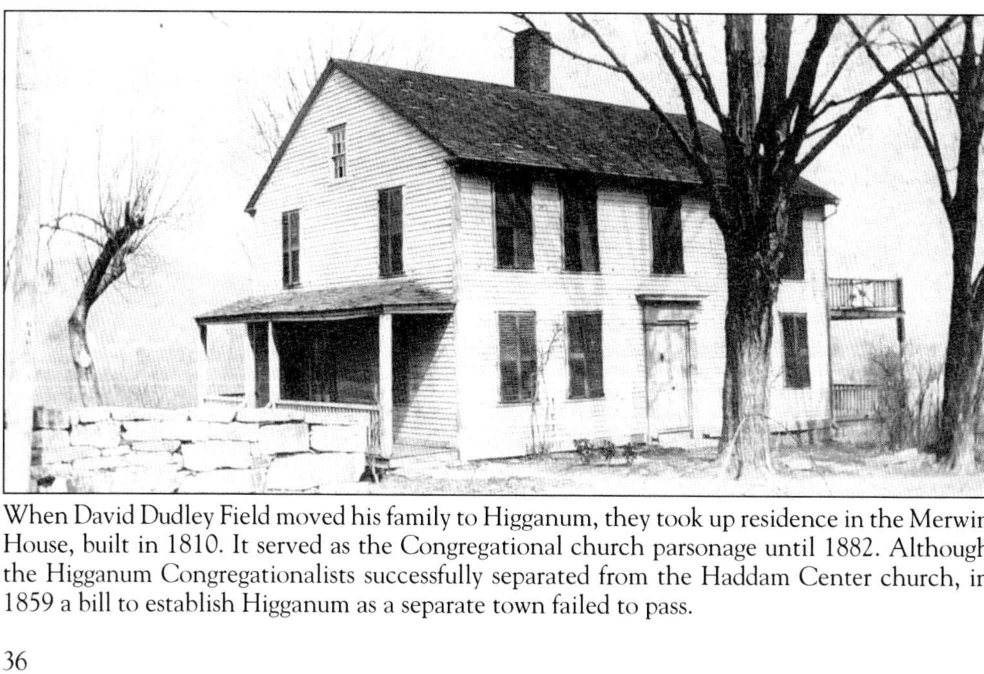

When David Dudley Field moved his family to Higganum, they took up residence in the Merwin House, built in 1810. It served as the Congregational church parsonage until 1882. Although the Higganum Congregationalists successfully separated from the Haddam Center church, in 1859 a bill to establish Higganum as a separate town failed to pass.

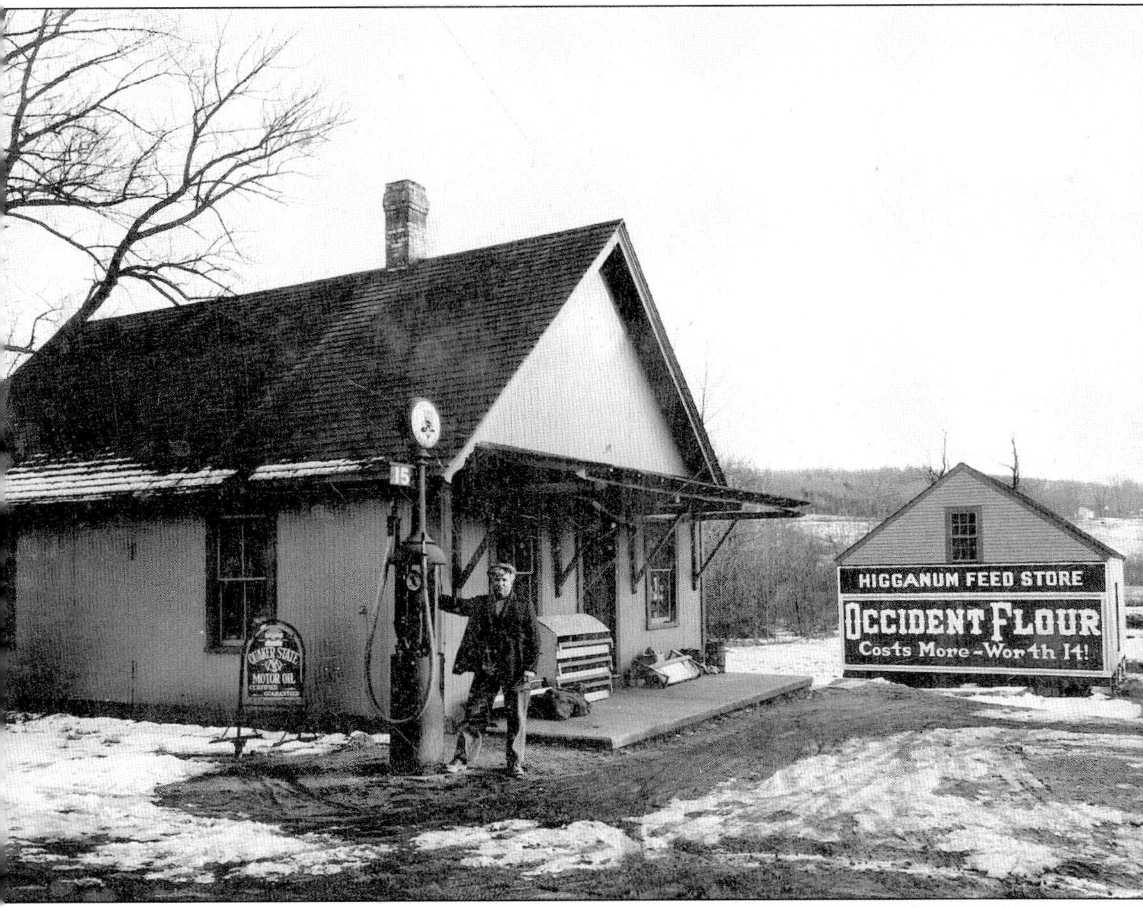

The Higganum gas station and feed store were both built sometime before 1888. Felix Petrofsky, shown here, was the owner from 1924 to 1945. Later, the gas station was closed and the building in the rear was torn down. The feed store is still in operation.

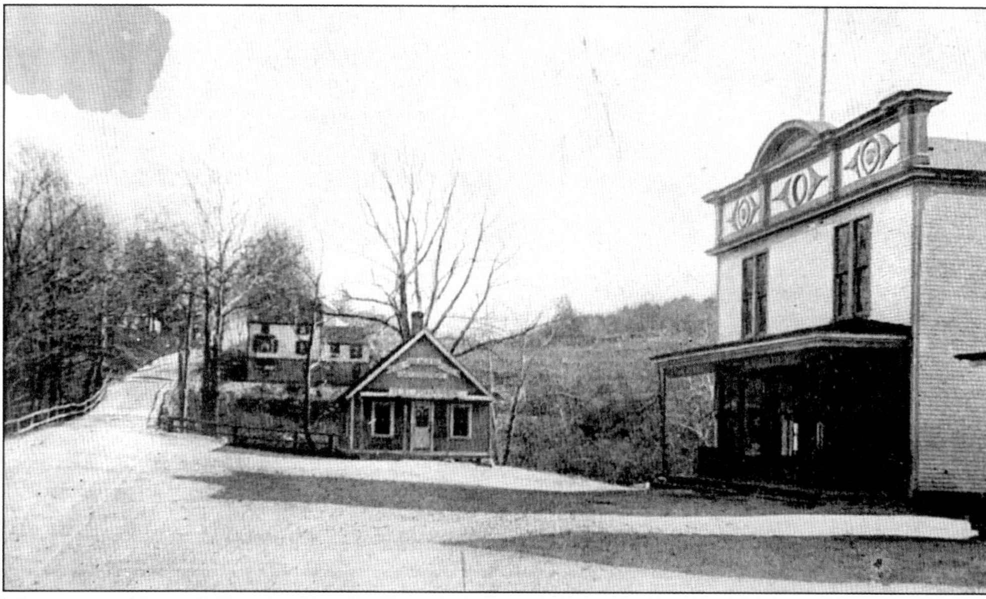

This view of Post Office Square, looking south, shows the Higganum Feed Store and Brainerd Hall. On the left, Saybrook Road extends up Big Hill. The road was lowered in 1929, when it was first paved.

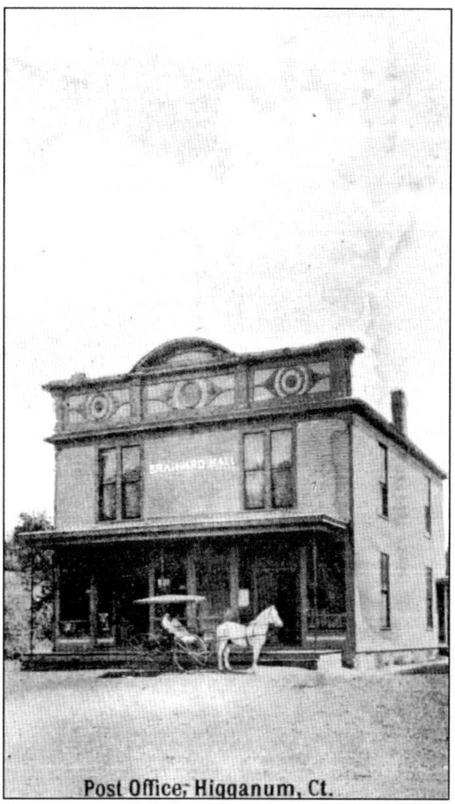

The first floor of this building housed the post office and a drugstore. Higganum Savings Bank, established by Cutaway Harrow to handle the company payroll, was on the second floor. Also on the second floor was a hall used for basketball games, high school graduations, and reunions, and, when the movies arrived, a cinema. Plays featuring local talent were produced here as well.

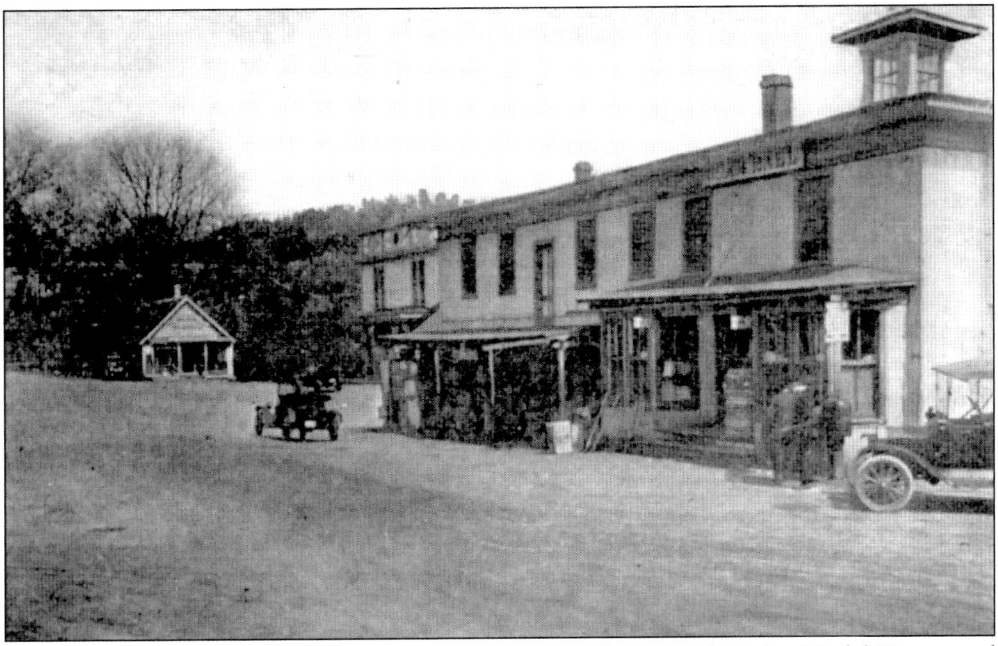

Early-20th-century Higganum was a bustling commercial center when this Model T traversed unpaved Middlesex Turnpike (today Saybrook Road). Parked outside Olsen's Store on the right is a 1915 Model T. The small building in the left background was then, as now, the Higganum Feed Store. Olsen's Store was torn down in the mid-1960s to make way for a bank and parking lot. (Courtesy Don Sampson.)

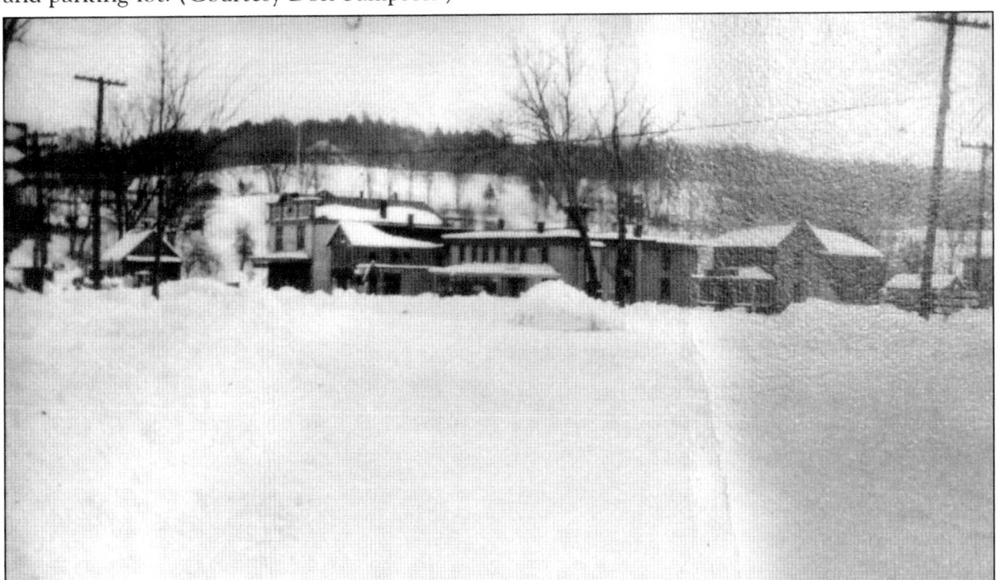

A snowfall appears to have discouraged traffic in this 1934 winter view of the same location seen in the previous image. Next to Brainerd Hall stands a dry goods store, which later became a package store and a small newsstand. Next to Olsen's Store is Walter Clark's Store, shown after it was moved to accommodate the widening of Saybrook Road. Behind it is the garage of a house that had burned down. (Courtesy Alan Webb.)

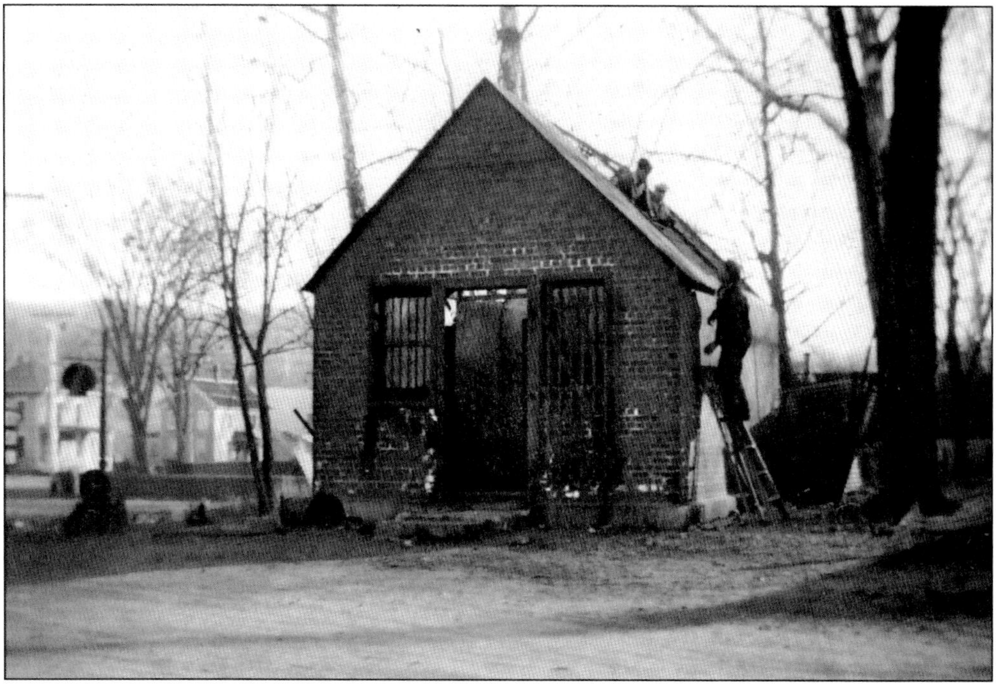

In 1907, the *Penny Press* described the new Higganum jail, located "east of the schoolhouse": "The lockup . . . is of brick, 15 by 18 with reinforced steel walls, metal roof and fireproof. It is fitted with two of the latest improved cells." In 1930, the town meeting voted to dismantle the jail after it had sat vacant for 12 years. The *Penny Press* stated, "Its removal is not any regret to residents." (Courtesy Alan Webb.)

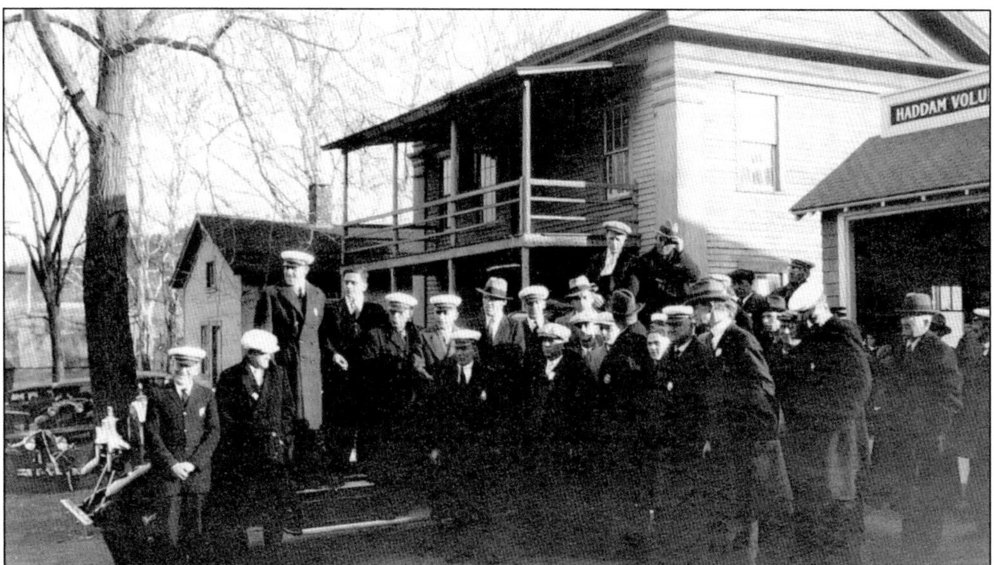

Firefighters pose in front of the old Higganum school in December 1930 at the dedication of Haddam's first firehouse. The school building was originally located on the green, near what became the site of the Higganum Union School in 1894.

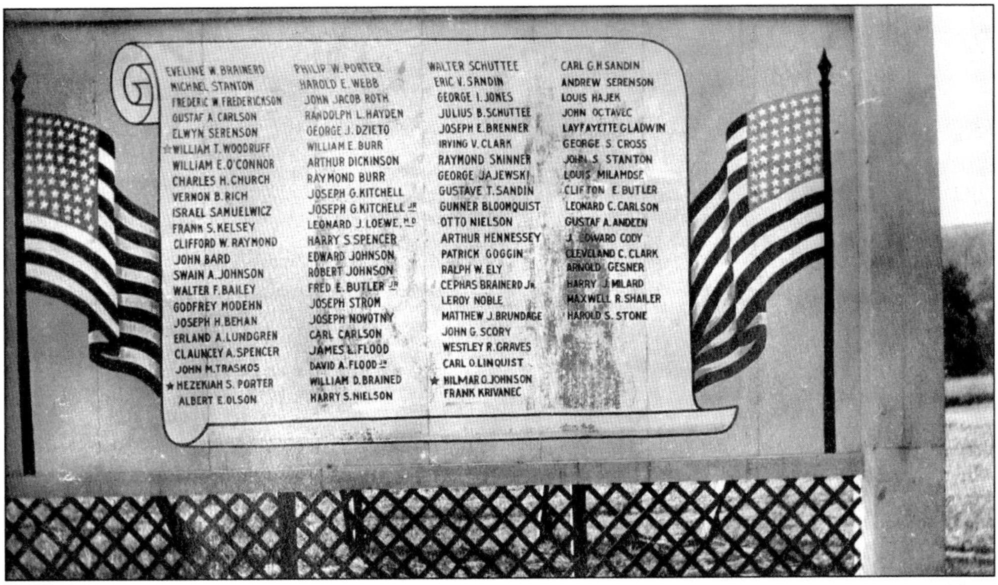

Eighty-three Haddam residents served in World War I; three died. During the war, Haddam organized the Town Council of Defence, later known as the War Bureau. Its major activities were to erect a billboard, shown here, listing those who served "to help make this world free and defend our interests in the present war," and to organize Welcome Home Days in 1919 for "the boys . . . who took part in the World War." (Courtesy Alan Webb.)

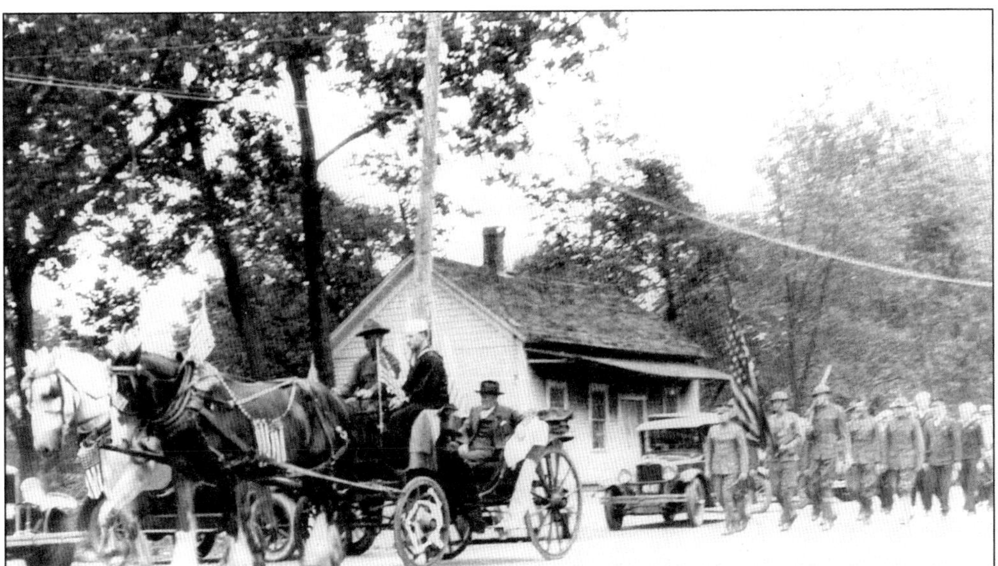

On Memorial Day 1930, World War I veterans, primarily marines and sailors, parade past Heger's Meat Market. In the front carriage, John Stanton and John Scory drive Civil War veteran Clayton "Grandpa" Hartman. Philip Porter, the only World War I pilot from town, leads the marchers, and Swain Johnson carries the flag.

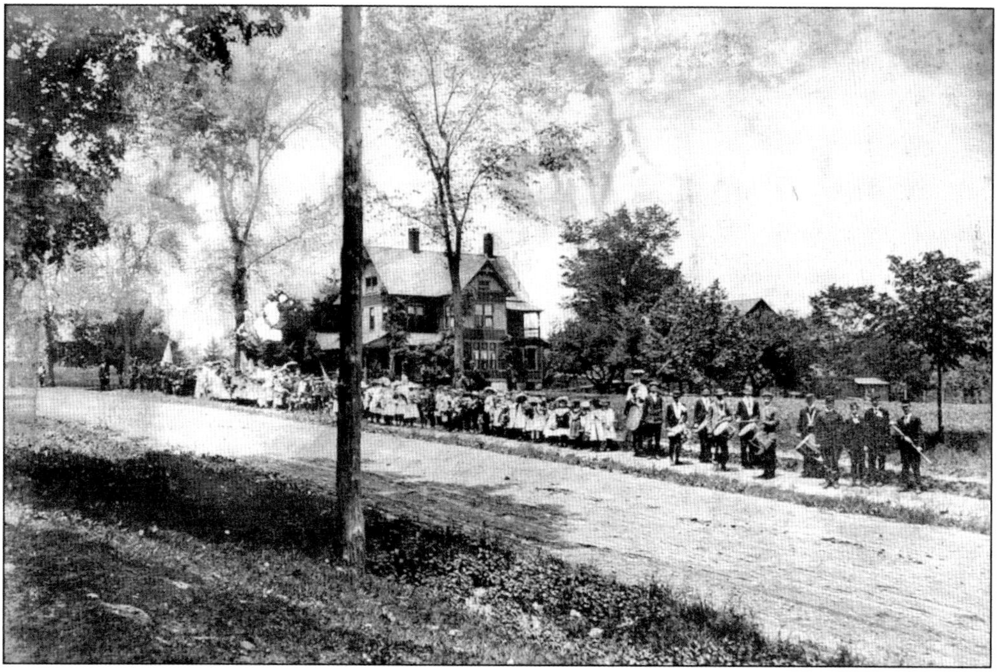

Schoolchildren, adults, and a fife and drum corps line up to honor veterans on Decoration Day, sometime in the late 19th century. In the background is Brainerd Farm, the present location of Haddam Elementary School.

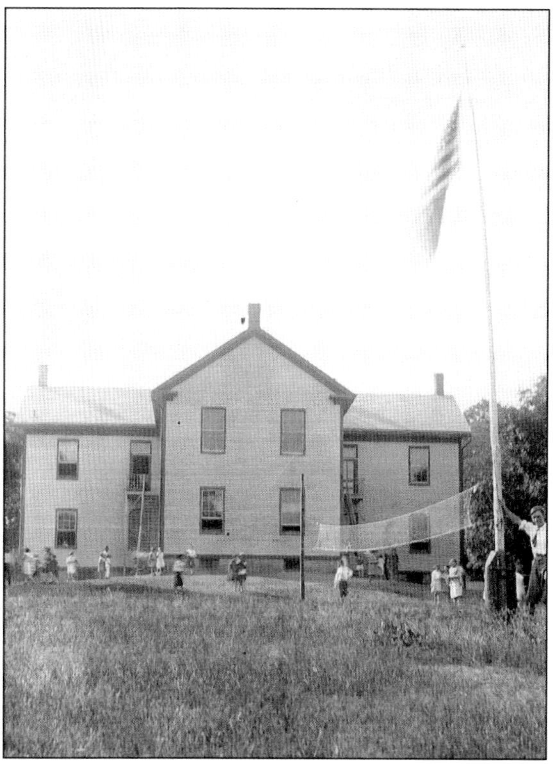

In 1894, the Higganum Union School replaced a four-room schoolhouse and several one-room schoolhouses at that end of town. All public one-room schools in Haddam were closed by the 1920s.

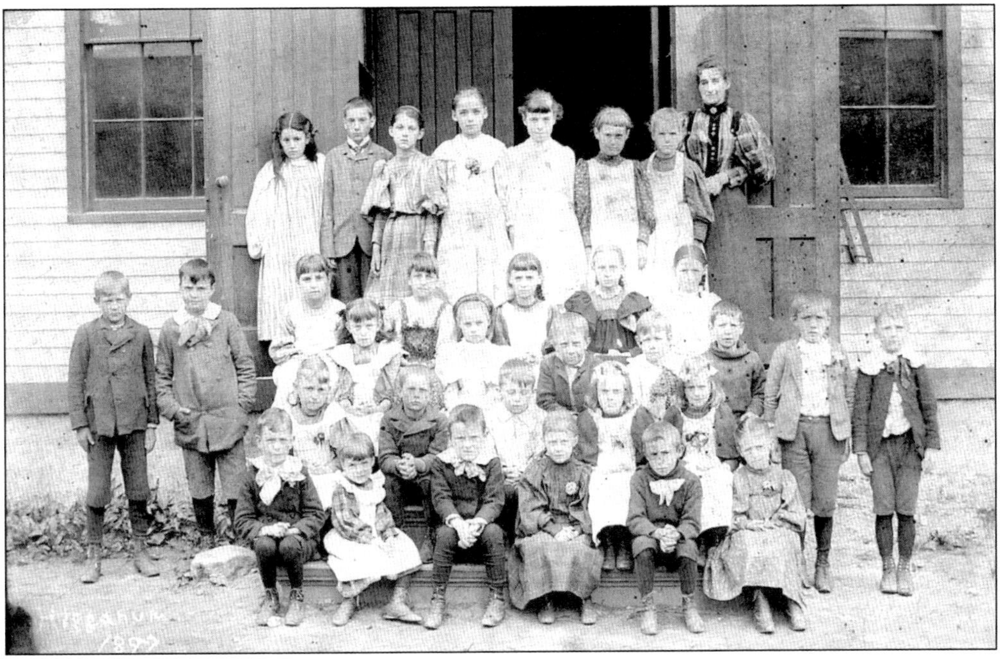

First- and second-grade students of Higganum Union School pose with their teacher in 1897.

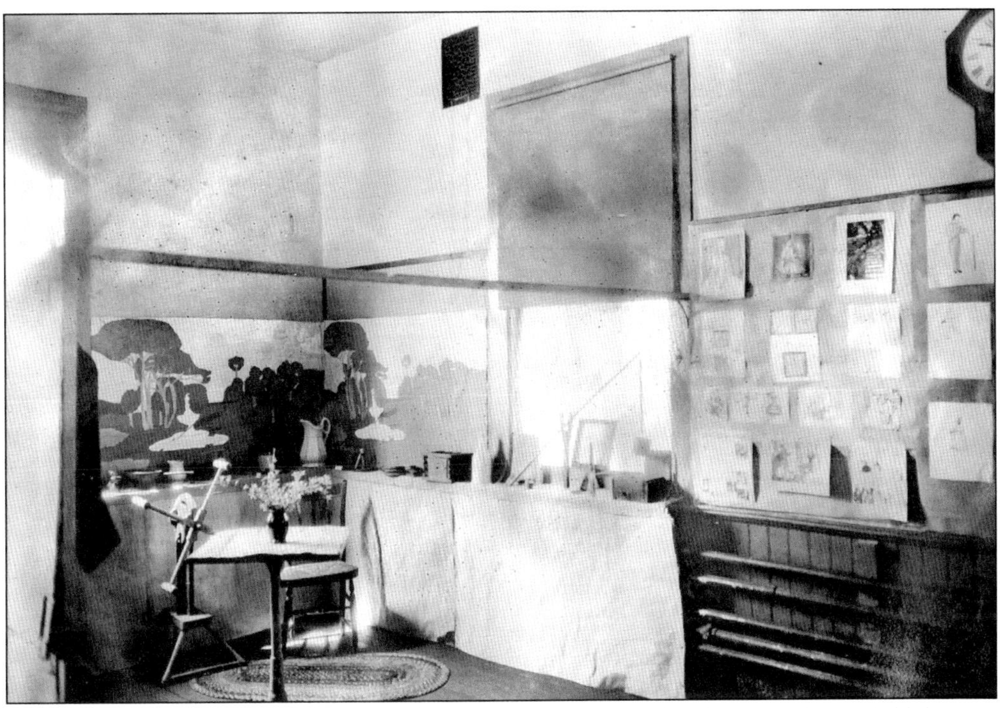

Room 4 of the Union School is shown here as it looked in 1931. (Courtesy Alan Webb.)

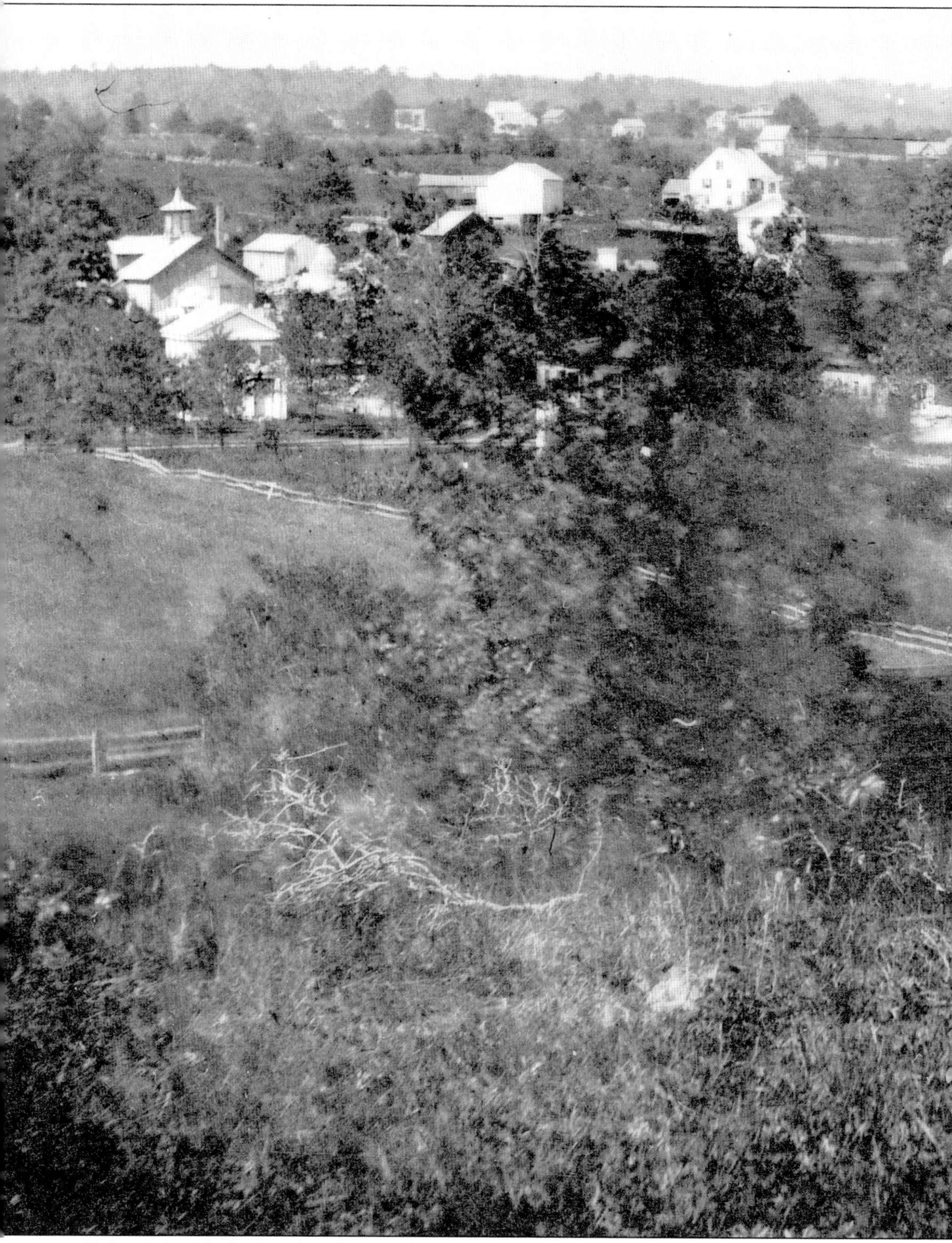

Behind the Methodist church, a path still leads to the summit of Swan Hill. Looking north toward Higganum from the top, this view shows the church in the background. The feldspar mill

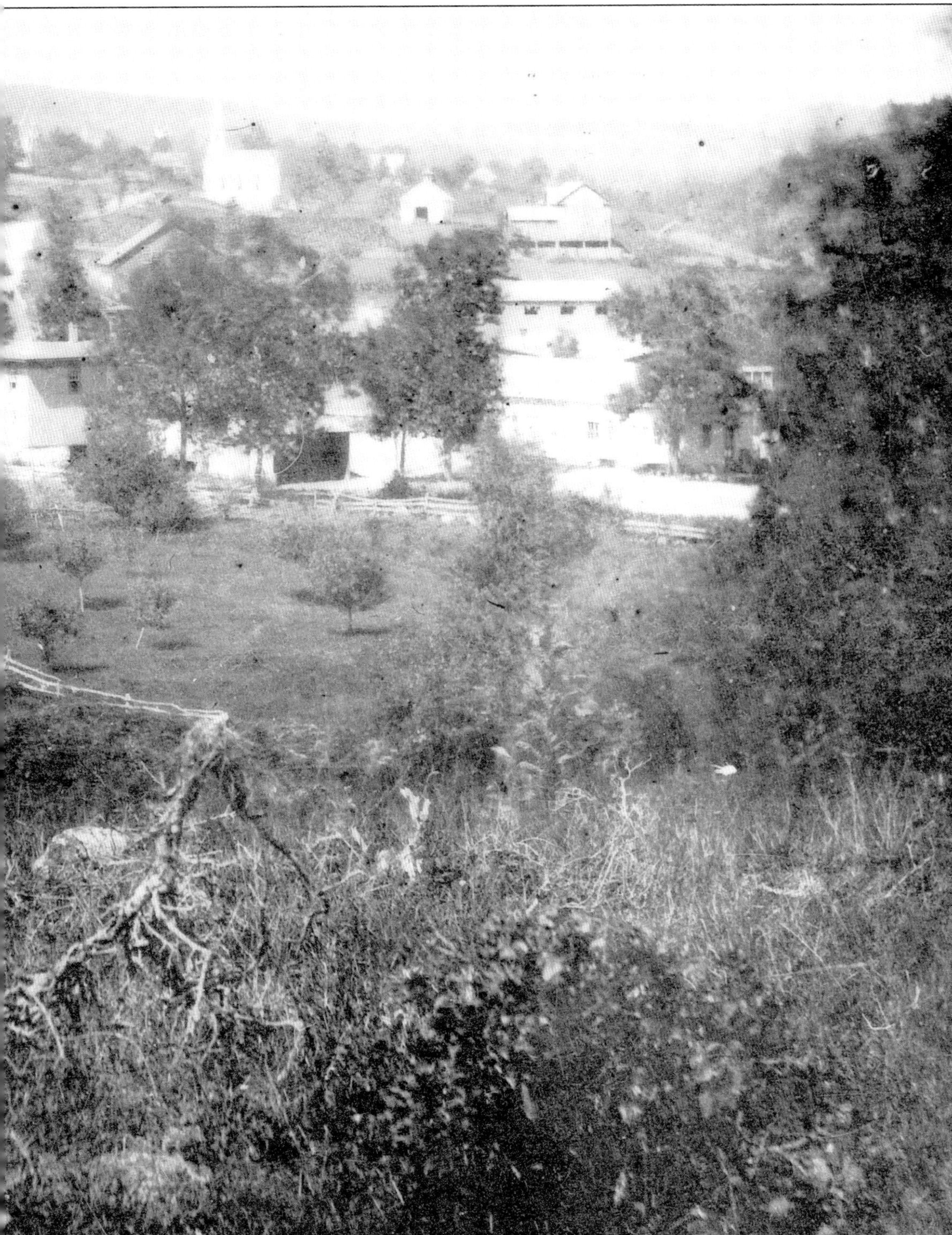

with cupola can be seen at the extreme left. (George Bradford Brainerd photograph, courtesy Brainerd Library.)

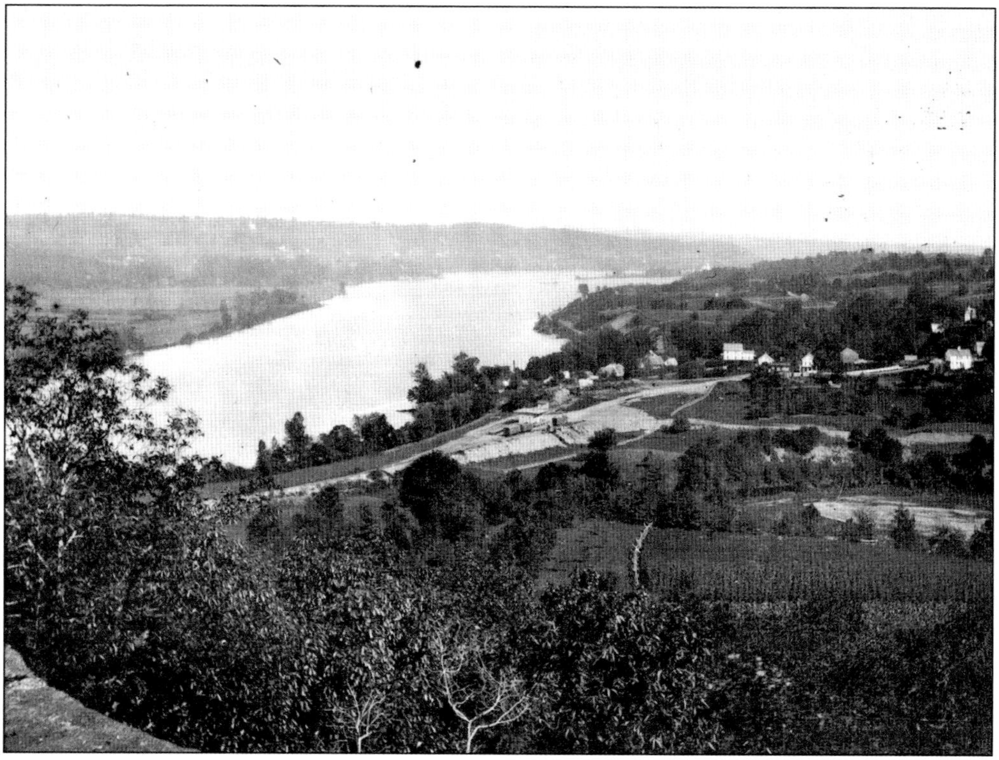

This 1877 view looks downriver. Railroad cars sit on the siding in front of the Higganum station. (George Bradford Brainerd photograph, courtesy Brainerd Library.)

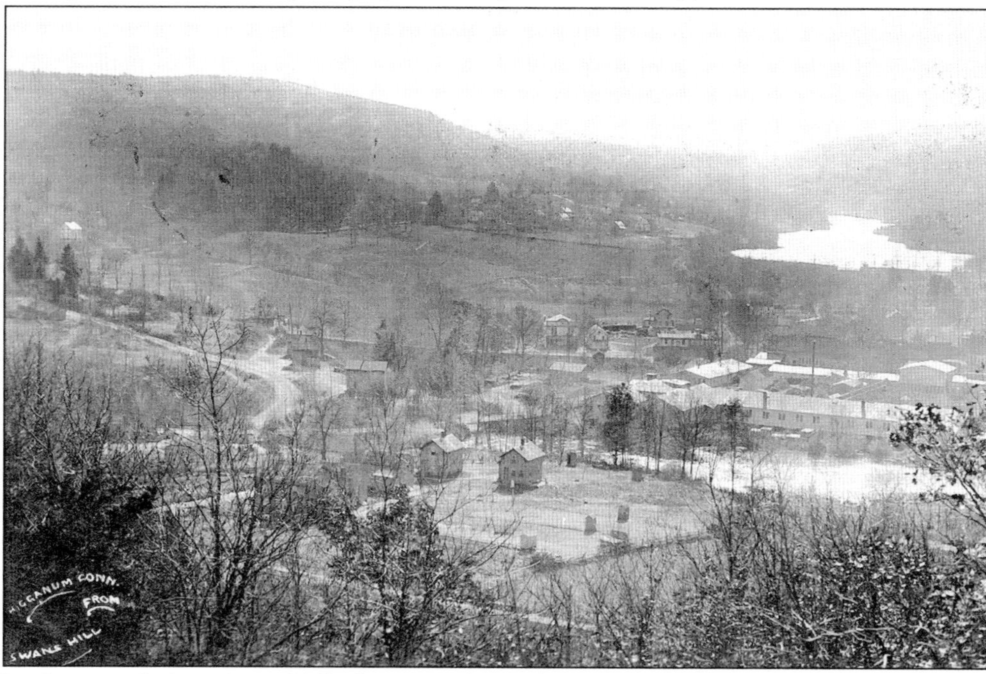

Looking south from Swan Hill, this view shows the reservoir for Higganum Manufacturing (later Clark Cutaway Harrow Company) in the background.

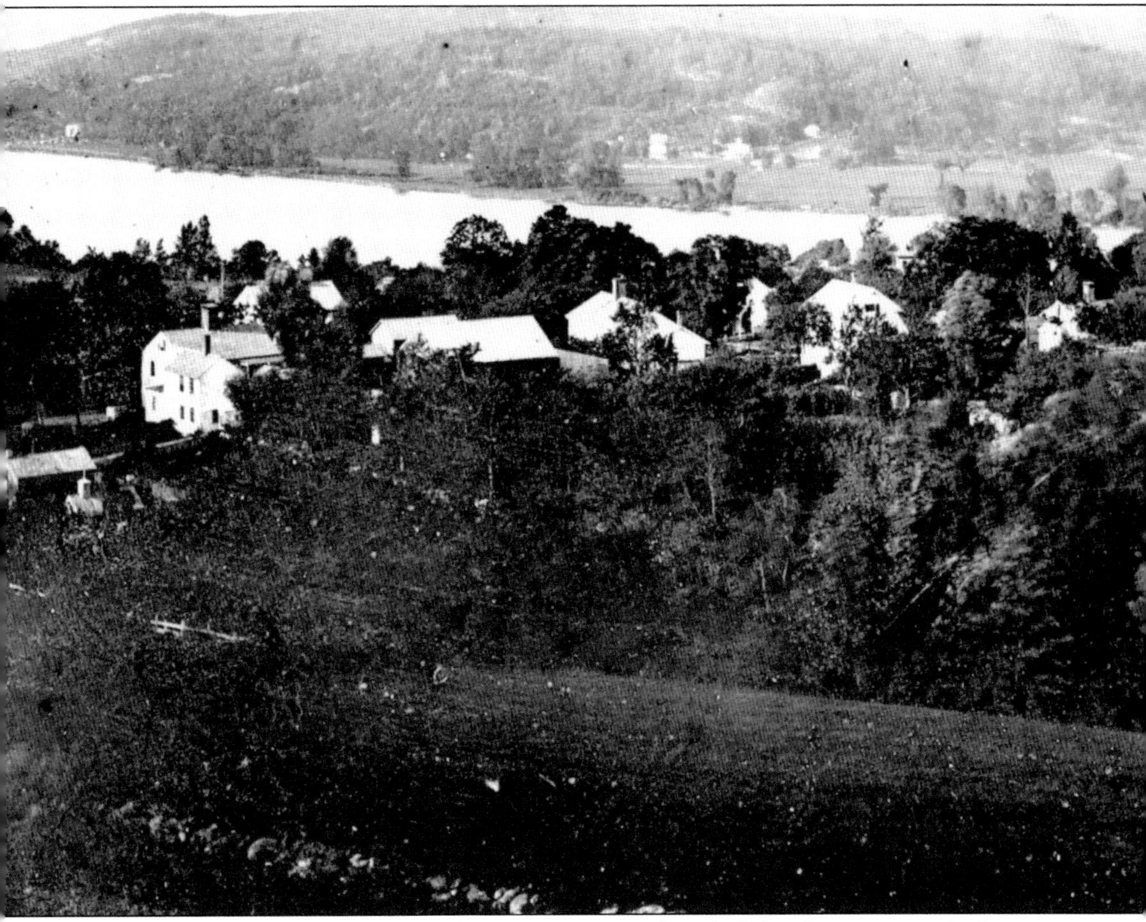

This view looks upriver from the same location in 1877. The Clark family mansion, which was later torn down, can be seen across the river in the background. (George Bradford Brainerd photograph, courtesy Brainerd Library.)

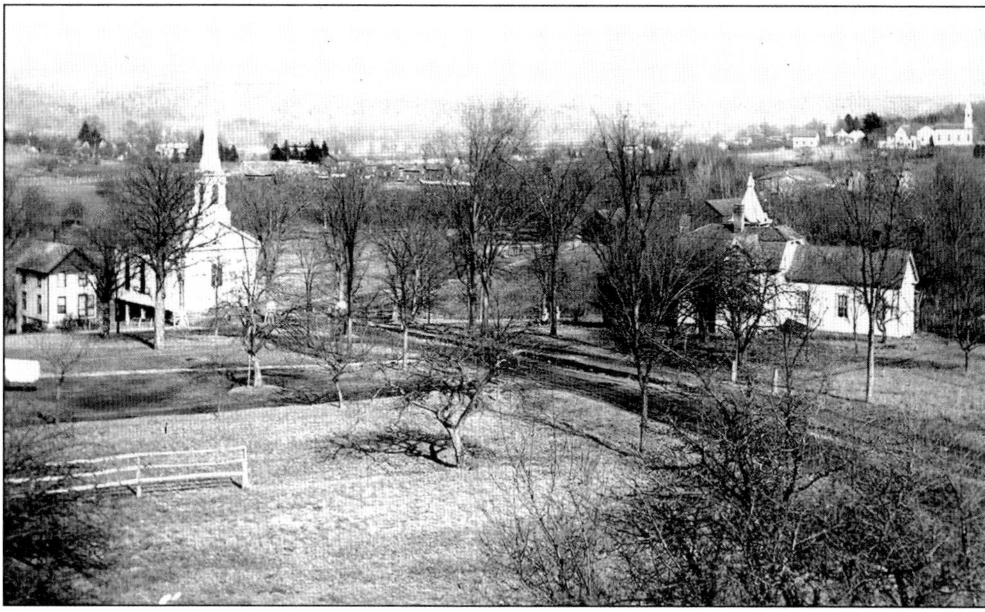

This view of Higganum, looking east from Christian Hill, shows the Methodist church at the left. The Methodist congregation was established in 1850. Factory housing can be seen in the background, and the Congregational church is at the upper right.

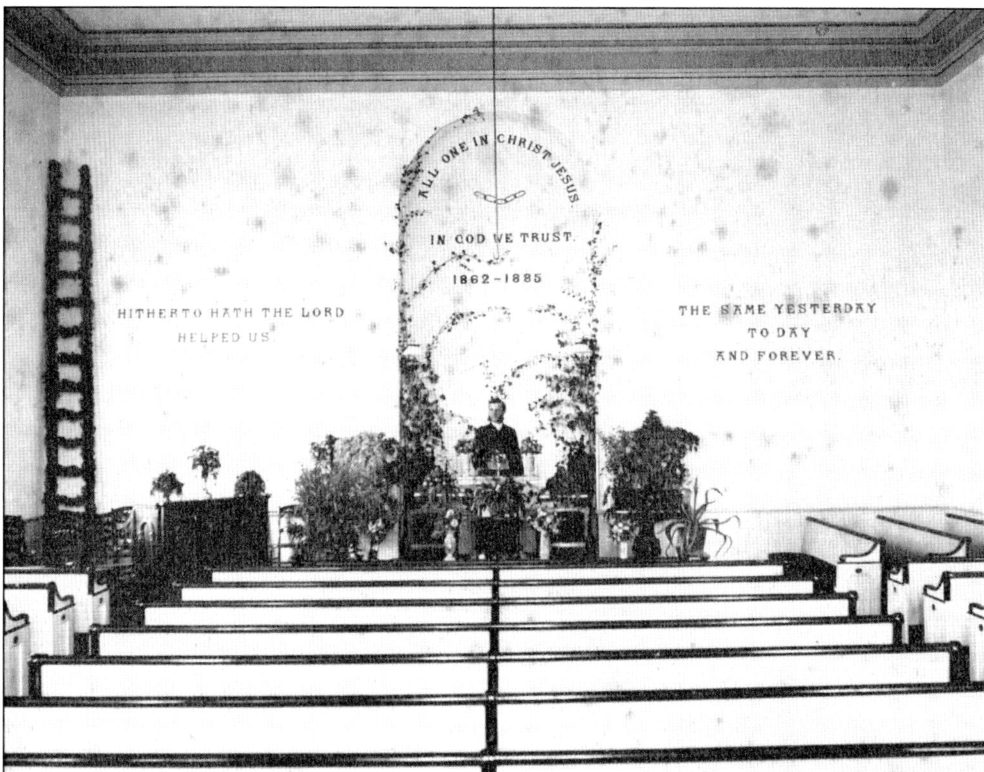

A look inside the Methodist church in 1885 reveals a plain interior and the Reverend C. W. Talmage, who was the minister from 1883 to 1887. (Courtesy Higganum United Methodist Church.)

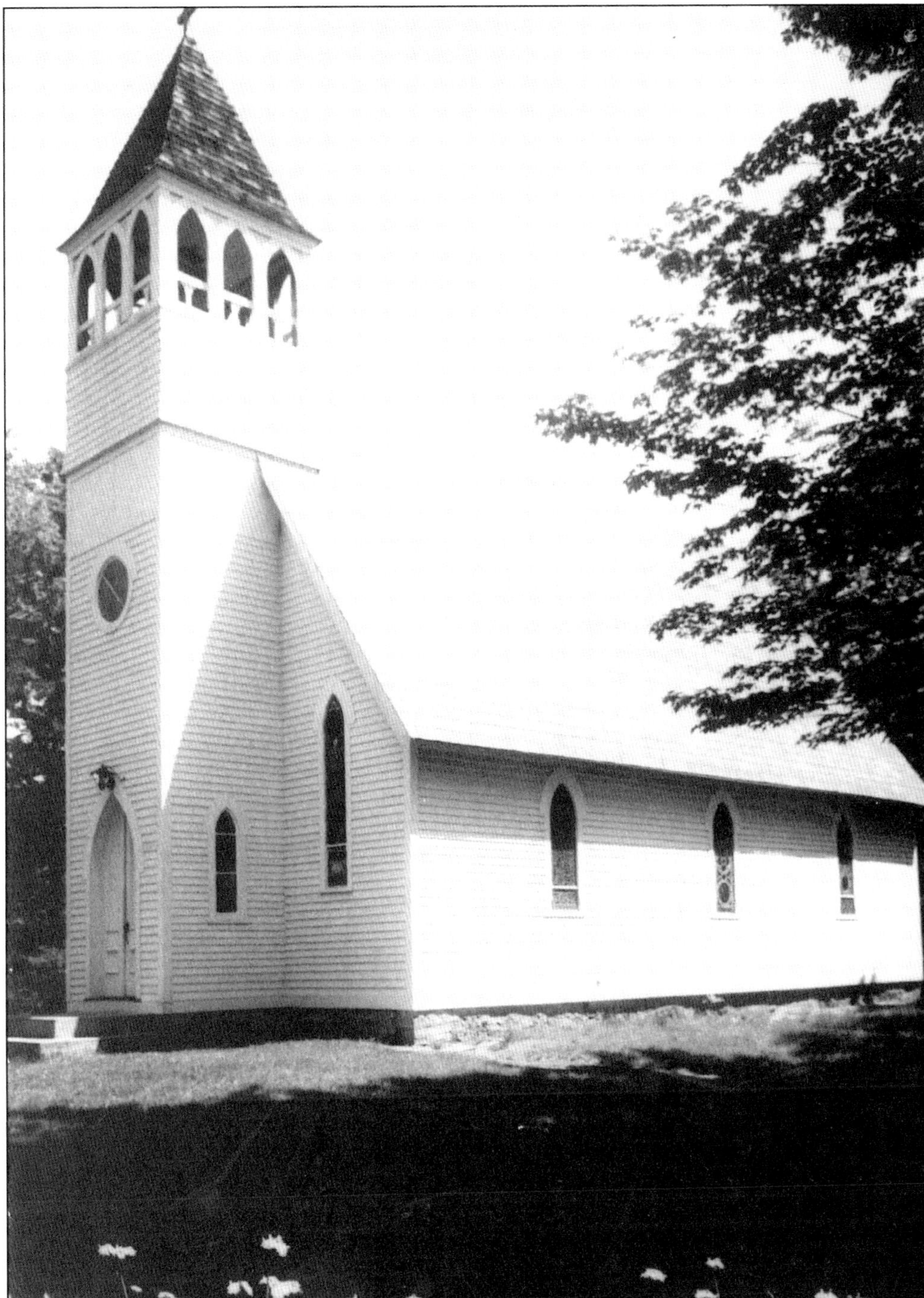

The original St. James Church stood on Saybrook Road in Higganum. Around 1850 the congregation moved to Killingworth Road in the Ponsett section, where the building shown here was constructed. In 1844, soon after the congregation was organized, the Episcopalians held the first Christmas celebration in Haddam. Other New England Protestant churches did not celebrate this holiday until after the Civil War.

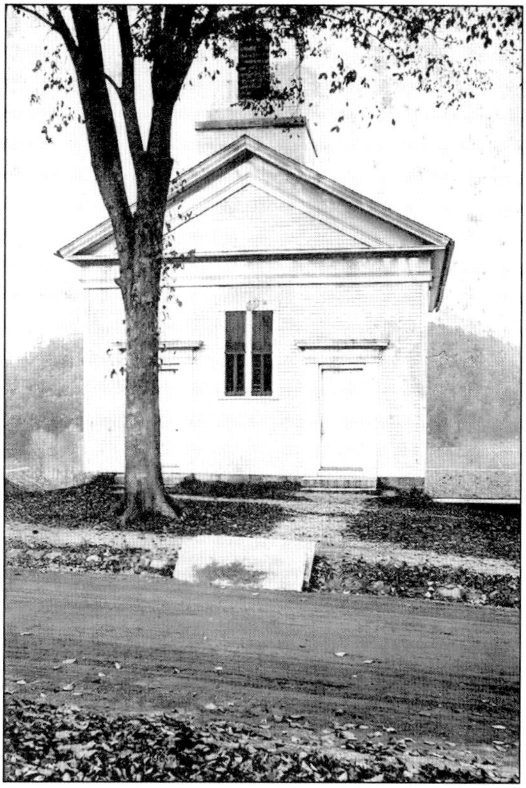

The following four photographs show views of the intersection of Christian Hill Road and Saybrook Road, looking south, north, west, and east before the road was paved in 1928. Note the same granite pavers in each photograph. This view, to the east, includes the Methodist church. In 1928 the Young People's Society raised $365 to replace the double windows with a stained-glass window showing the "Good Shepherd."

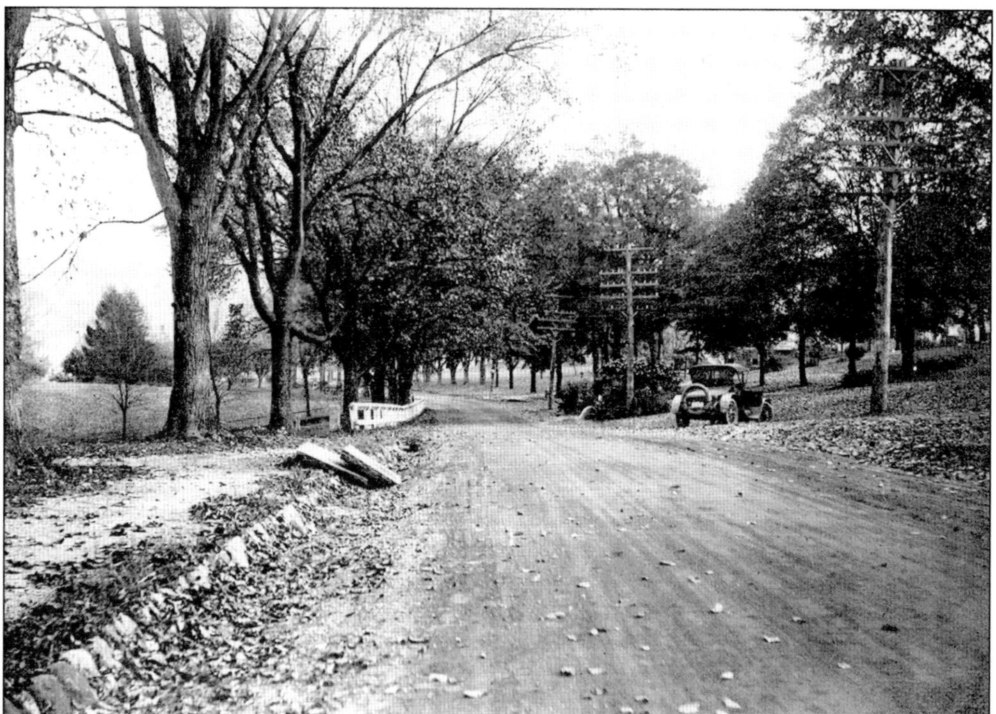

The photograph, looking south, shows an early automobile.

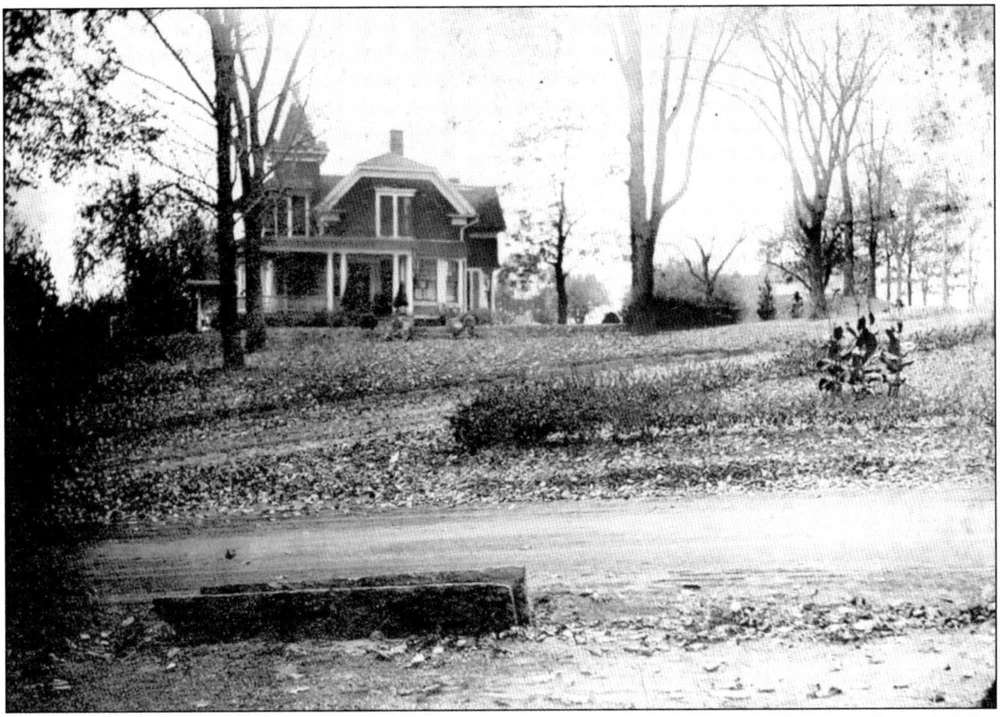

This view looks west toward the Jesse Smith House, built in the Queen Anne style in 1875.

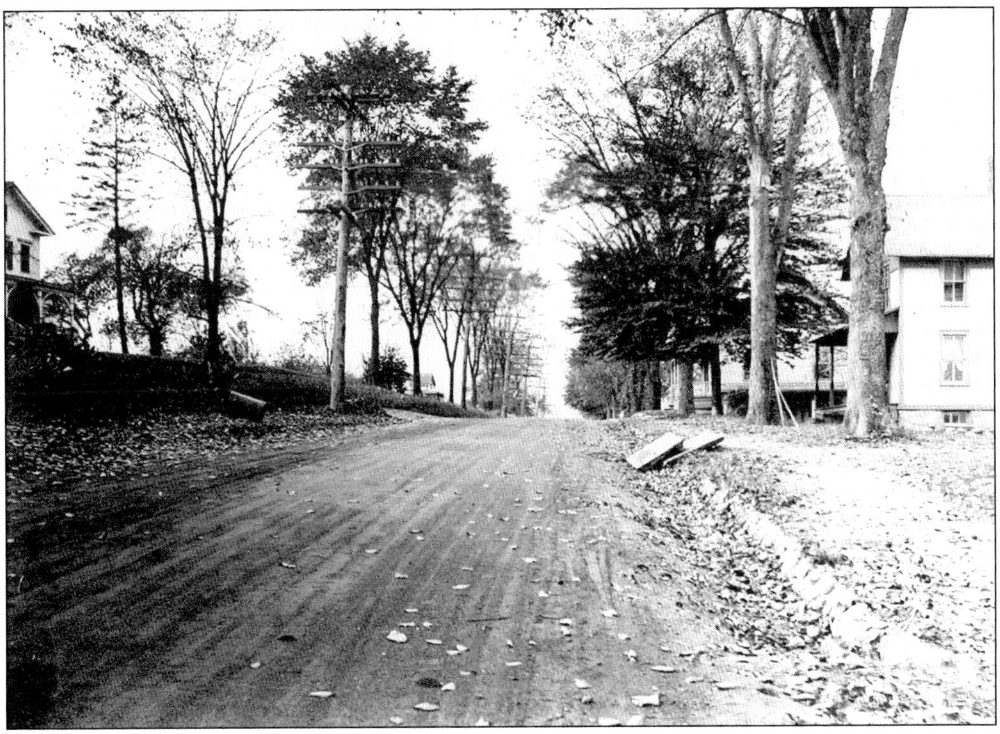

This photograph looks north up Saybrook Road, away from Higganum.

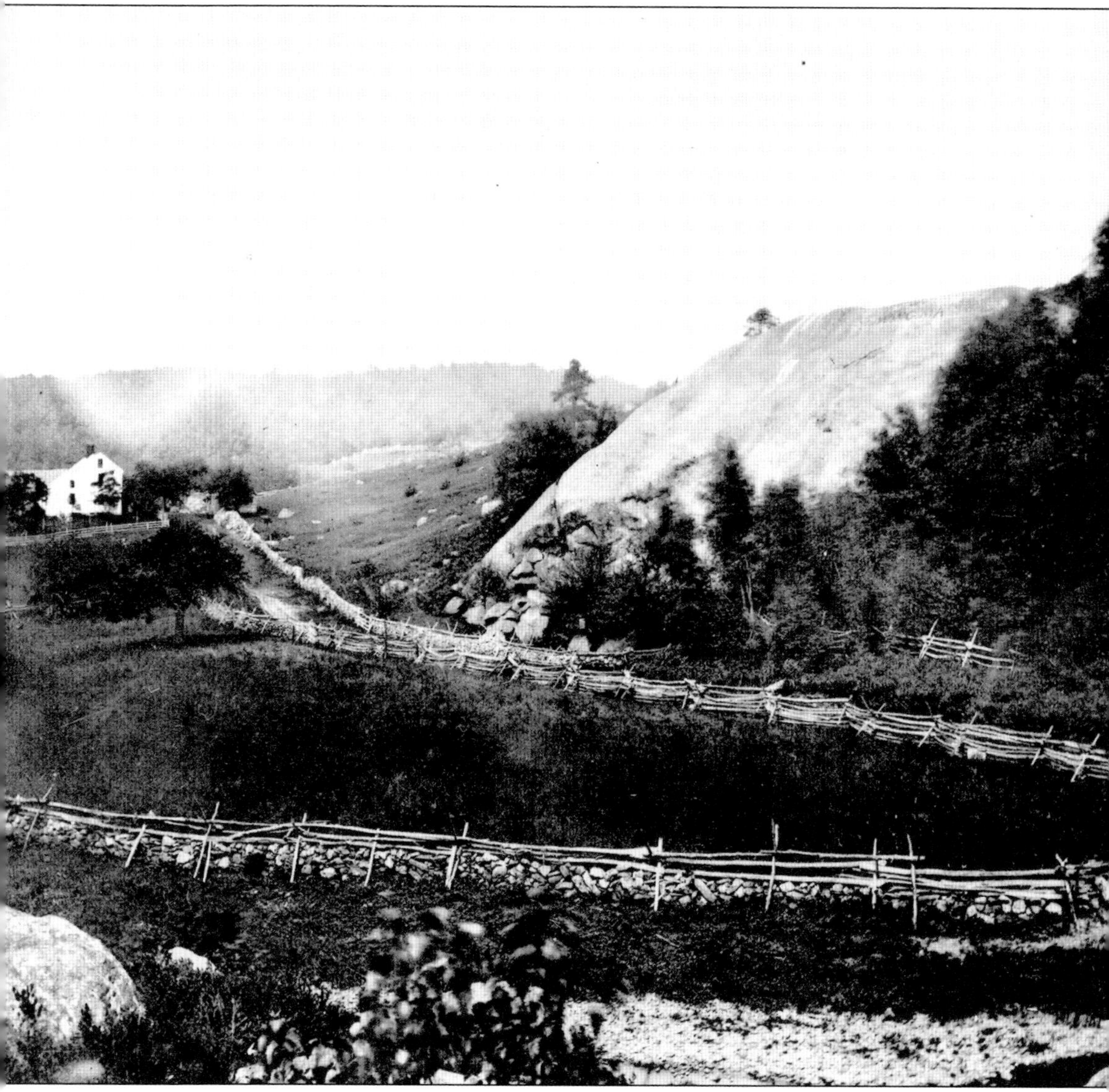

Travelers might have spent a few minutes contemplating Shopboard Rock, also called Devil's Slide, when this photograph was taken in 1877. The exposed portion measures 65 feet high and 75 feet wide, making it possibly the largest glacial erratic in New England. The story of the tailor who used the rock as a cutting board is probably apocryphal. The 1759 Preston Arnold House stands in the background. (George Bradford Brainerd photograph, courtesy Brainerd Library.)

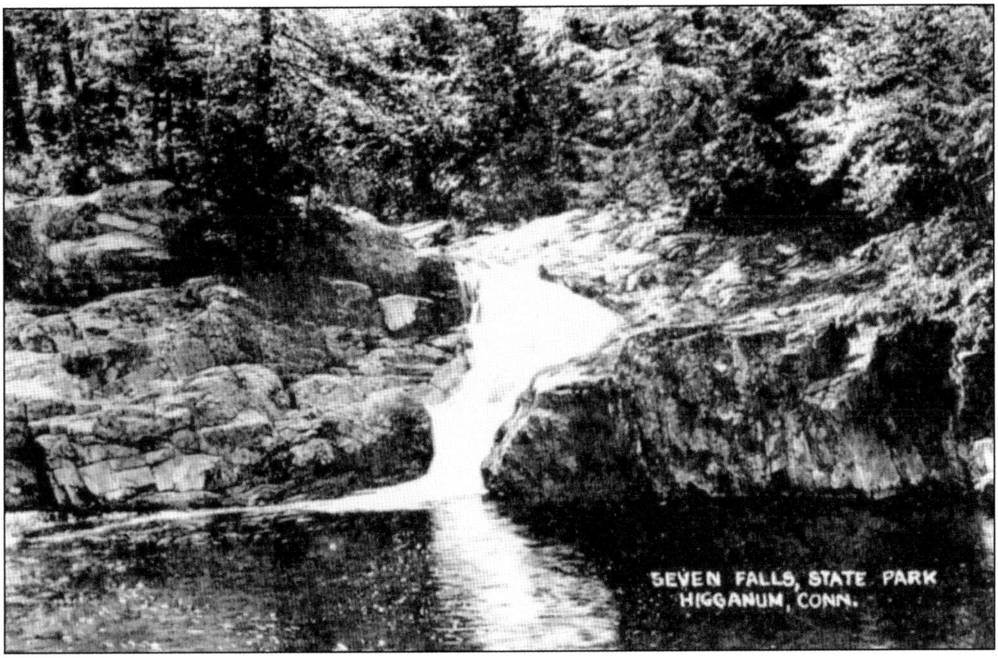

Seven Falls was established sometime prior to 1928 as the first Connecticut roadside park. Sunday drives were popular about this time, after the price of automobiles became within the reach of the middle class.

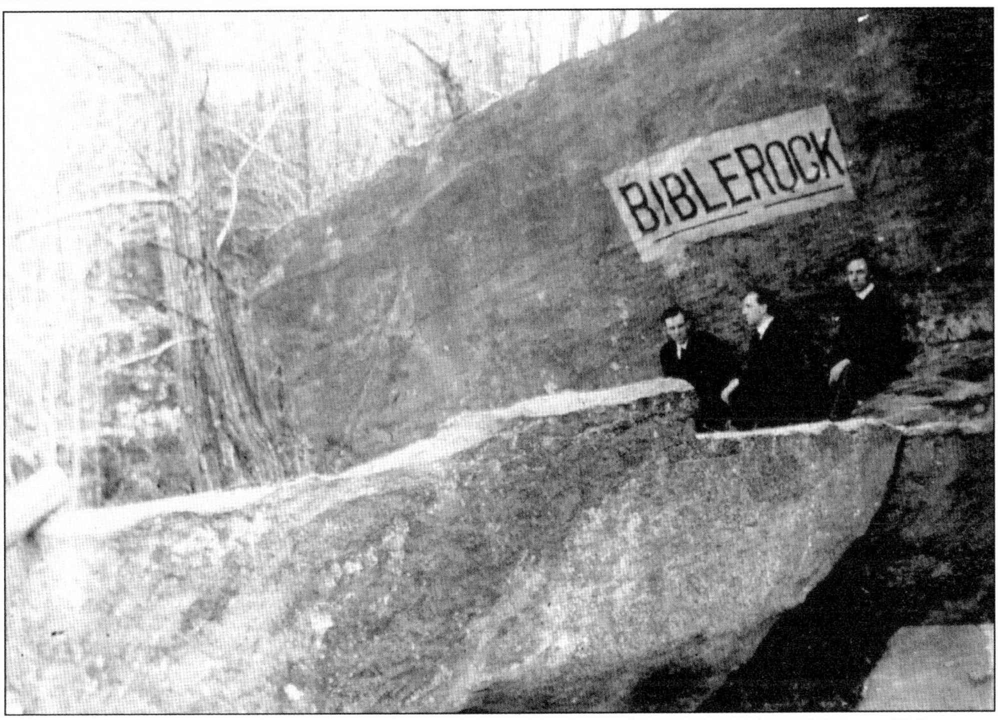

George Bradford Neuman (left), Ernest Frederick Neuman (center), and Carl Samuel Neuman pose about 1906 at the center of Bible Rock, so called because its split shape suggested the pages of an open book.

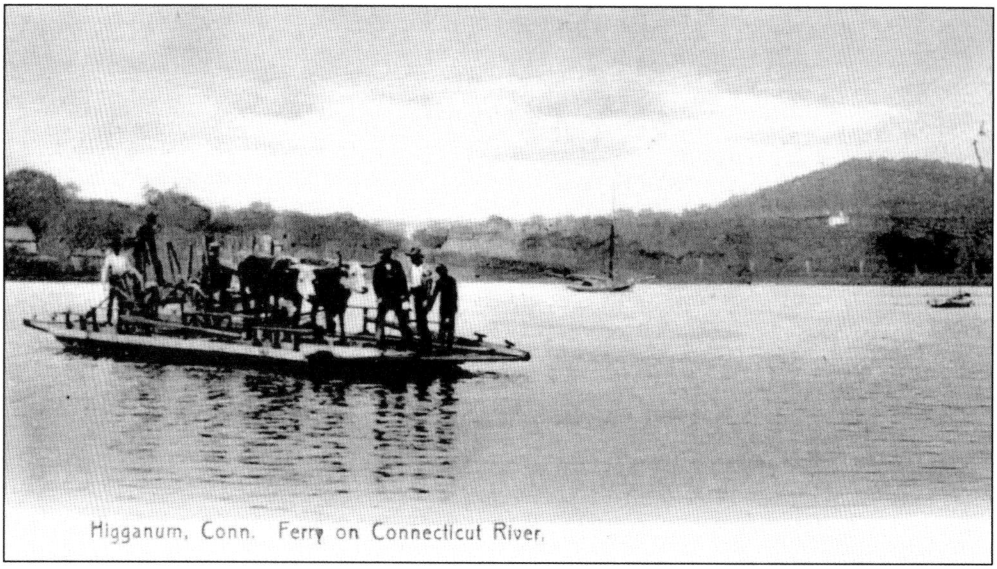

Until the early 20th century, ferries provided transportation across the Connecticut River at five different locations. In this 1907 photograph, an oxcart makes the trip from Higganum to Haddam Neck.

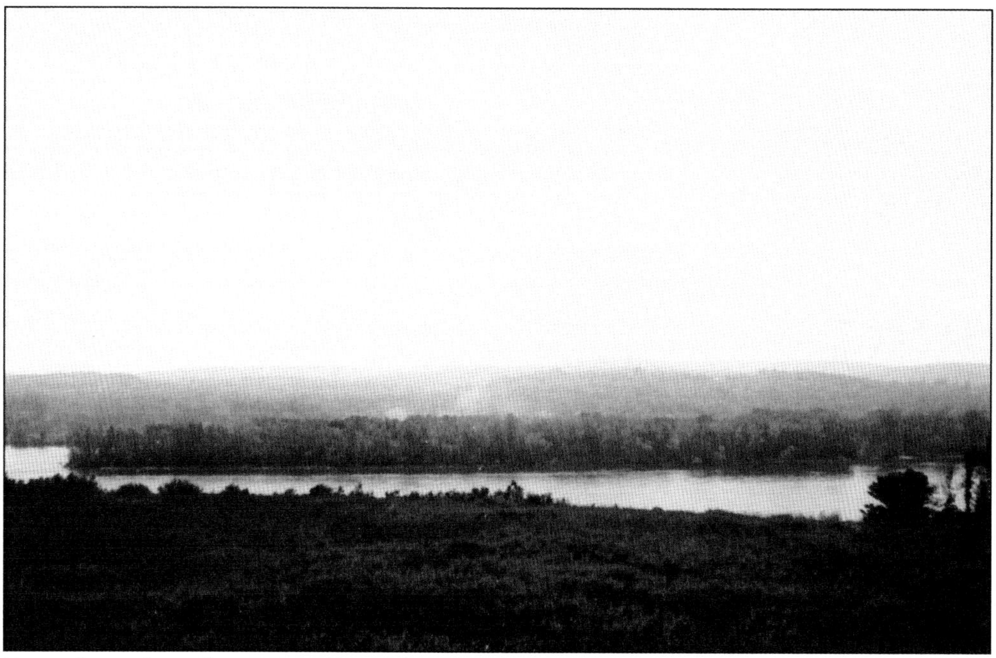

From the earliest days of Haddam's founding, the Connecticut River was the outstanding geographical feature of the town. From its origins in the Connecticut Lakes of northern New Hampshire, the river descends along the Vermont/New Hampshire border, through Massachusetts and Connecticut, to end at Long Island Sound. The river's level rises and falls according to the tides as far as Windsor Locks, located 65 miles upstream, hence the origin of its Algonkian name, "long tidal river."

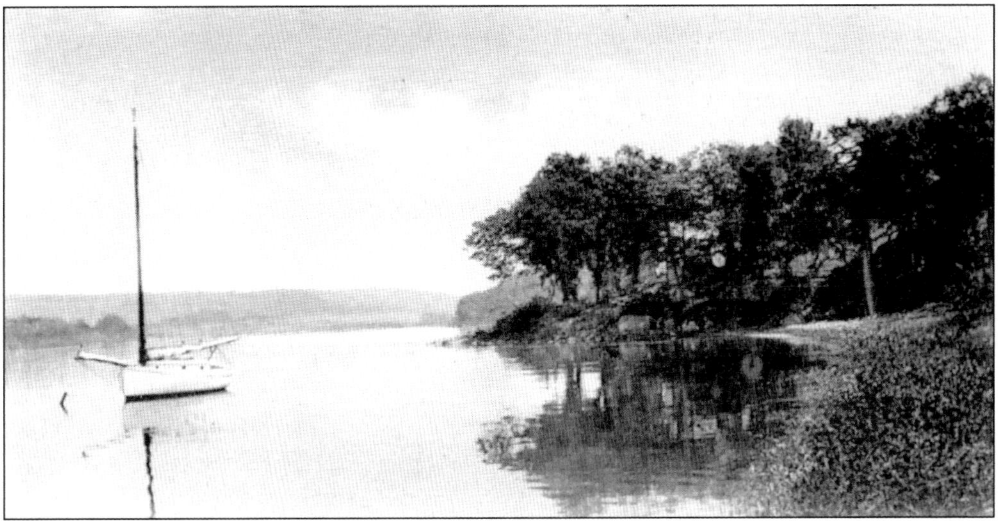

For the people of Haddam, the Connecticut River has always been an economic resource, a means of transportation, and a place for relaxation. This photograph of Higganum Cove was taken about 1907.

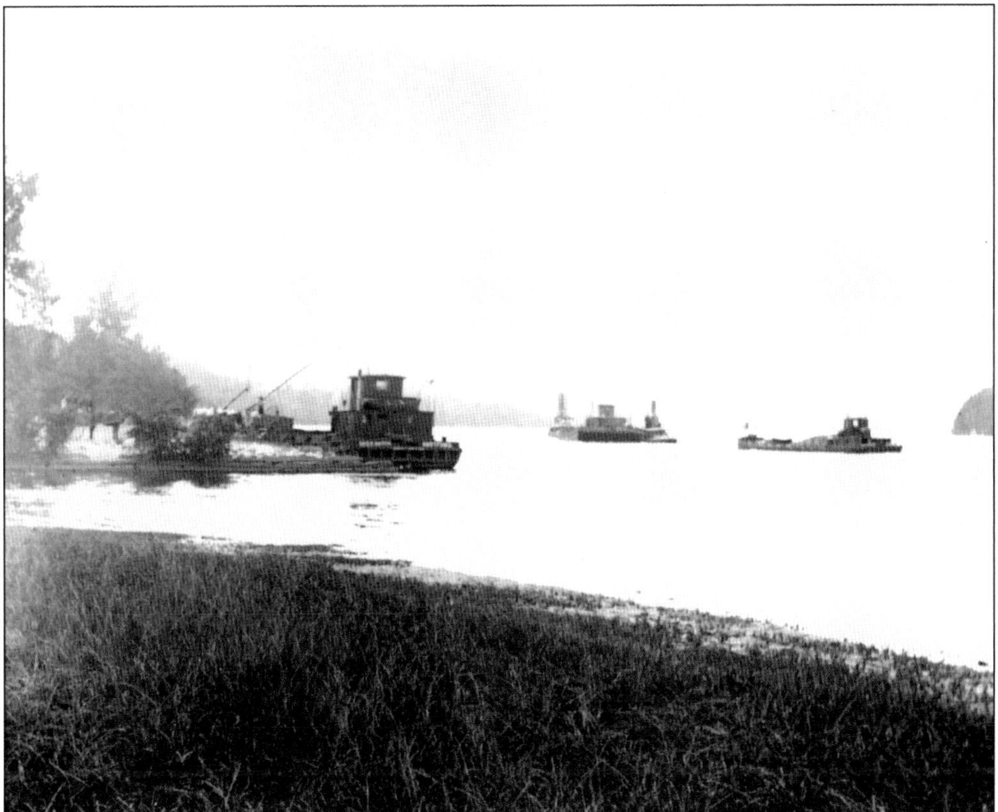

Horse carts line up to meet barges at the Scovil dock in this *c.* 1903 photograph. Coal for the Higganum factories was an important product off-loaded here. (Charles Church photograph.)

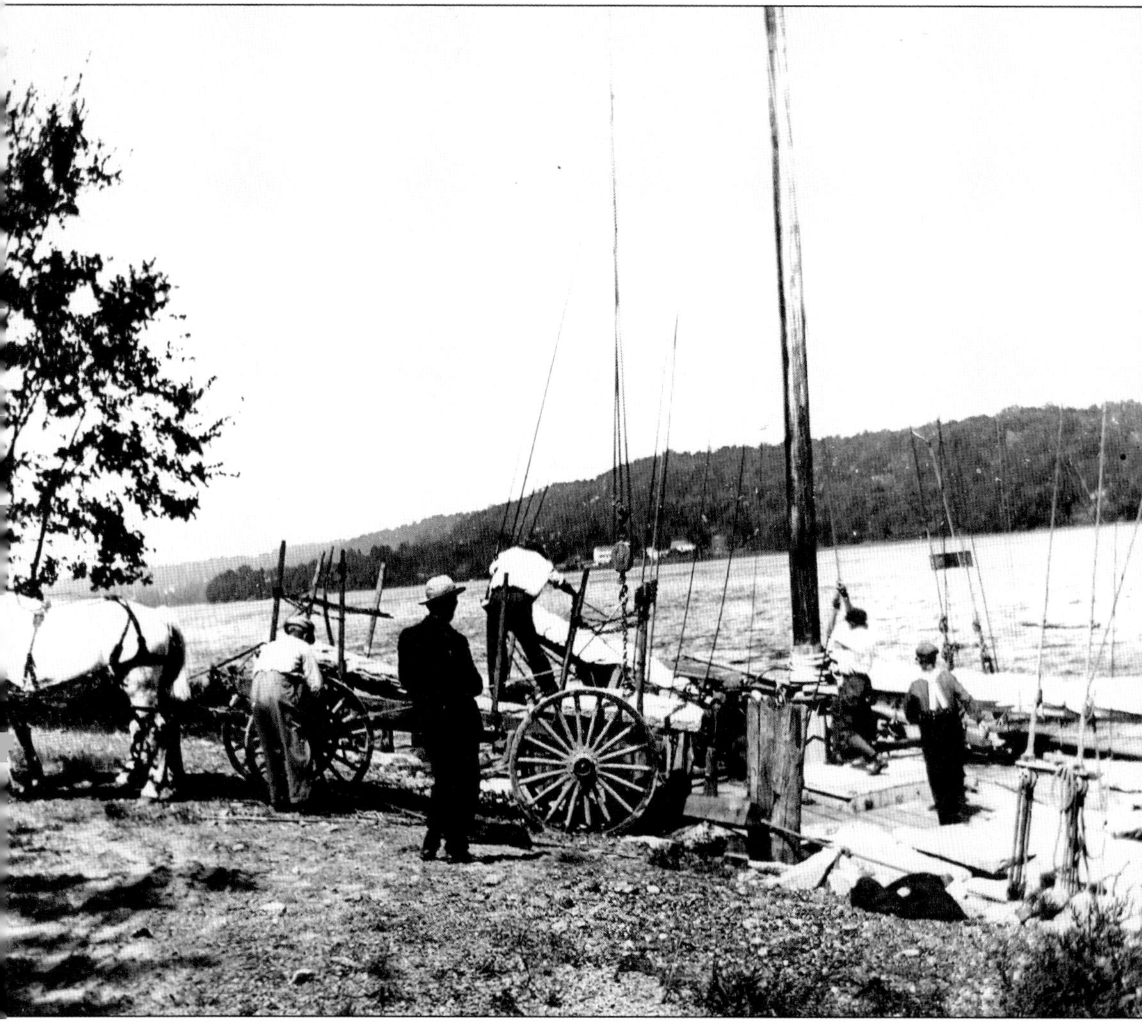

Men load a schooner with granite at Arnold's Landing, near Mill Creek, in 1905. Quarrying was an important local industry since 1762, when Ezra Brainerd of Haddam Neck opened a quarry. Outcroppings of granite dot the Haddam landscape, and many local families made a living cutting and selling stone, both locally and to customers in New York, Philadelphia, and New Orleans. Small amounts of Haddam granite are still cut and sold today. (Charles Church photograph.)

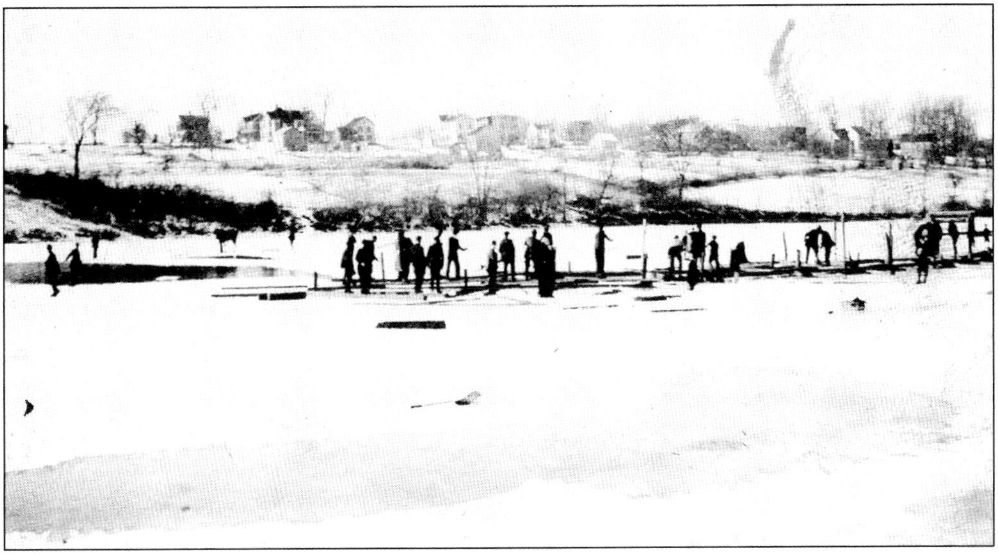

A fine winter's day in 1913 provided the opportunity for cutting ice on Mill Creek, at the Connecticut River. Cutting and selling ice provided farmers with winter income and was a common practice until World War II. Stored in icehouses that had thick walls insulated with sawdust, the ice was covered with hay and could be preserved in this way through the summer and even until the following winter. (Charles Church photograph.)

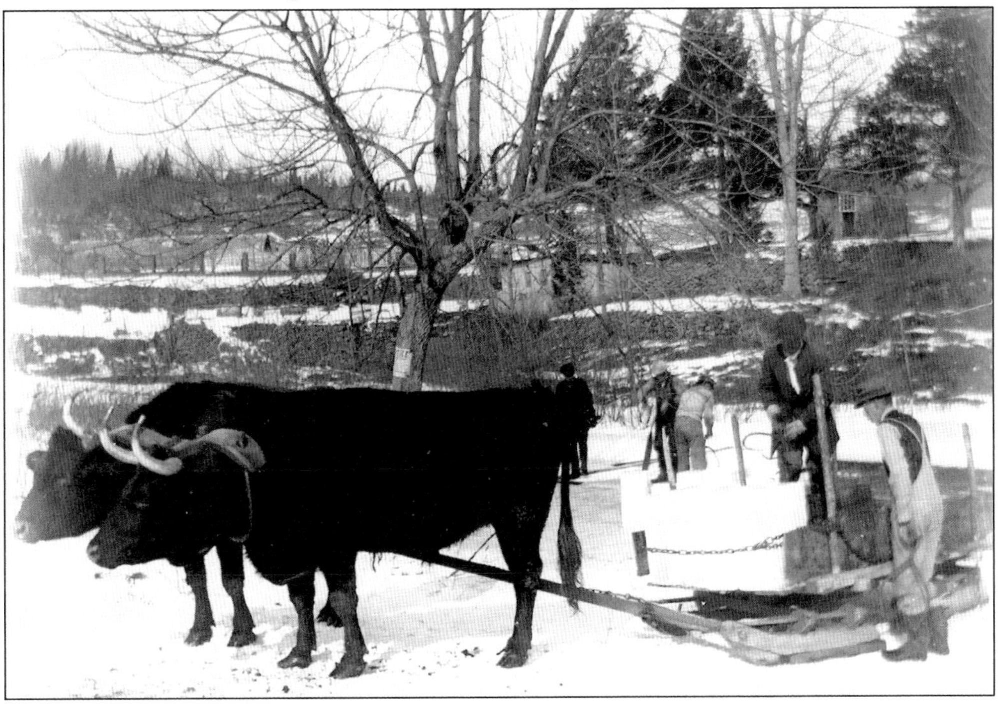

These men are cutting ice from Kreiger Pond West off Walkley Hill. They are using ice tongs to load the ice onto sleds. Ice was sold locally to Clark's ice factory in Higganum. The fishing industry was also a large consumer of ice. When the concrete was poured during the construction of the Connecticut Yankee atomic power plant in 1968, tons of ice were used to keep the concrete at the proper temperature for curing.

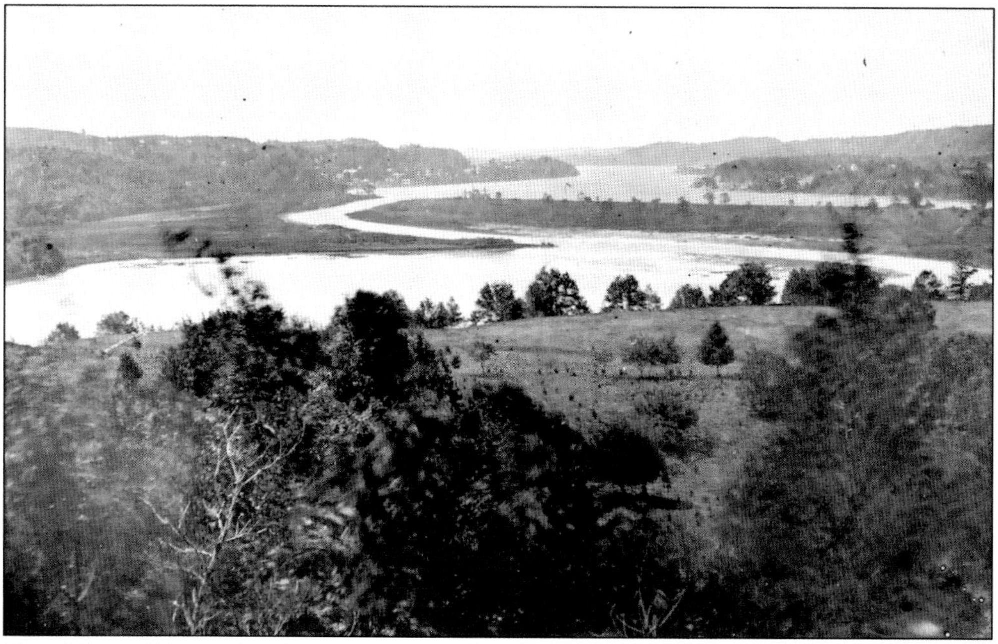

The Salmon River joins the Connecticut River south of Haddam Neck. By the time this photograph was taken in 1878, the fish that gave this river its name had disappeared, the paths to their spawning grounds blocked by dams constructed on Connecticut River tributaries. About a century later, the state began efforts to reintroduce salmon to the river. These efforts have been only partially successful. (George Bradford Brainerd photograph, courtesy Brainerd Library.)

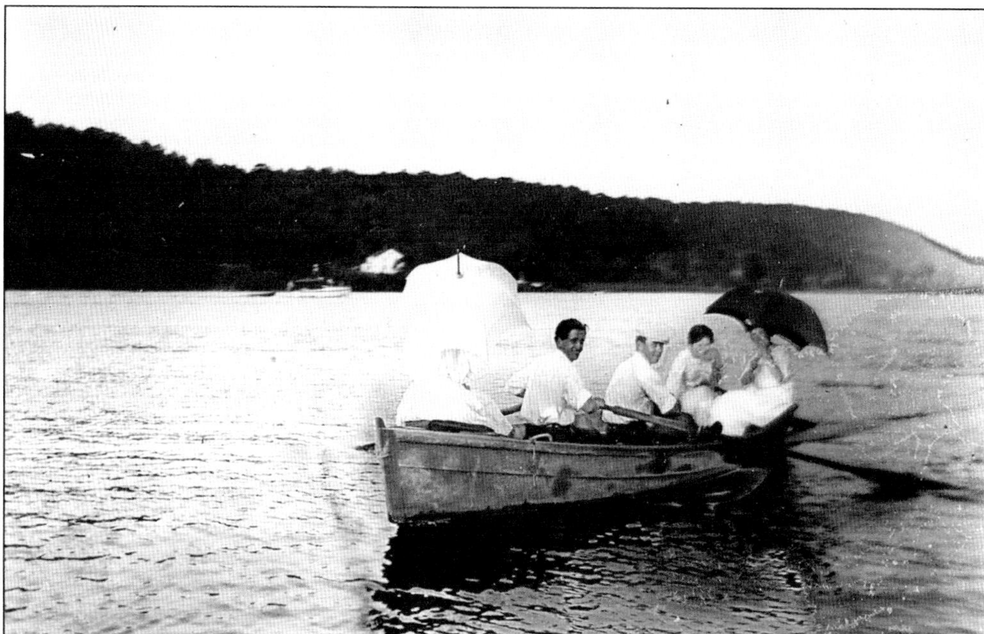

Enjoying a boat ride on the Connecticut River, these couples are typical of the "summer people" who made Haddam a vacation destination after the Civil War. Some were former residents or their descendants who had gone to New York City or farther to seek their fortunes.

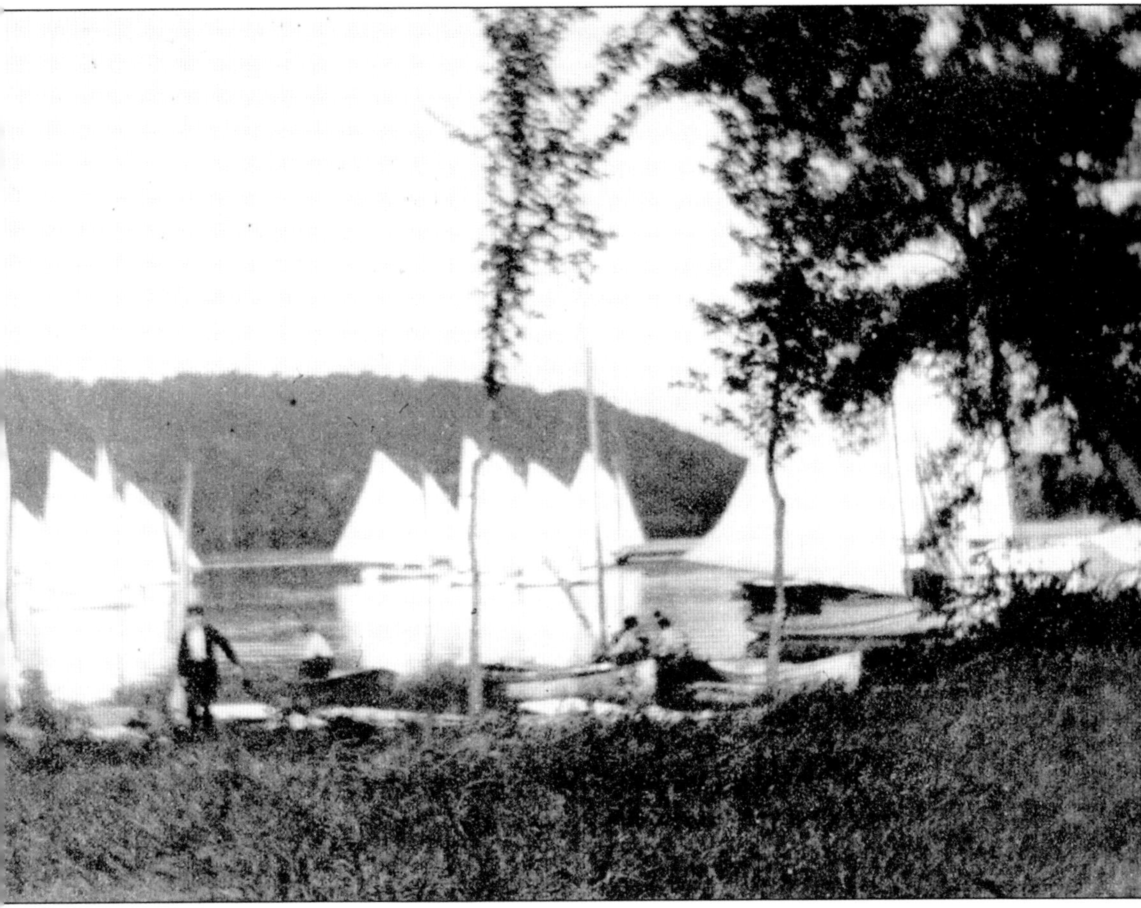

Photographer George Brainerd captured a yacht race in progress on the Connecticut River in 1885. This photograph was probably taken at the beginning of the race. The dark object on the right may be the committee boat, from which the starting gun was fired. (George Bradford Brainerd photograph, courtesy Brainerd Library.)

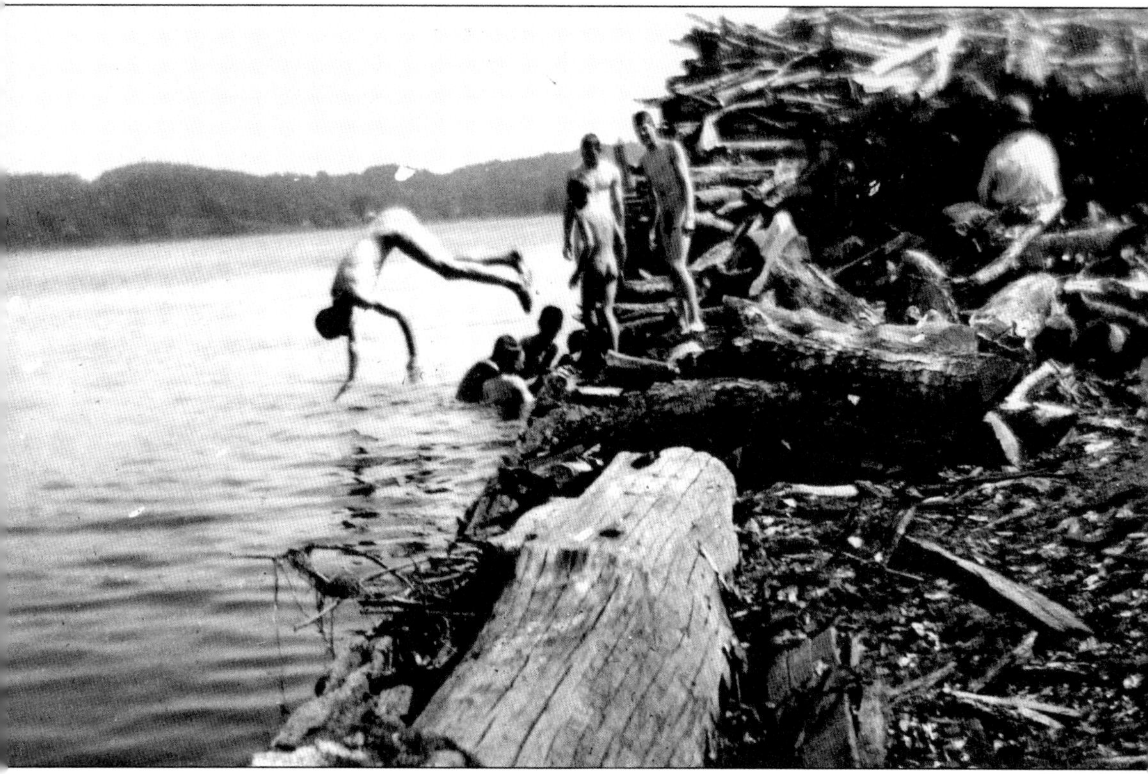

On a summer afternoon in 1885, George Brainerd photographed this scene of local boys enjoying a swim in the river. (George Bradford Brainerd photograph, courtesy Brainerd Library.)

Three

HADDAM NECK TO TYLERVILLE

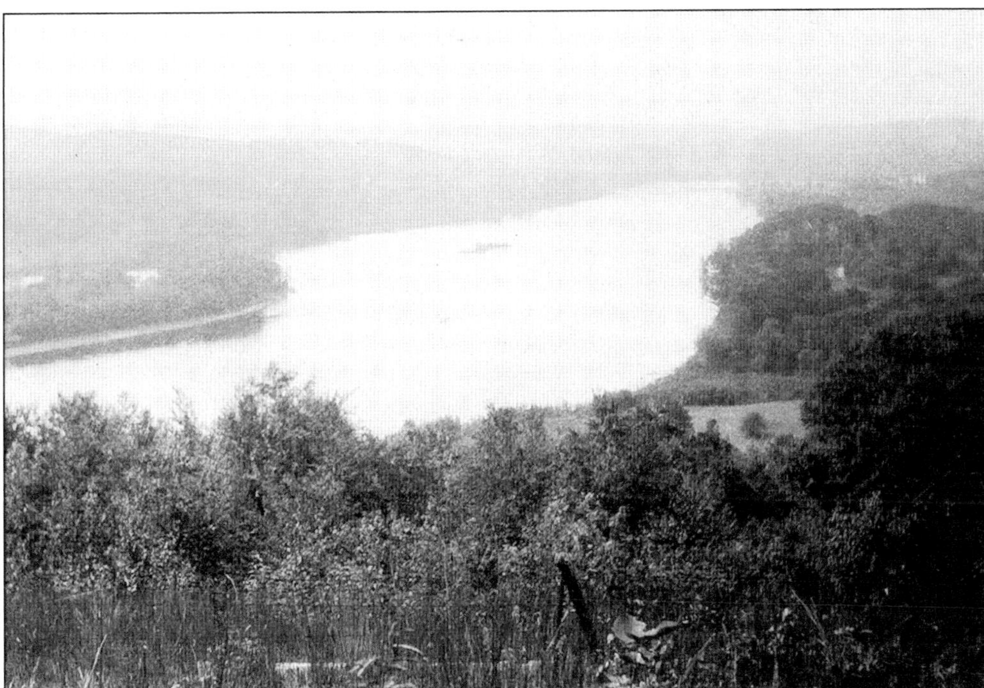

Isolated from the rest of the town by the Connecticut River, Haddam Neck developed a unique identity. Even today, certain Haddam Neck families trace their roots to the original settlers, who moved here between 1710 and 1712 from Middle Haddam, Saybrook, and Haddam. Because this area lacked arable land, its inhabitants turned to fishing, quarrying, and shipbuilding to supplement farming. This photograph was taken from Brainerd Quarry, opened in 1762, overlooking Thirty Mile Island (Haddam Island). (Courtesy Kruger family.)

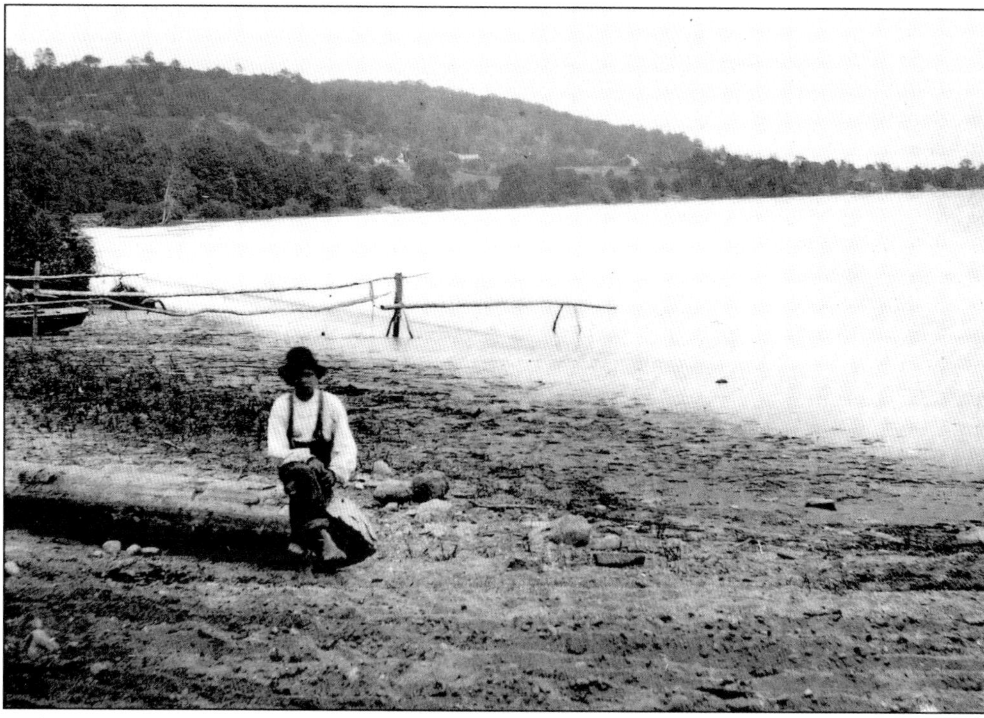

In this view downriver, a young boy rests on a log on the Rock Landing shore in 1875. (George Bradford Brainerd photograph, courtesy Brainerd Library.)

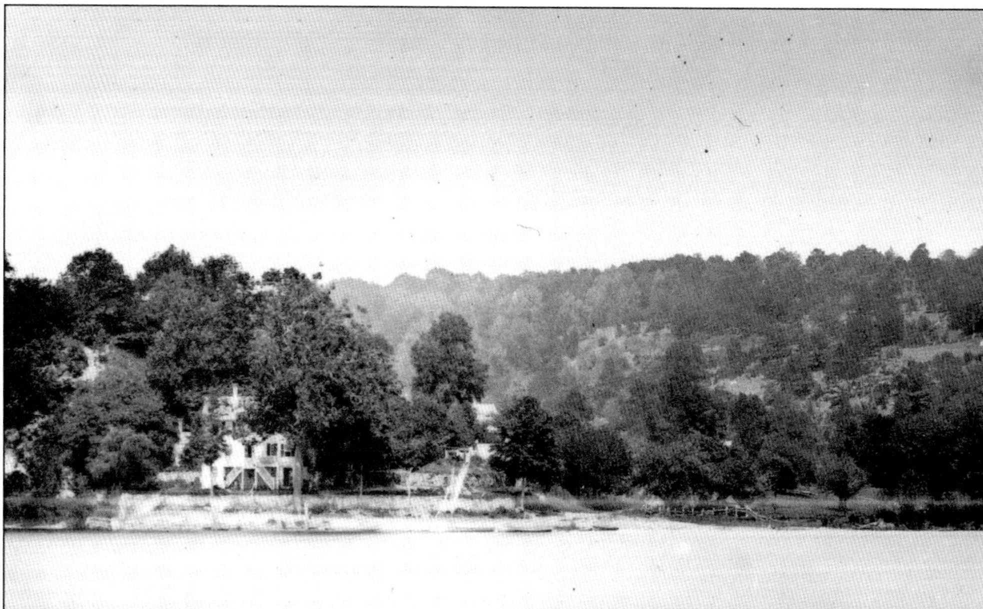

This Rock Landing landmark was originally Brainerd's store. At the dock in front, ships took on Connecticut River fish to be sold in New York, and Haddam Neck lumber to be sold in the Caribbean. The structure acquired its Second Empire style when it was converted to an inn by Charles Russell in the 1870s. It housed guests until steamboat service to Hartford and New York was discontinued in 1931. (George Bradford Brainerd photograph, courtesy Brainerd Library.)

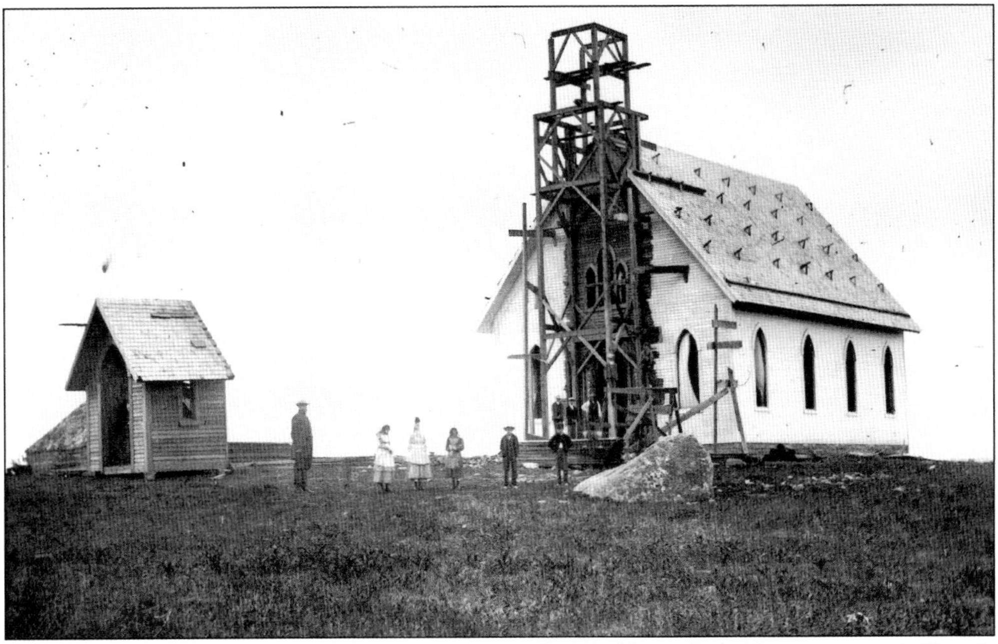

When this photograph was taken in June 1874, the Haddam Neck Congregational Church building was under construction. Its Gothic Revival architecture is typical of the period. Church members had been without a building since their meetinghouse on Hog Hill Road in Middle Haddam had collapsed. (George Bradford Brainerd photograph, courtesy Brainerd Library.)

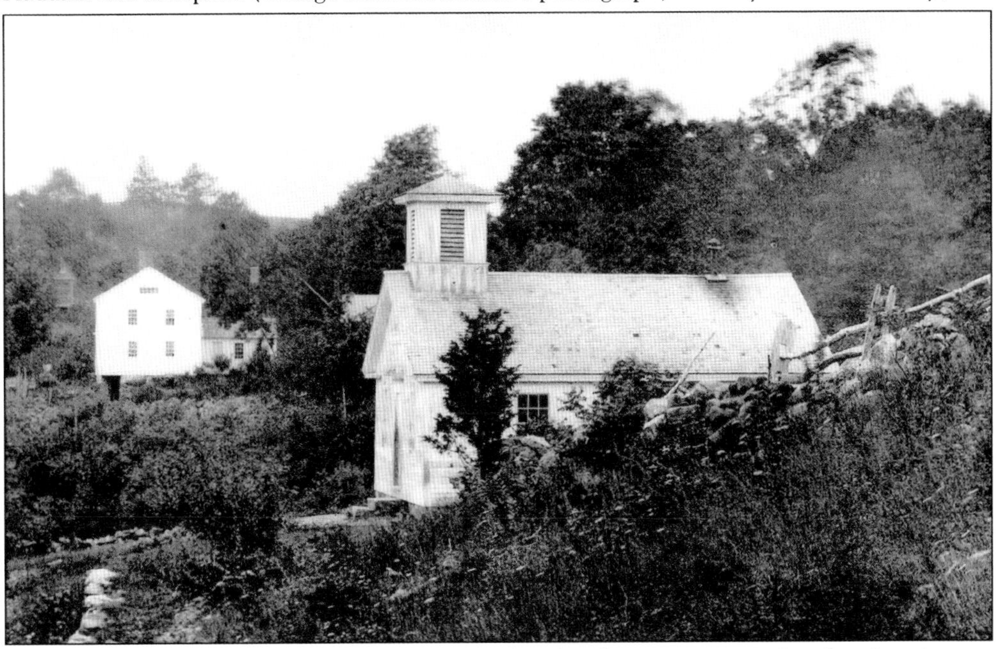

This 1874 photograph shows the Haddam Neck schoolhouse opposite the church, where it was originally built in 1822. When the school closed in 1925, the building was donated to the church for use as a parish house and was moved across the road and placed next to the church. The children of Haddam Neck attended elementary school in Middle Haddam until 1978. (George Bradford Brainerd photograph, courtesy Brainerd Library.)

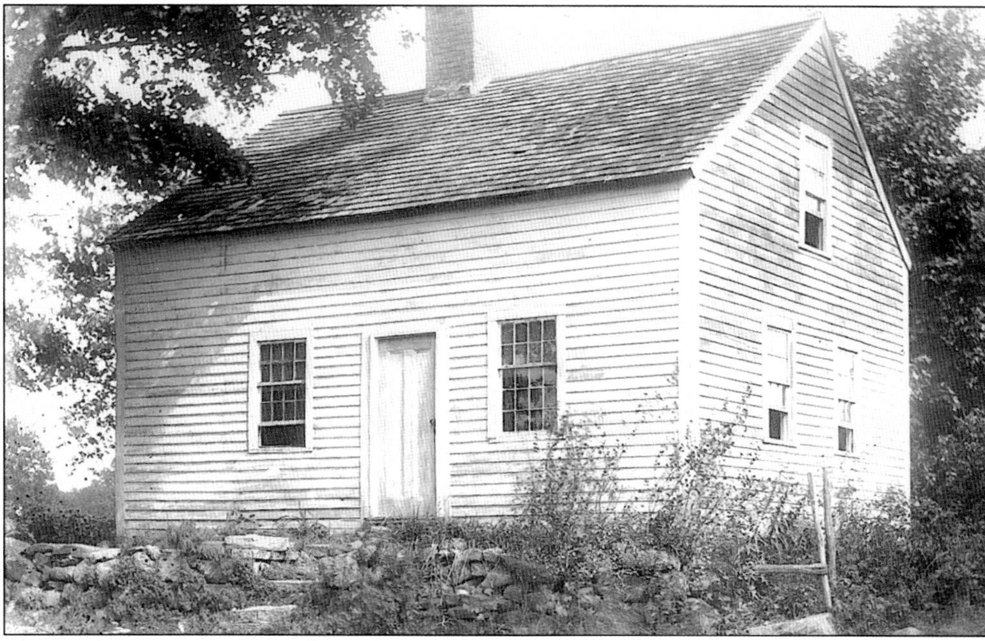

The pox house on Quarry Hill Road quarantined smallpox sufferers. Some had received a mild case of the disease from inoculation. In 1930, Dr. Kate C. Mead was instrumental in organizing the Haddam Public Health Association to combat the unusually high incidence of disease in Haddam due to lack of health education. The nurses reported that they had found several cases of typhoid that "were truly preventable" if the symptoms had been identified early. (Courtesy Middle Haddam Library, Olsen Collection.)

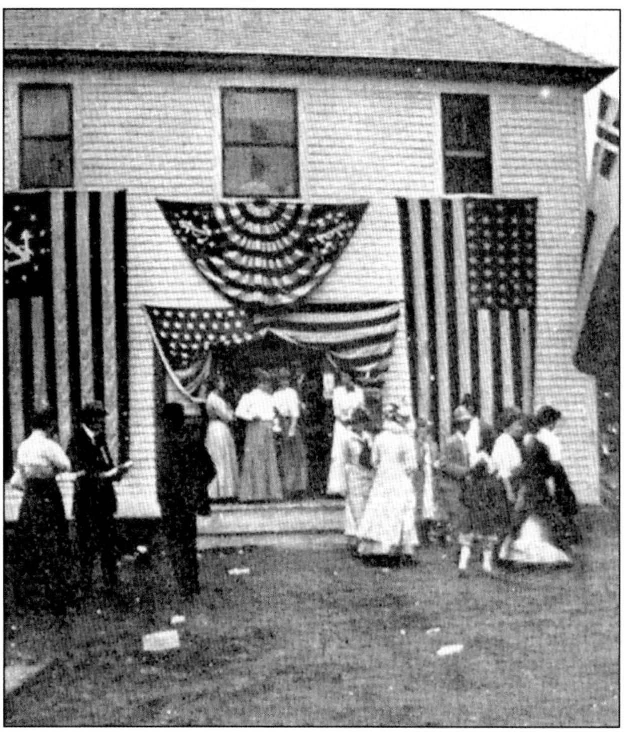

A year after its founding in 1910, the Haddam Neck Grange No. 177 P. of H. held its first country fair on the premises of Bailey's Garage on Haddam Neck Road. (The garage has since burned.) In 1914, the Grange purchased land and built this hall and horse barn about a quarter of a mile down the road to the south.

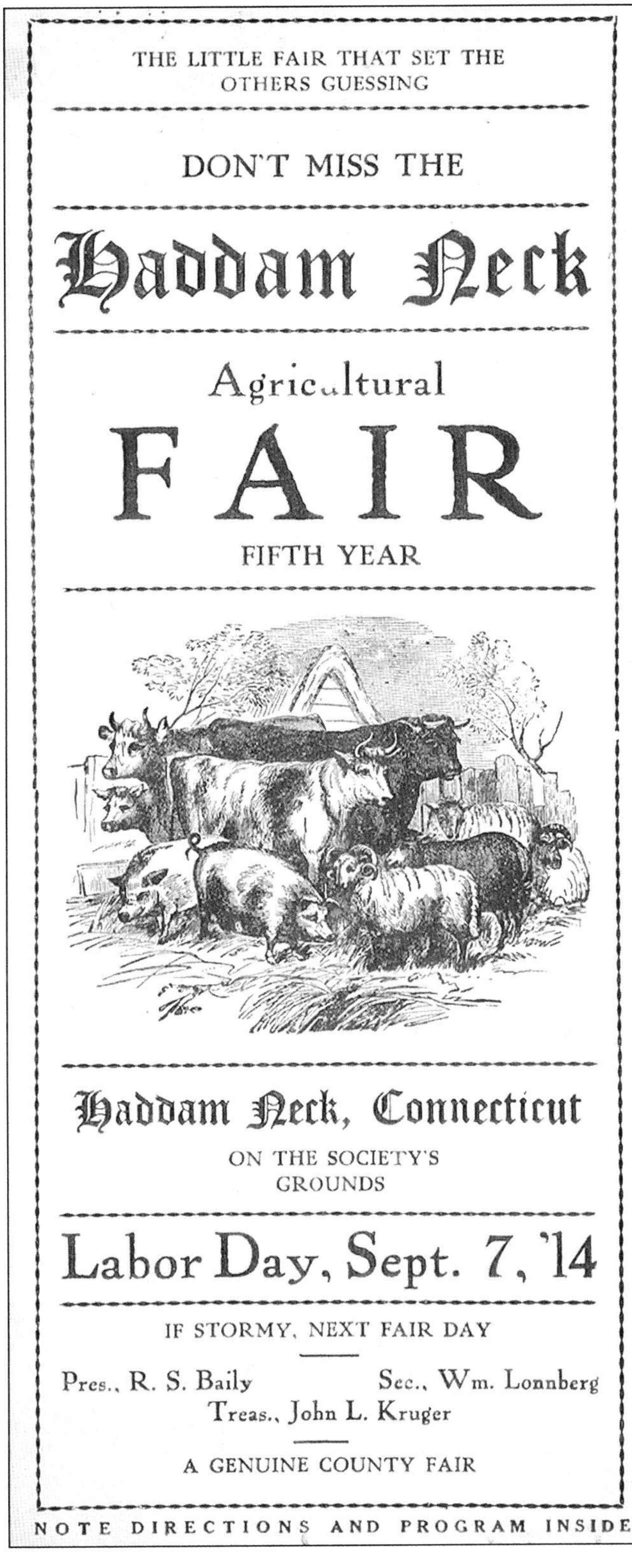

Today the three-day Haddam Neck Fair is the signature community event, drawing fairgoers from across the state. (Courtesy Kruger family.)

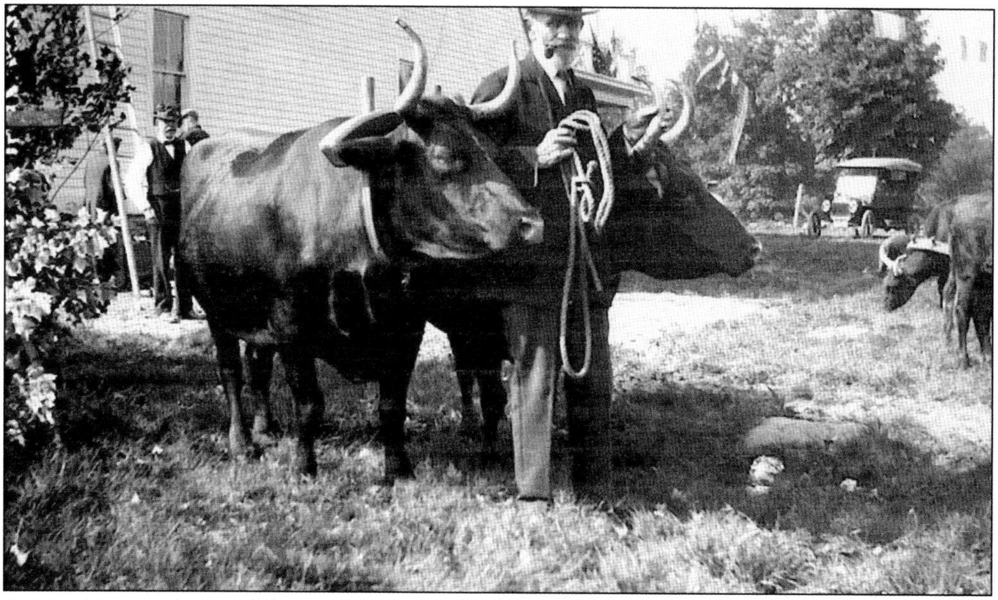

A proud owner shows off his prize oxen at the fair in the early 20th century. A 1914 Model T can be seen in the background. (Courtesy Kruger family.)

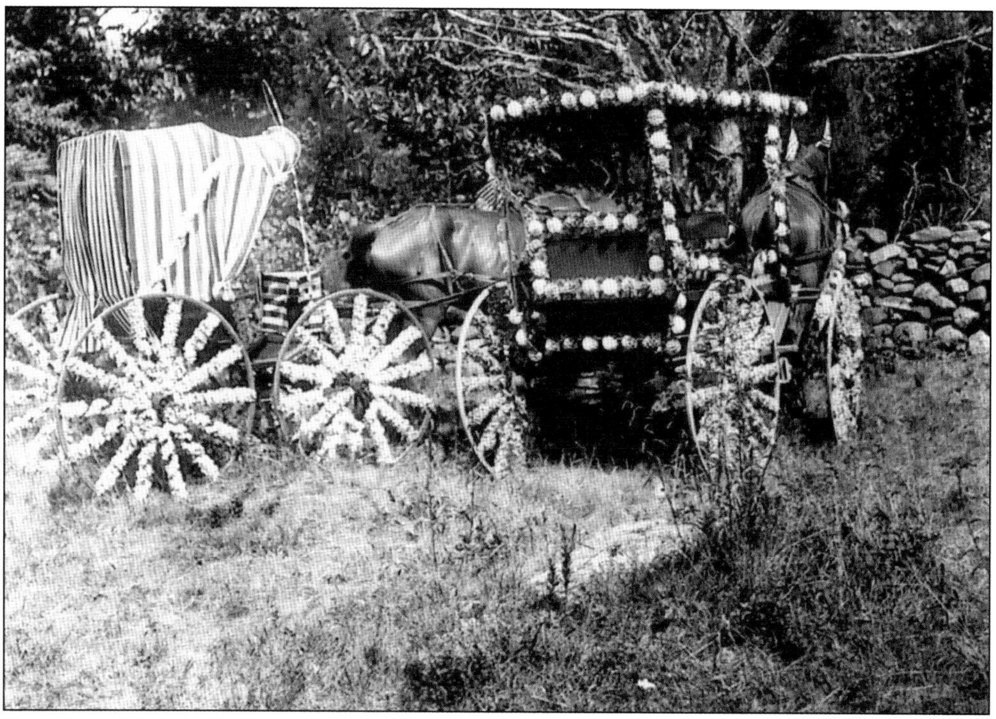

Carriages decorated with flowers prepare to parade to the fairgrounds. (Courtesy Middle Haddam Library, Olsen Collection.)

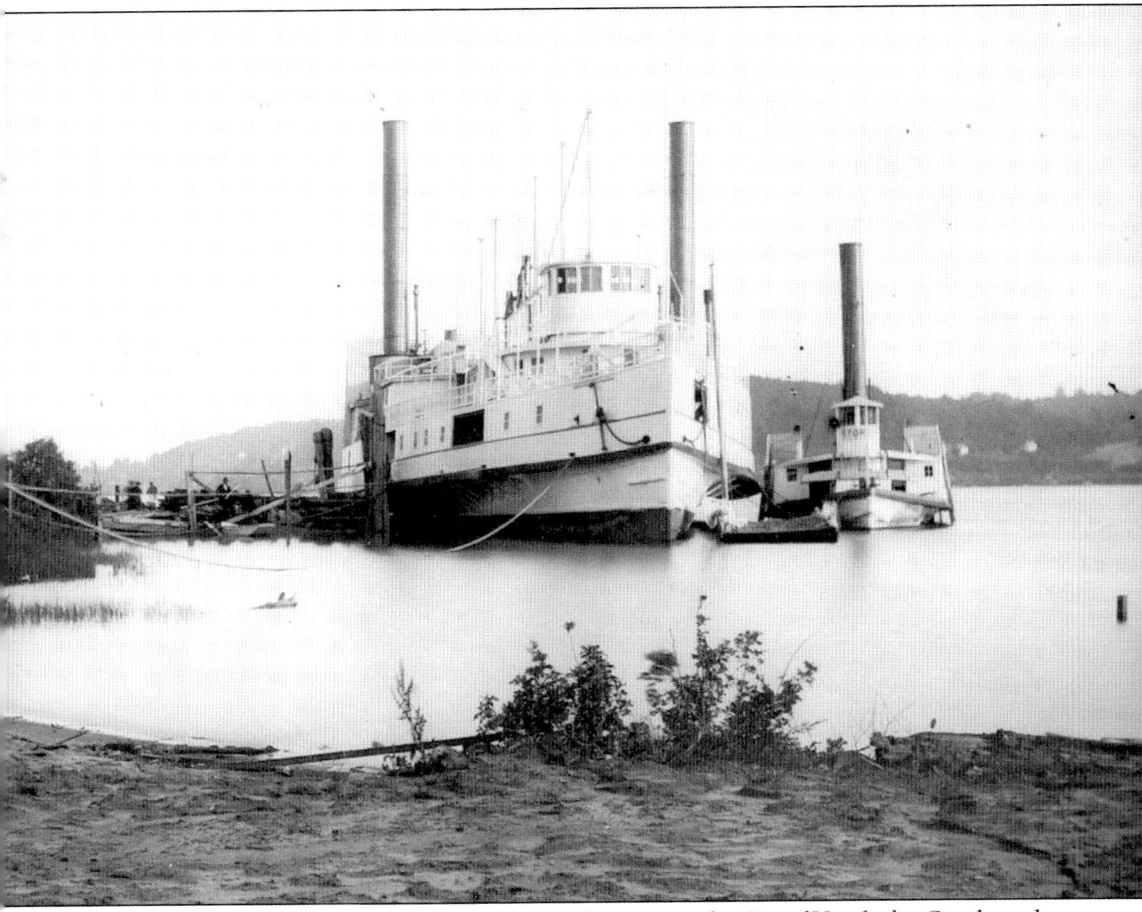

On a late-June day in 1878, a small side-wheel steamboat assists the *City of Hartford* at Goodspeed Landing in East Haddam. Shifting sandbars make river navigation dangerous for larger boats; even today, commercial ships are required to hire a Connecticut River pilot when navigating on the waterway. (George Bradford Brainerd photograph, courtesy Brainerd Library.)

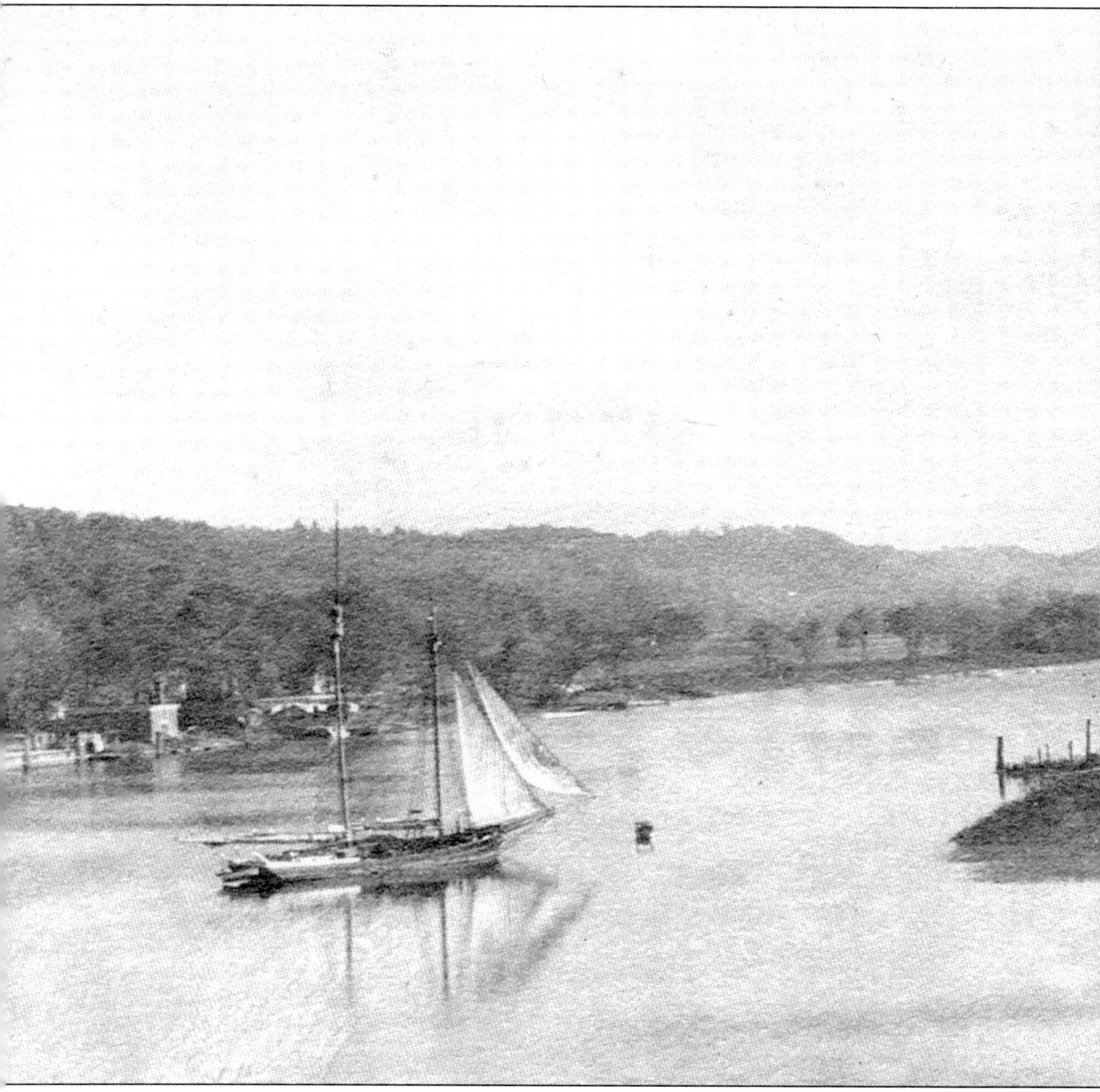

In this painterly photograph, a sailboat proceeds upriver at Goodspeed Landing sometime

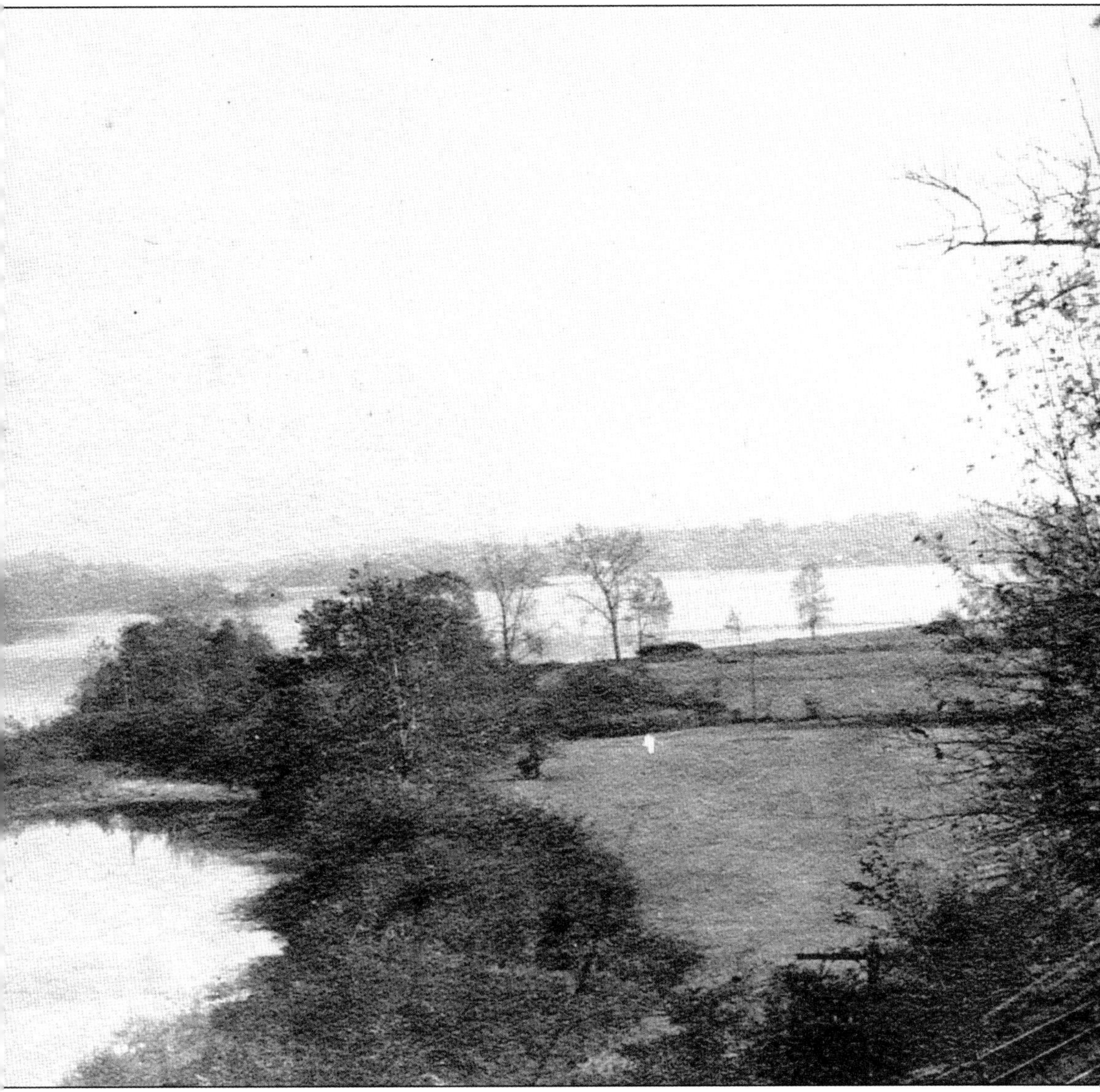

before the swing bridge was opened in 1913.

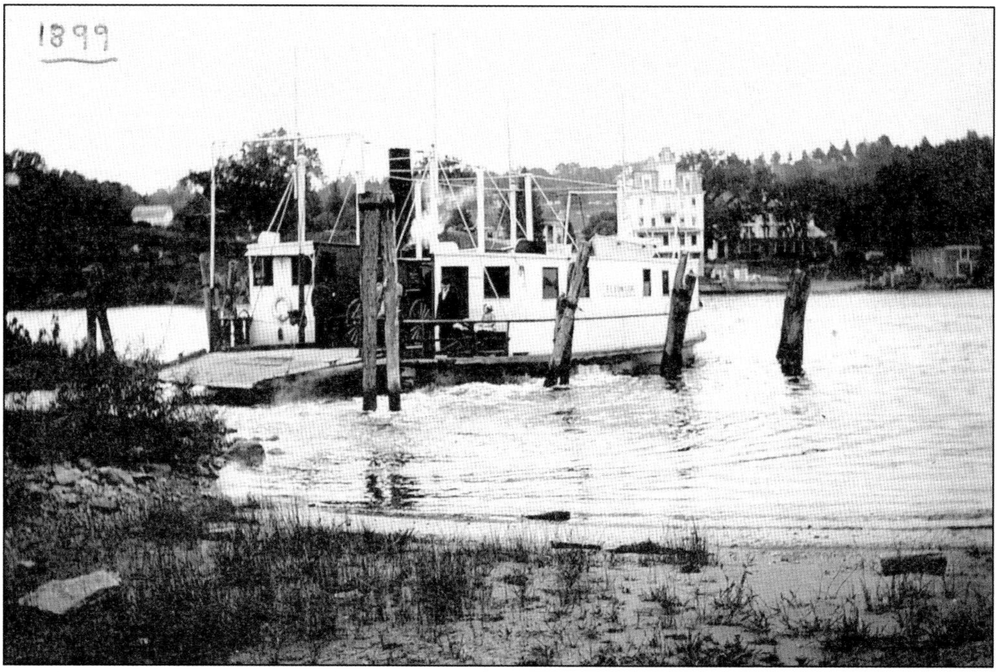

The East Haddam ferry proceeds across the Connecticut River toward the Goodspeed Opera House in 1899. (Courtesy Camp Bethel.)

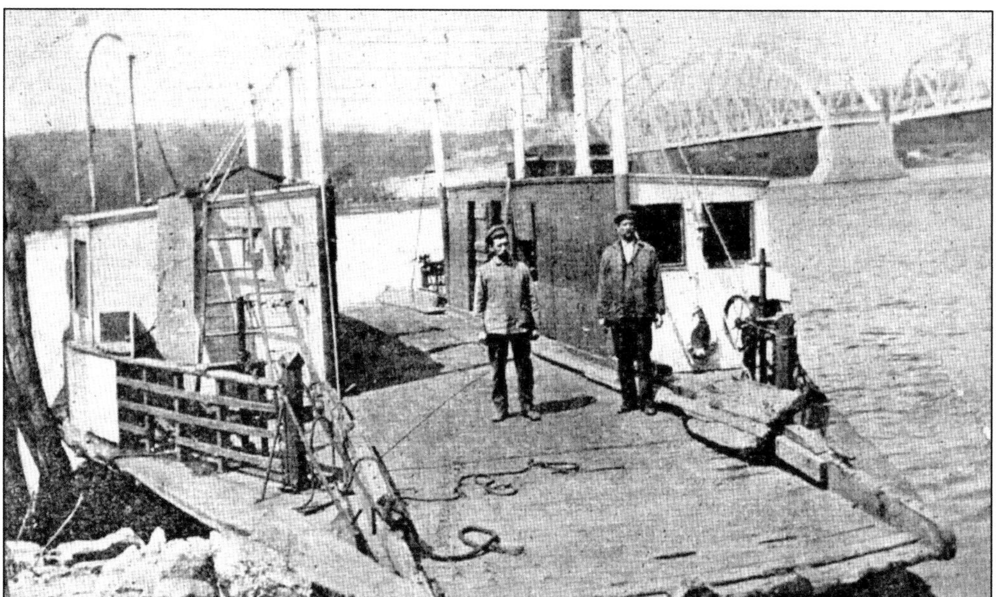

The ferry boat *General Spencer* was soon to be made obsolete by the bridge at Goodspeed Landing, seen under construction in the background of this photograph. (Courtesy Camp Bethel.)

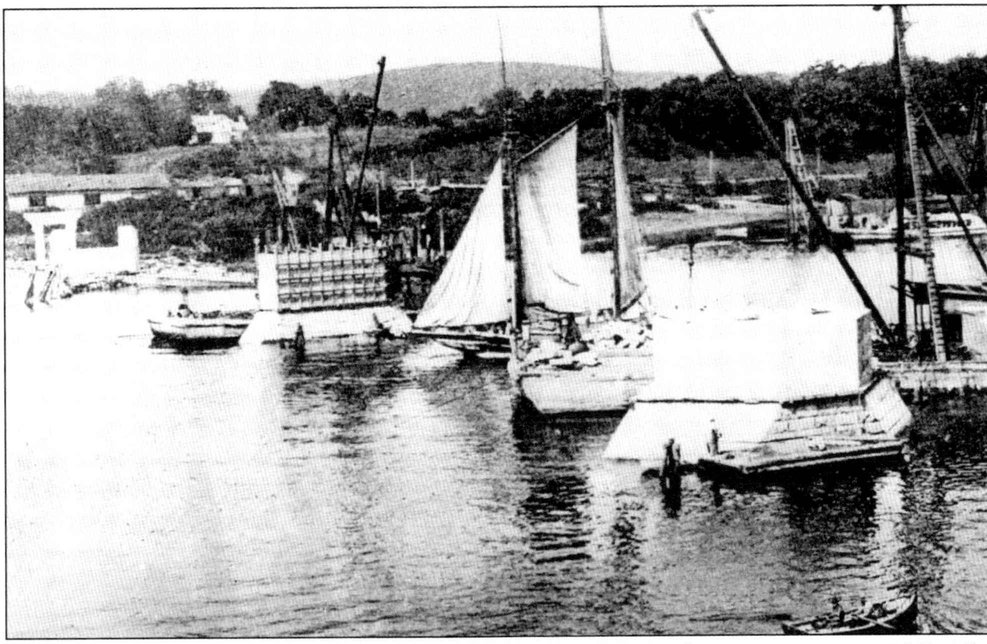

A sailboat navigates the piers for the swing bridge, seen here under construction in 1912. The tracks of the Connecticut Valley line of the New York, New Haven and Hartford Railroad can be seen on the Haddam shore in the background. (Courtesy Max Miller.)

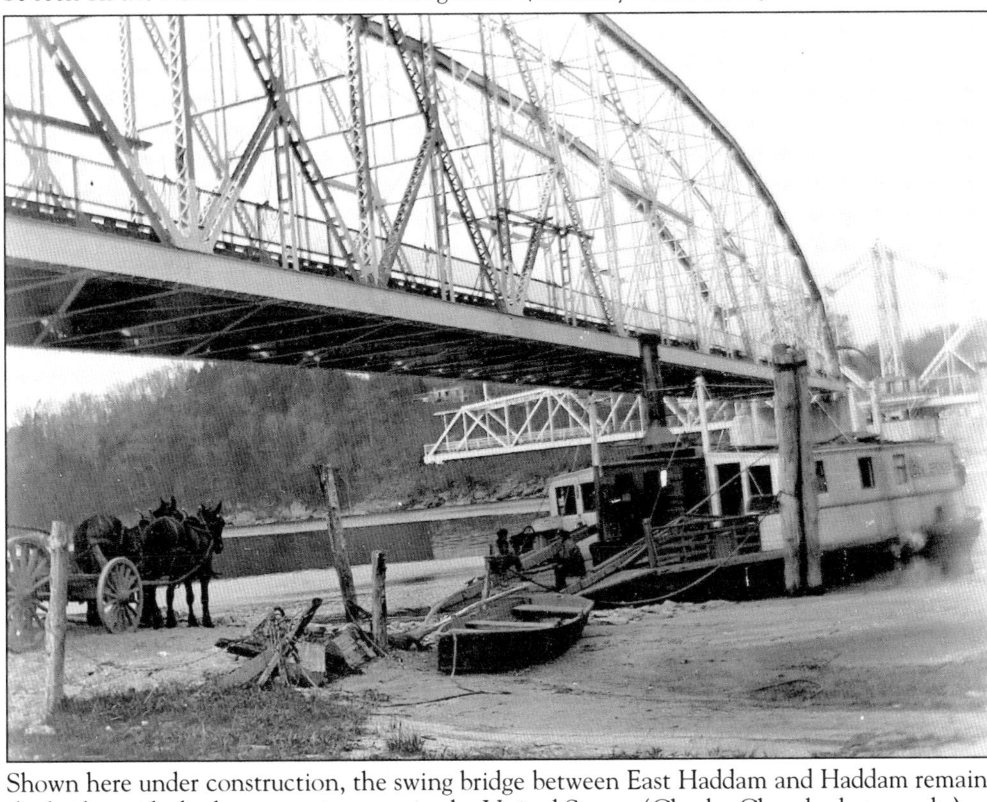

Shown here under construction, the swing bridge between East Haddam and Haddam remains the bridge with the longest swing span in the United States. (Charles Church photograph.)

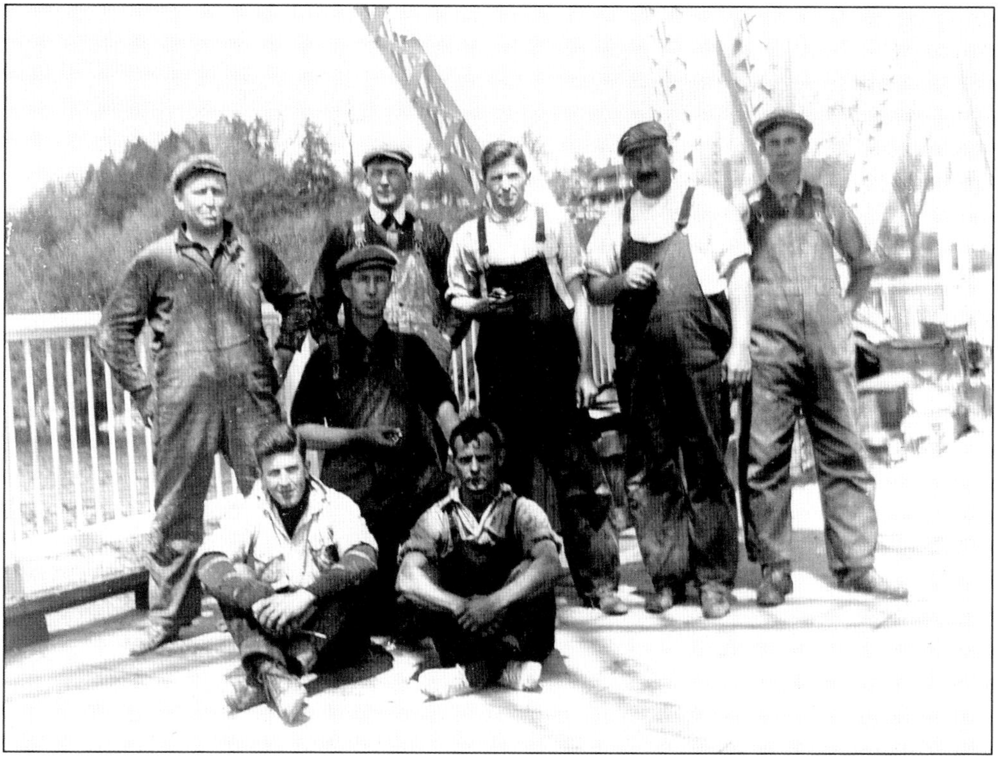

The bridge construction crew poses around 1913. (Charles Church photograph.)

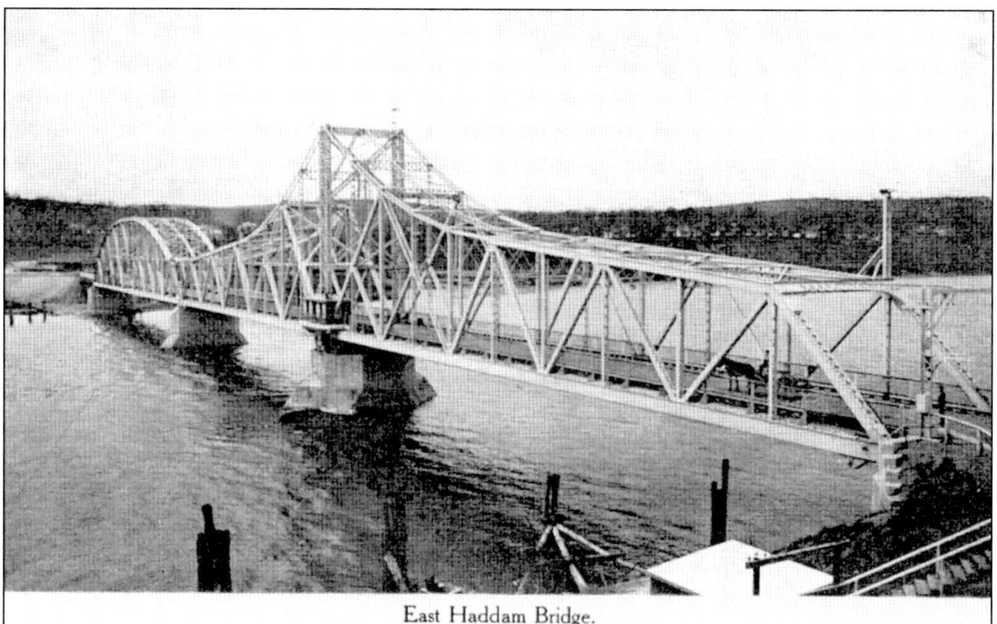

The bridge was dedicated on May 29, 1913. Here a horse-drawn wagon crosses over to the Haddam side of the river. Camp Bethel is in the distance.

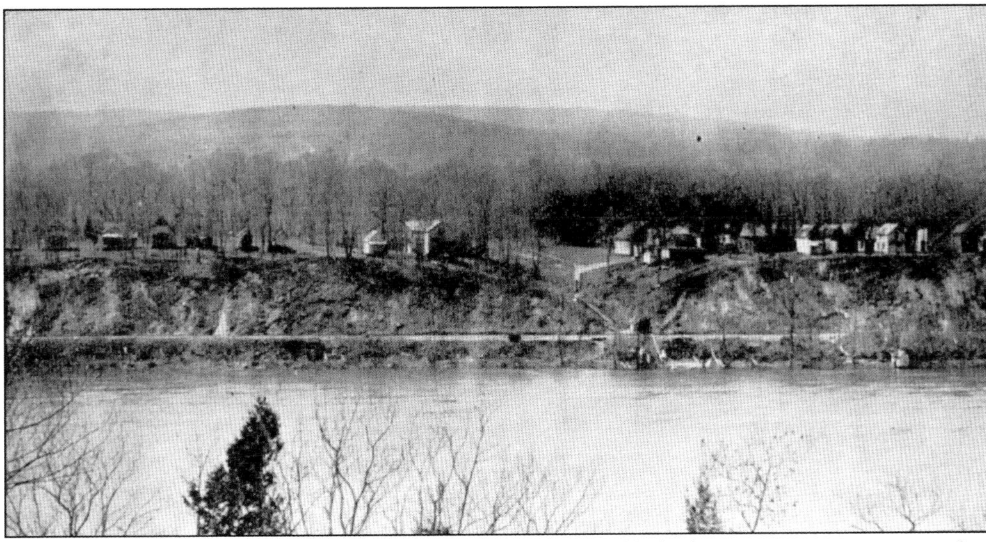

In 1878, members of the Advent Christian Church established a camp meeting ground in Tylerville overlooking the Connecticut River. Since then, families have gathered there each summer for fellowship and worship. (Courtesy Camp Bethel.)

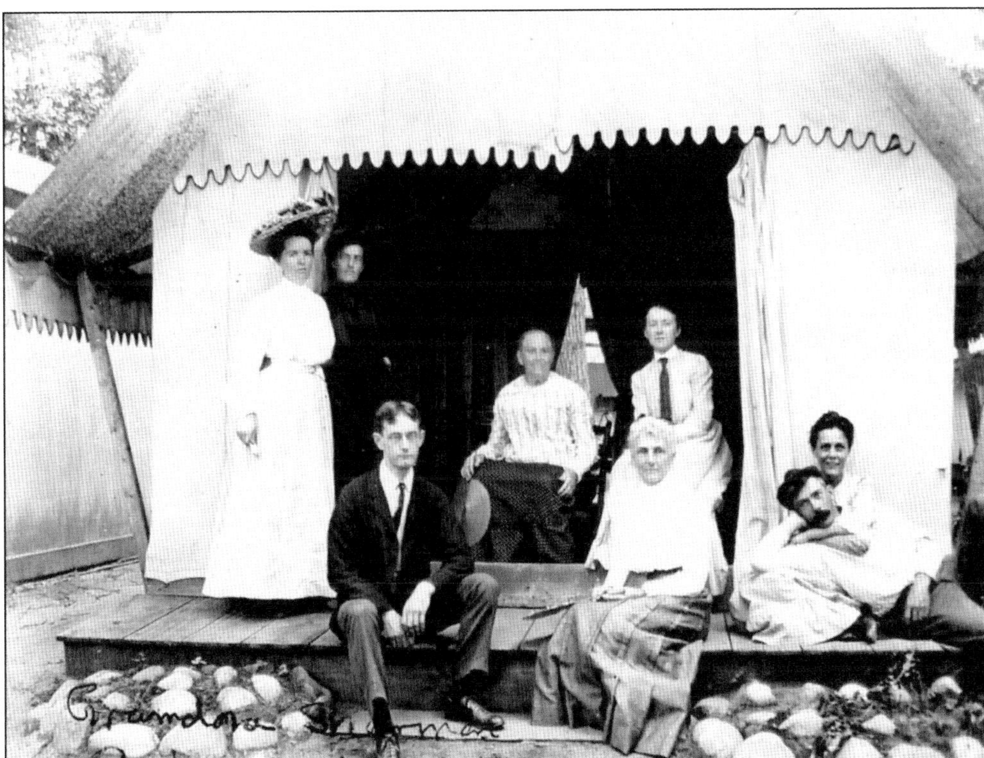

During the camp's early years, campers lived in closely spaced tents arranged in a semicircle. In 1927, Mabel Miner recalled, "The white tents with their red bindings were a delight to the eye" in spite of the general lack of conveniences. (Courtesy Camp Bethel.)

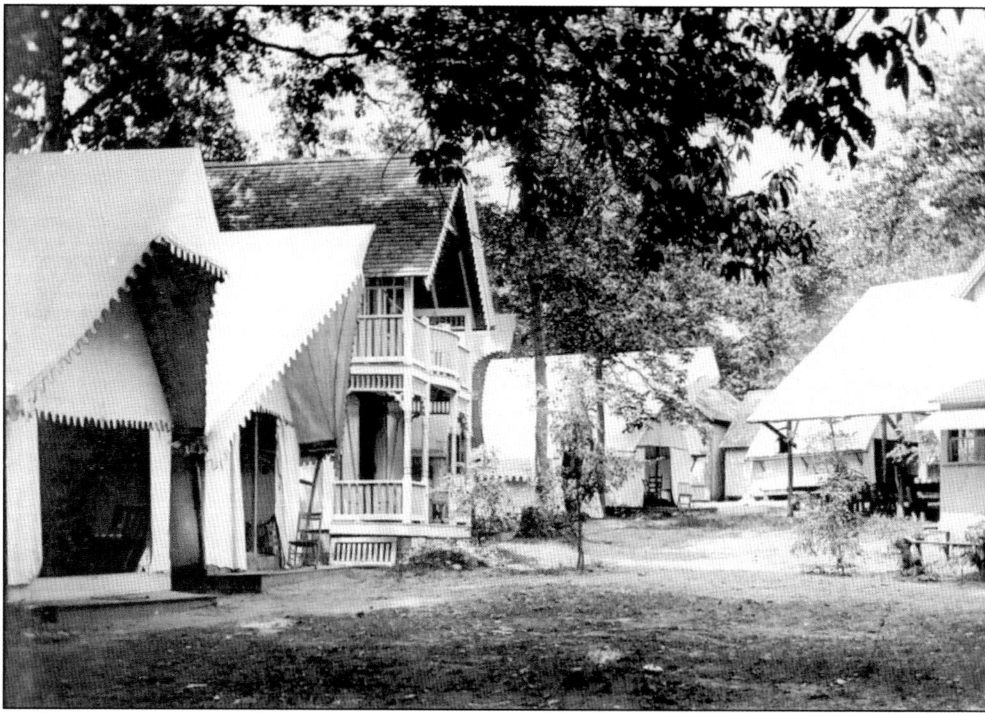

In time, the tents were replaced by one-and-a-half-story cottages built in the Carpenter Gothic style. The small size and close proximity of the cottages were determined by the tent sites that they were built on. In 1963, the Camp Bethel Association split from the Advent Christian Church. Today it is a nondenominational organization. (Courtesy Camp Bethel.)

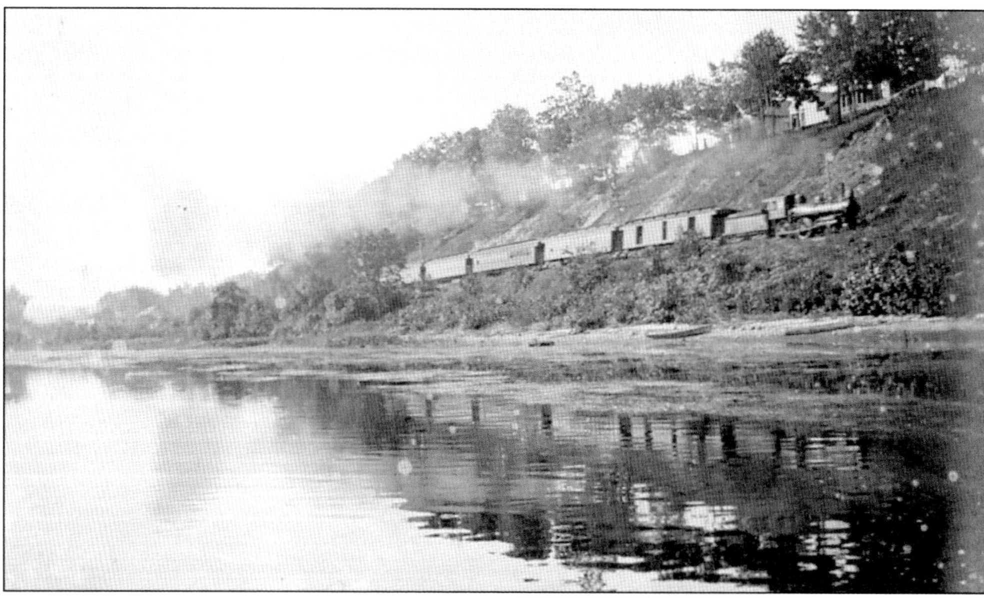

The Connecticut Valley Railroad charged campers half price to ride the train if their tickets were signed by the president of the camp meeting association. Here a passenger train steams north upriver past Camp Bethel. The railroad ran from Old Saybrook to Hartford. (Courtesy Camp Bethel.)

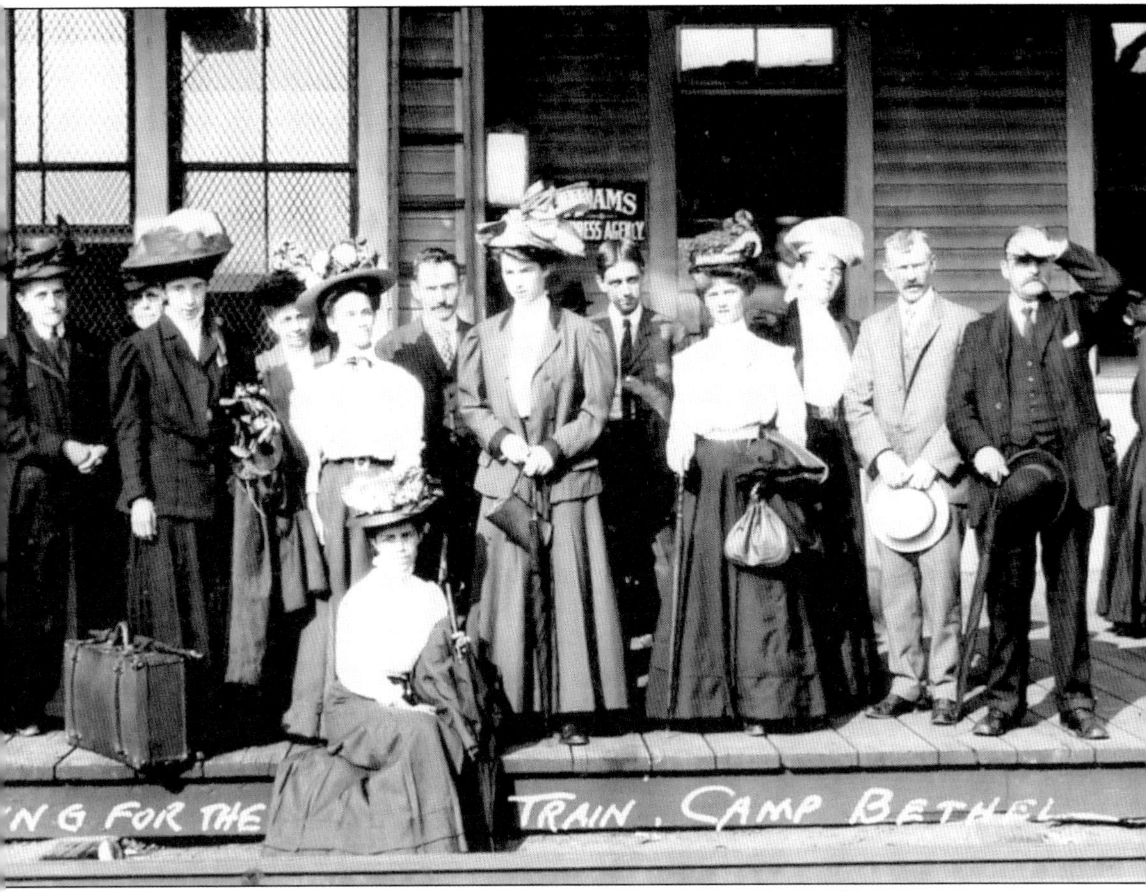

Following a petition by prominent local taxpayers, in August 1869 the Haddam town meeting voted to buy $40,000 worth of railroad stock to help finance the construction of the Old Saybrook to Middletown leg of the Connecticut Valley Railroad. Prominent Haddam citizens and business owners stood to benefit from the rail line's construction. Here a group from Camp Bethel waits at Goodspeed Station in Tylerville about 1904. The seated woman is Helen S. L. Lockward, the wife of photographer Lynn G. Lockward. (Courtesy Camp Bethel.)

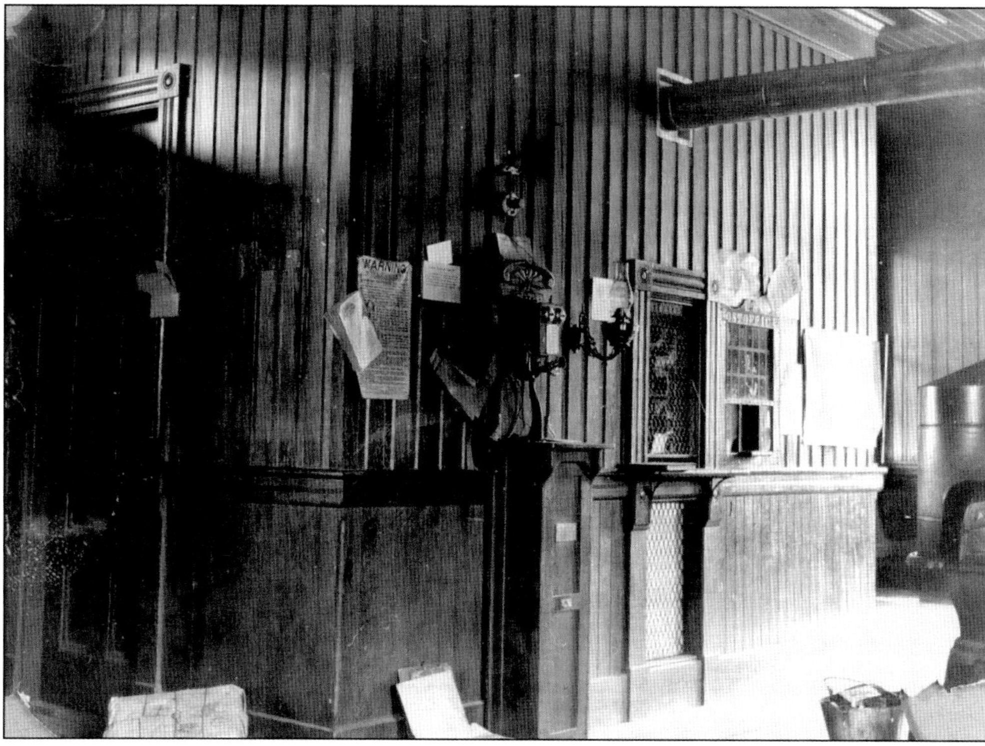

This view of the waiting room at Goodspeed Station reveals that the station did double duty as the Tylerville post office. Patrons could also make calls from the pay phone by the light of a kerosene lamp. A coal stove provided warmth. This building replaced one that burned on February 5, 1897. (Courtesy Max Miller.)

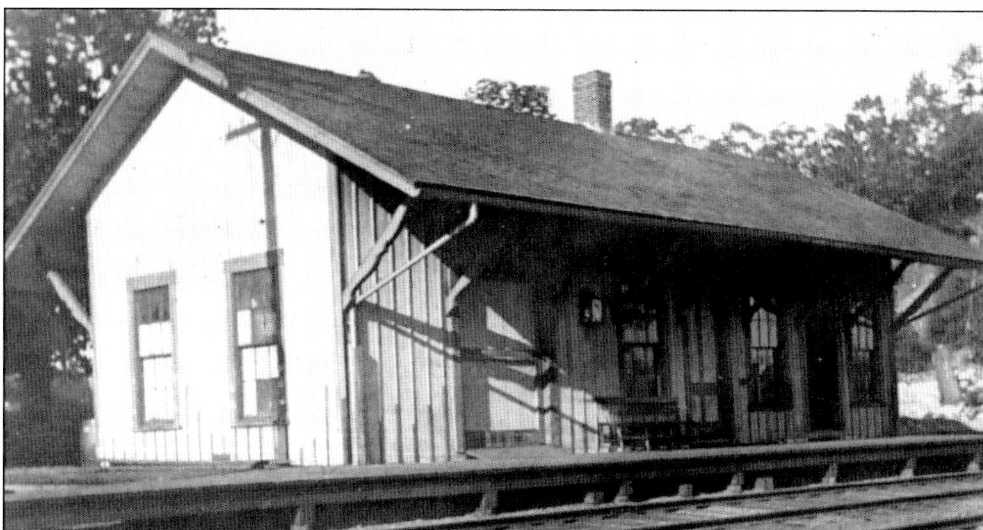

There were five railway stations in Haddam. Goodspeed Station was at the south end of town; moving north, the second station in town, shown in this 1902 photograph, was Arnold's Station. It was built at the personal expense of Isaac Arnold Sr., a Haddam resident and a director of the railroad company, who was later reimbursed by the company for building costs of $2,000. (Courtesy Max Miller.)

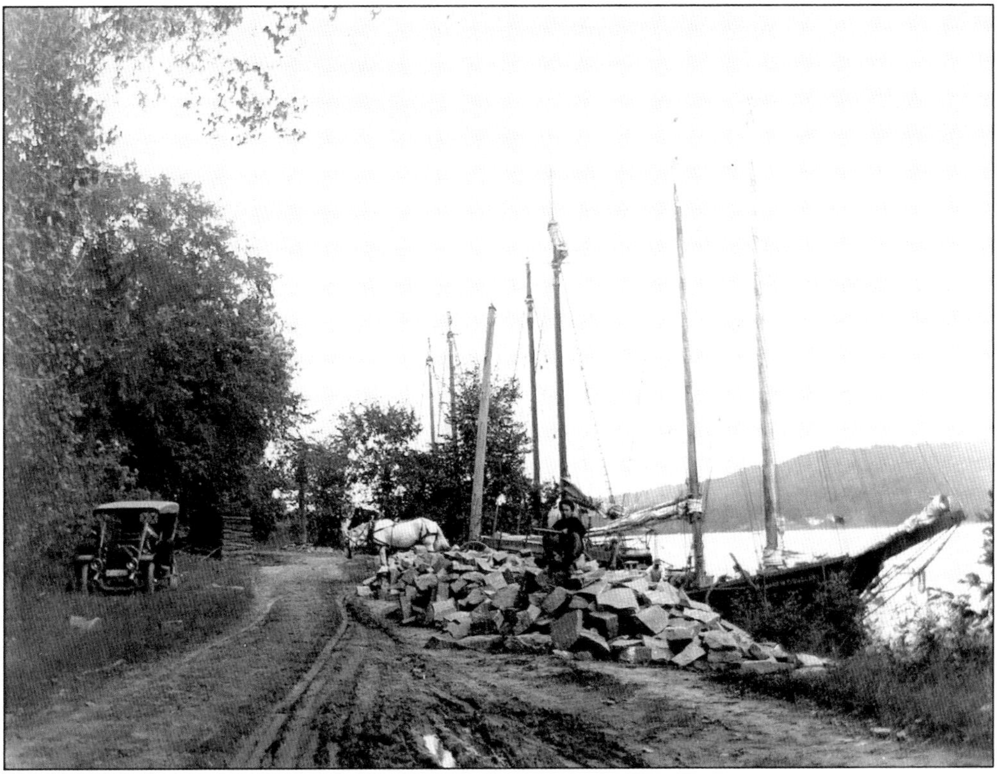

Isaac Arnold's diverse businesses benefited from their proximity to a railway stop. As a young man in the 1830s, Arnold began his career dealing in quarry stone. The stone was shipped downriver, as shown in this early-20th-century photograph.

HADDAM QUARRY & LUMBER CO.,

—AT—

HADDAM, MIDDLESEX CO., CONN.

—ALL KINDS OF—

Hardwood & Lumber, Ship Plank & Frame Timber,

Hickory and Ash Plank, Rail Road Ties &c.

KEPT ON HAND AND SAWED TO ORDER.

—ALSO—

Curb, Gutter & Cross Walk Stone, Flag Stone,

Paving Blocks &c. kept on hand & quarried to order.

ISAAC ARNOLD, PRES.

Capitalizing on the arrival of the railroad, Arnold and others incorporated an expanded Haddam Quarry and Lumber Company in 1882 to deal in stone, lumber (including railroad ties), grain, flour, and feed. The company also sold waterpower and land.

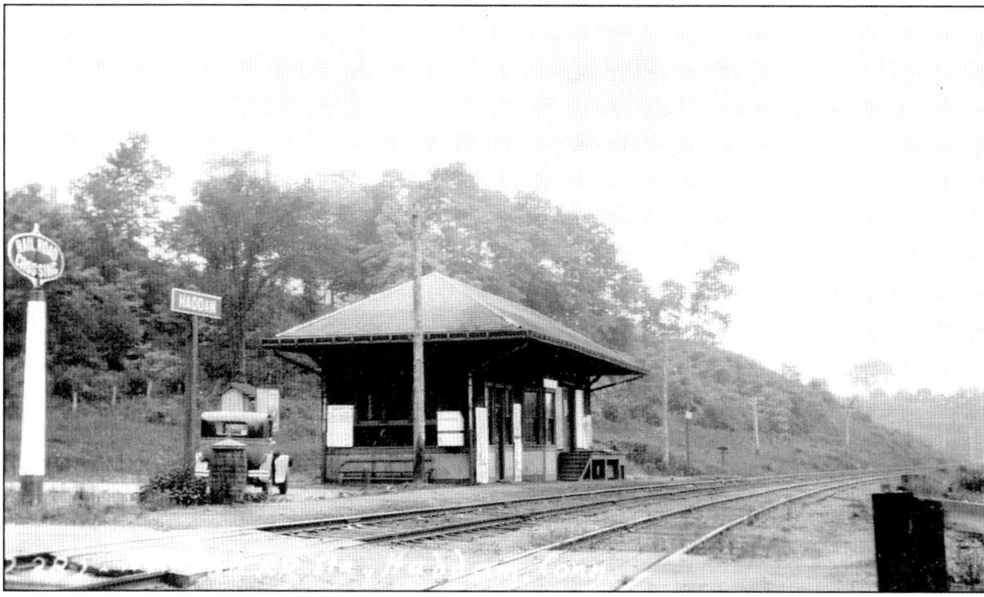

Situated just one mile north of Arnold's Station, Haddam Station was constructed after Haddam Center residents petitioned the state railroad commissioners for a stop of their own. The depot is shown here as it looked in 1930. (Courtesy Max Miller.)

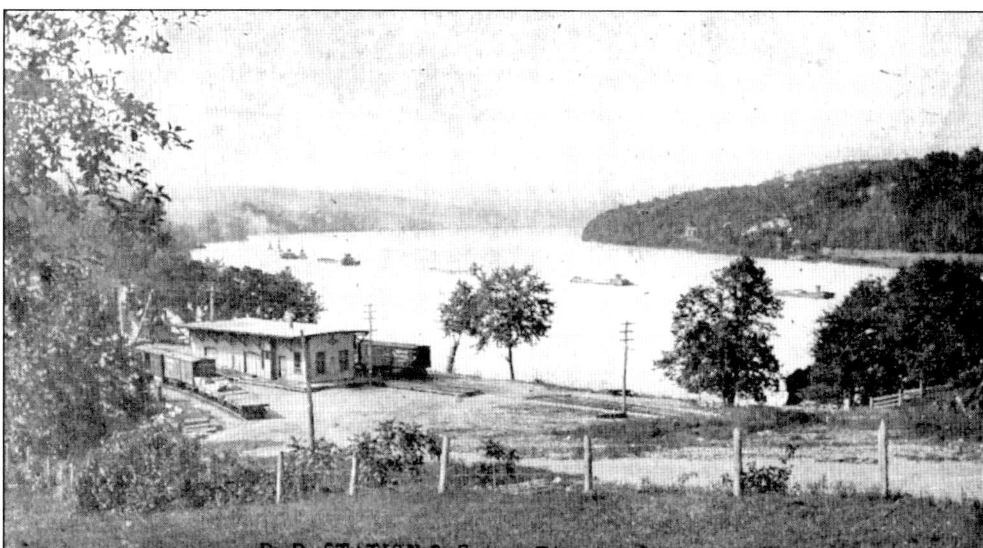

No photographs exist of Walkley Station, which was located approximately halfway between Haddam Center Station and Higganum Station, pictured here.

Four

MAKING A LIVING

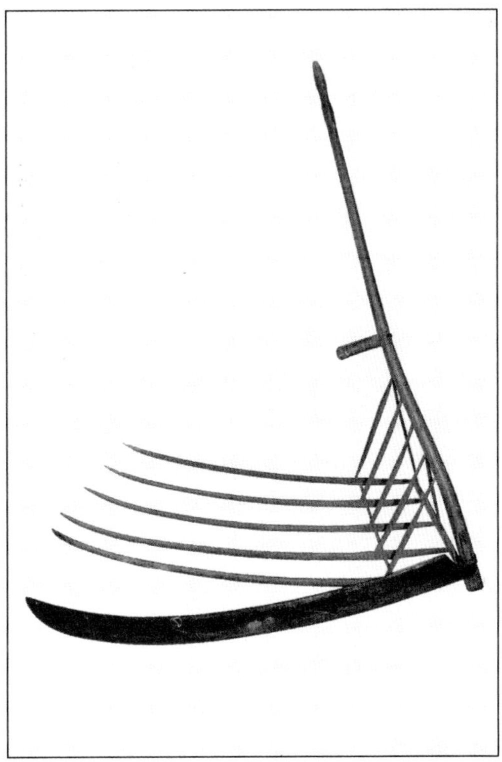

The scythe was a common agricultural tool. In the years between 1870 and 1930, economic life in Haddam changed. Immigrants and new employment opportunities represented by enterprises such as the D&H Scovil Hoe Company and Clark Cutaway Harrow transformed the economic and social landscape. Making money for its own sake replaced rural ideals of self-sufficiency. Cultural and religious diversity replaced social homogeneity. Old and new ways of making a living coexisted as residents sought prosperity by exploiting the town's natural resources and geographical location.

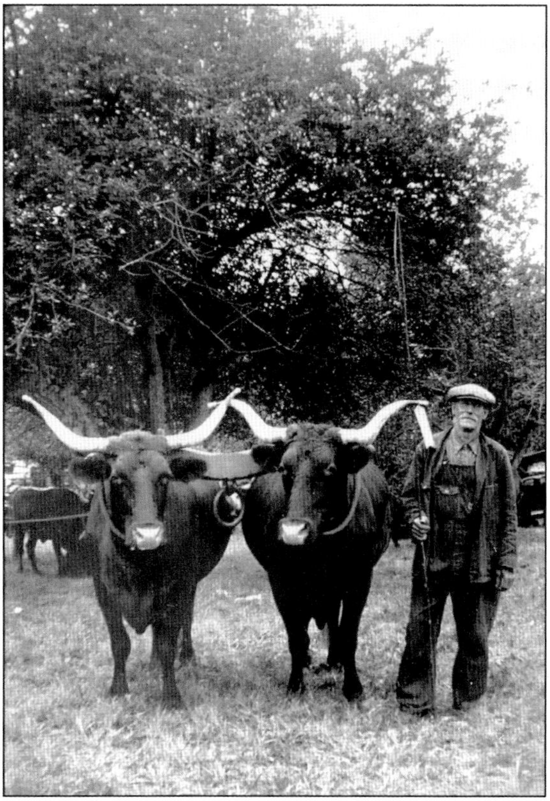

Harley Peck, a bachelor farmer on Candlewood Hill Road, poses with his oxen in this undated photograph. Ox teams were the "trucks" of the day. Farmers sometimes hired out their teams to haul freight. Augusta Chadsey remembered that "as many as seventy ox teams plodded through muddy roads . . . in a single day, loaded with goods." Candlewood Hill's name derives from the nearby trees whose pitch was used as a candle substitute.

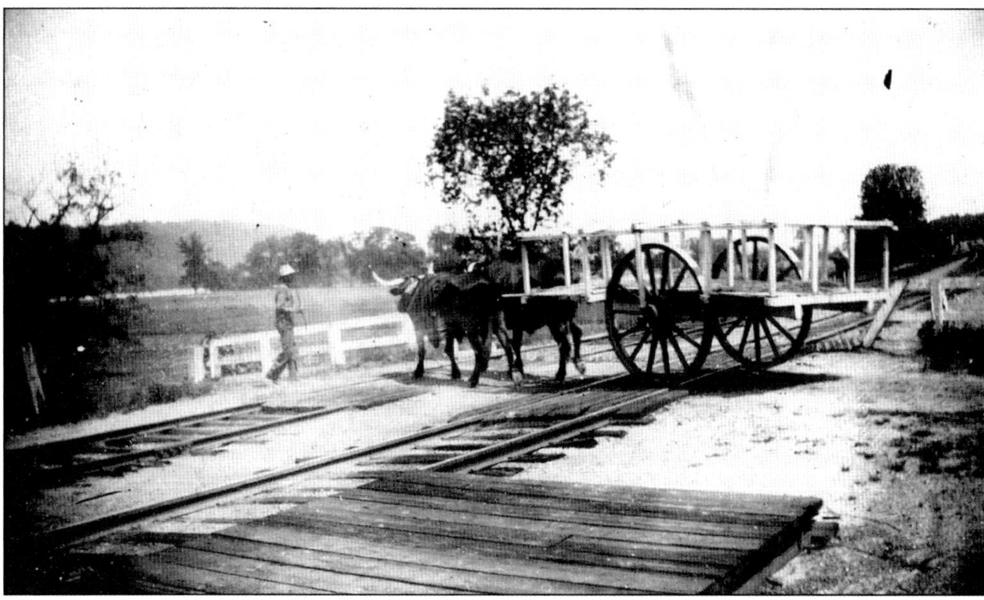

In this Clark family photograph, an ox team crosses the railroad tracks on Station Hill near the Connecticut River, just south of the Haddam railroad station. Managing an ox team required extensive training of the animals beginning at a young age, but a farmer could earn a return on this investment. In 1917, the town meeting voted to pay $4 a day to a man with an ox team.

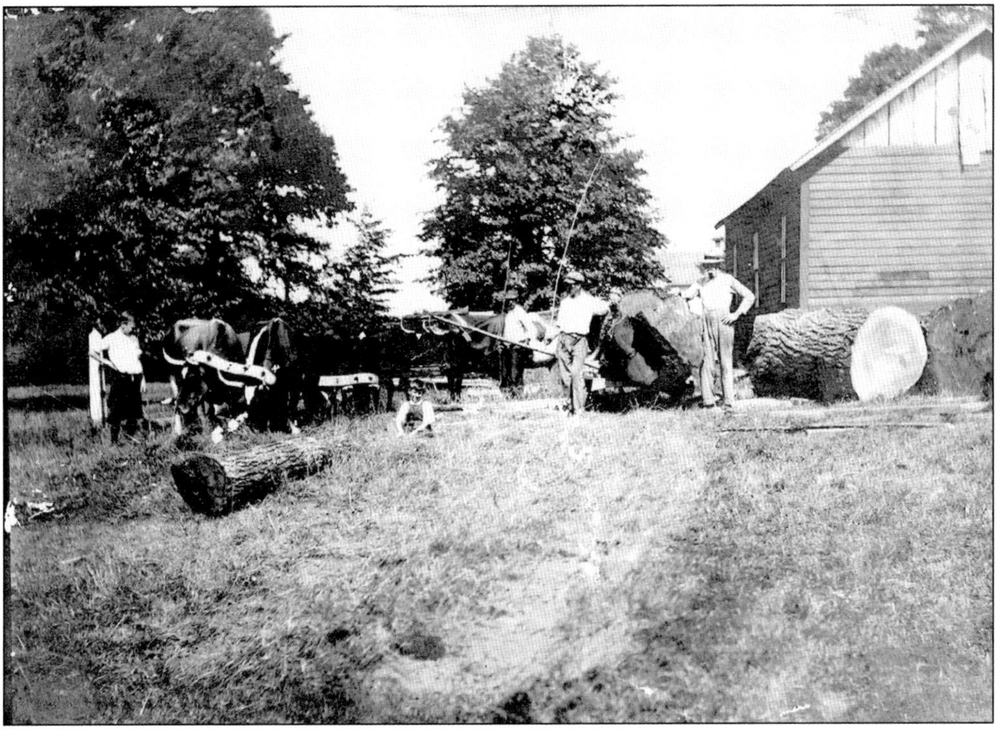

A team of oxen assists in cutting and hauling a massive log at Frank House's sawmill on Quarry Hill Road in Haddam Neck. House, the man standing on the right, also owned the Pine Brook Paper Mill. (Courtesy Kruger family.)

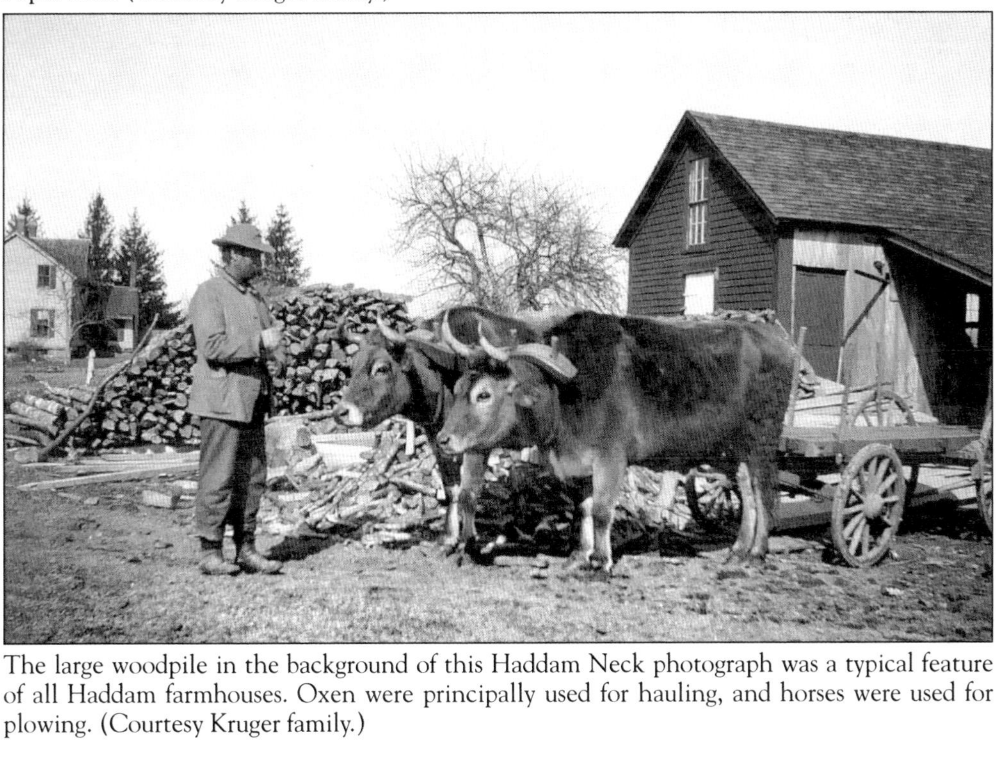

The large woodpile in the background of this Haddam Neck photograph was a typical feature of all Haddam farmhouses. Oxen were principally used for hauling, and horses were used for plowing. (Courtesy Kruger family.)

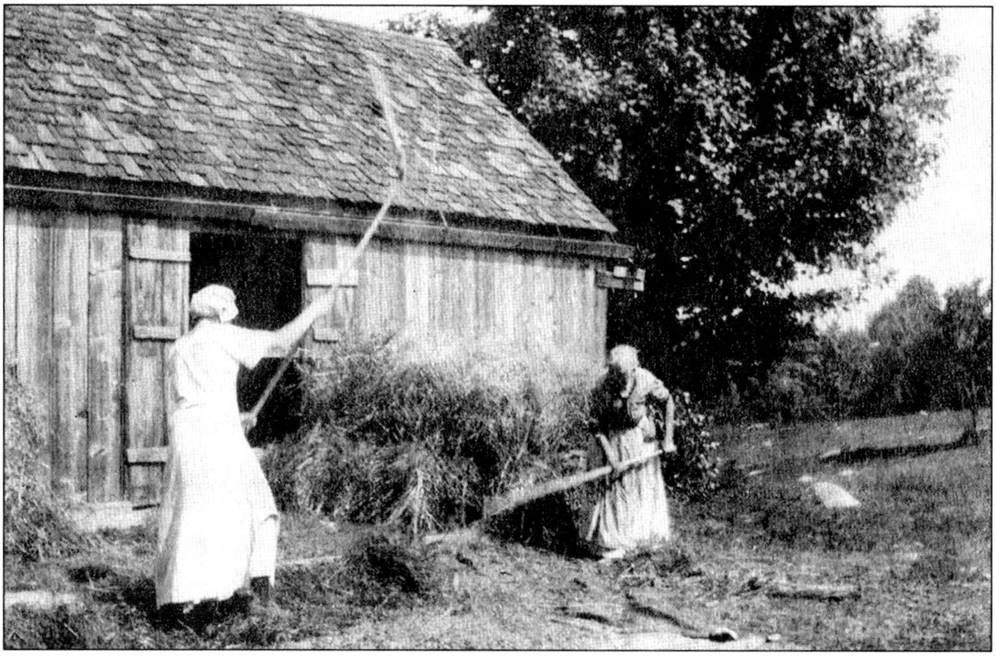

Agnes and Mary Pokorny thresh wheat behind their barn on Pokorny Road sometime in the 1920s.

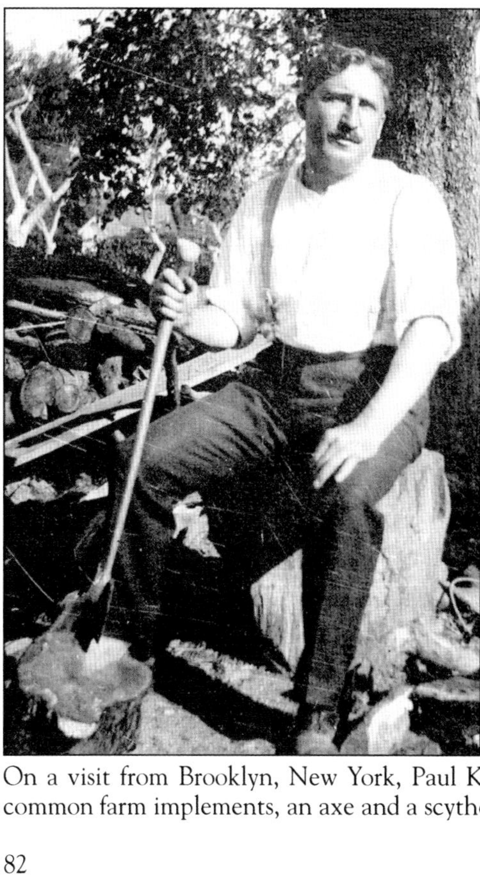

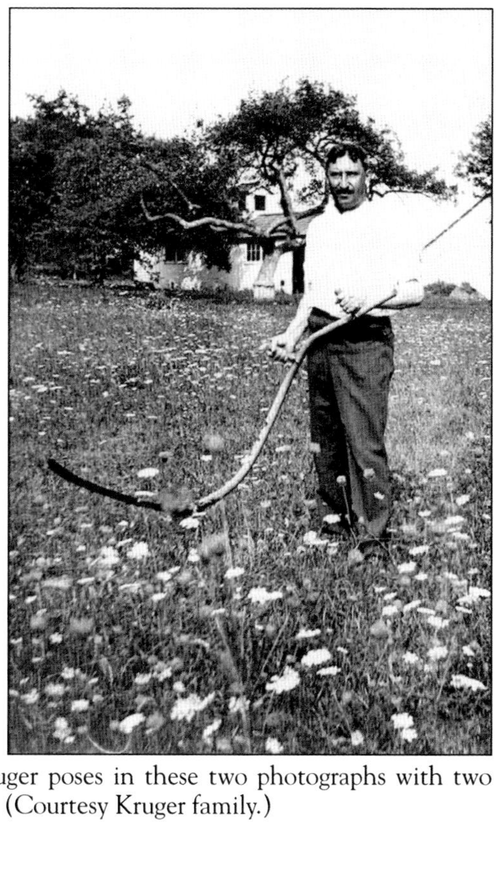

On a visit from Brooklyn, New York, Paul Kruger poses in these two photographs with two common farm implements, an axe and a scythe. (Courtesy Kruger family.)

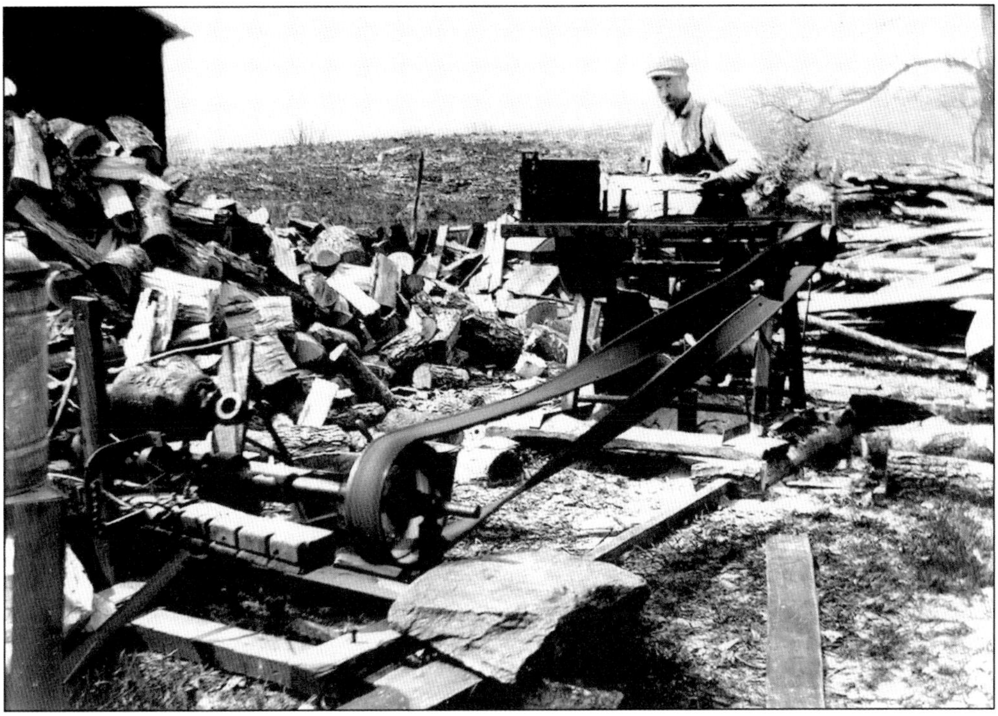

Frank Pokorny described procuring firewood in the early 20th century: "We cut wood (no chain saws, only axes and cross-cut saws). It would be brought in and cut into stove lengths. John Knowles . . . had a wagon with a circular saw on the back and an engine in the front that drove the saw by a long belt. He cut our wood until my father built a rig of his own."

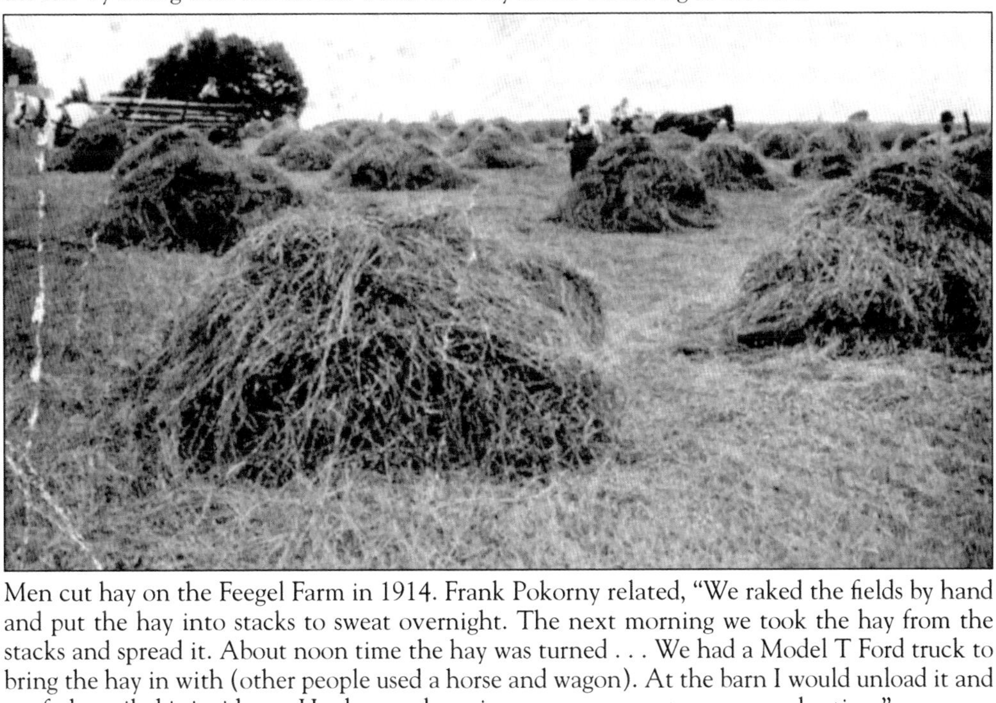

Men cut hay on the Feegel Farm in 1914. Frank Pokorny related, "We raked the fields by hand and put the hay into stacks to sweat overnight. The next morning we took the hay from the stacks and spread it. About noon time the hay was turned . . . We had a Model T Ford truck to bring the hay in with (other people used a horse and wagon). At the barn I would unload it and my father piled it inside . . . He threw salt on it to prevent spontaneous combustion."

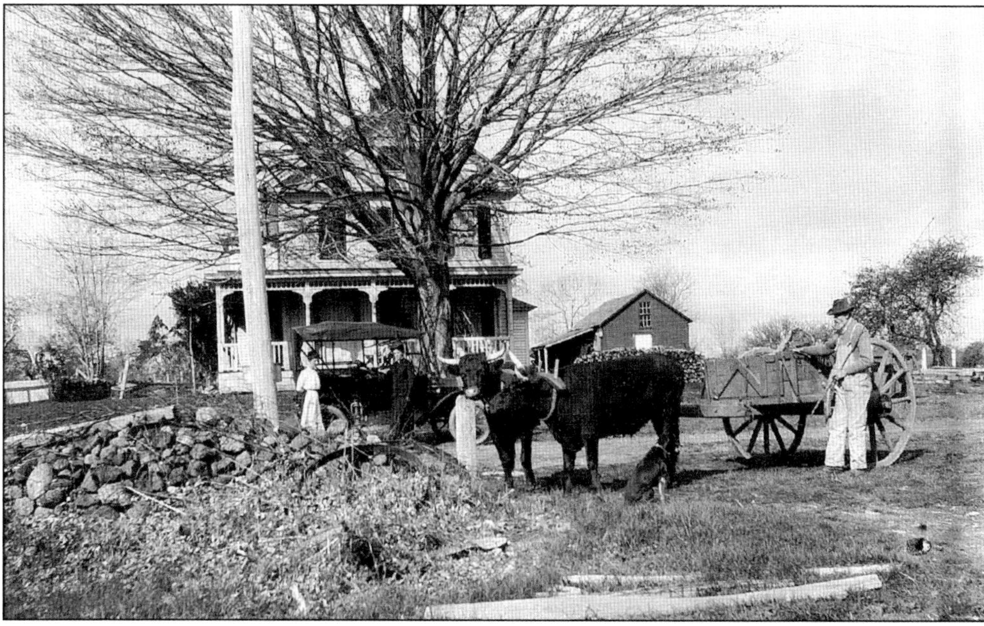

This family photograph depicts a classic farmstead, including a farmhouse, a barn, a woodpile, oxen, and an orchard. Apples were a staple crop that were picked in the fall. They were stored fresh in wooden barrels, sliced and dried, or made into cider, much as had been done since the Colonial days. Some families bought cider. In the early decades of the 20th century, Joseph Kalweit operated a cider mill on Killingworth Road. (Courtesy Kruger family.)

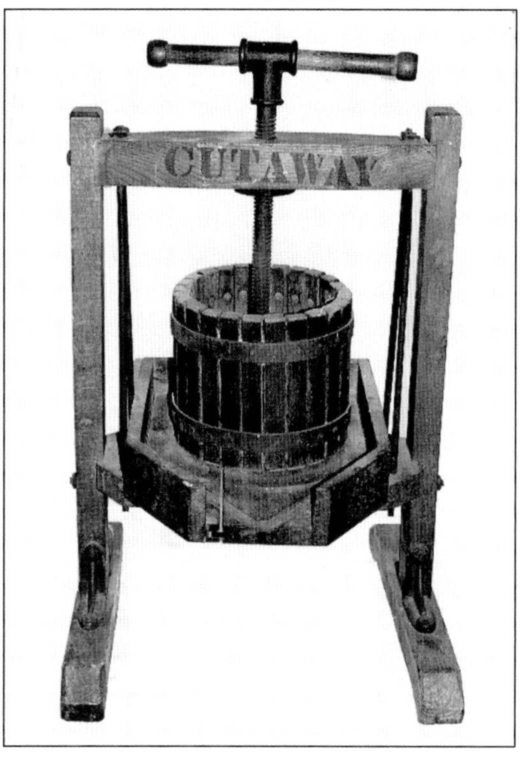

Some people made more exotic drinks from other fruits. Frank Pokorny remembered, "My father had a small press that he used to squeeze the juice out of grapes, elderberries, and wild cherries to make wine. We also made dandelion wine. This was expensive to make because we added sugar and oranges. It was stronger than the others." (Courtesy Dave Lenzi.)

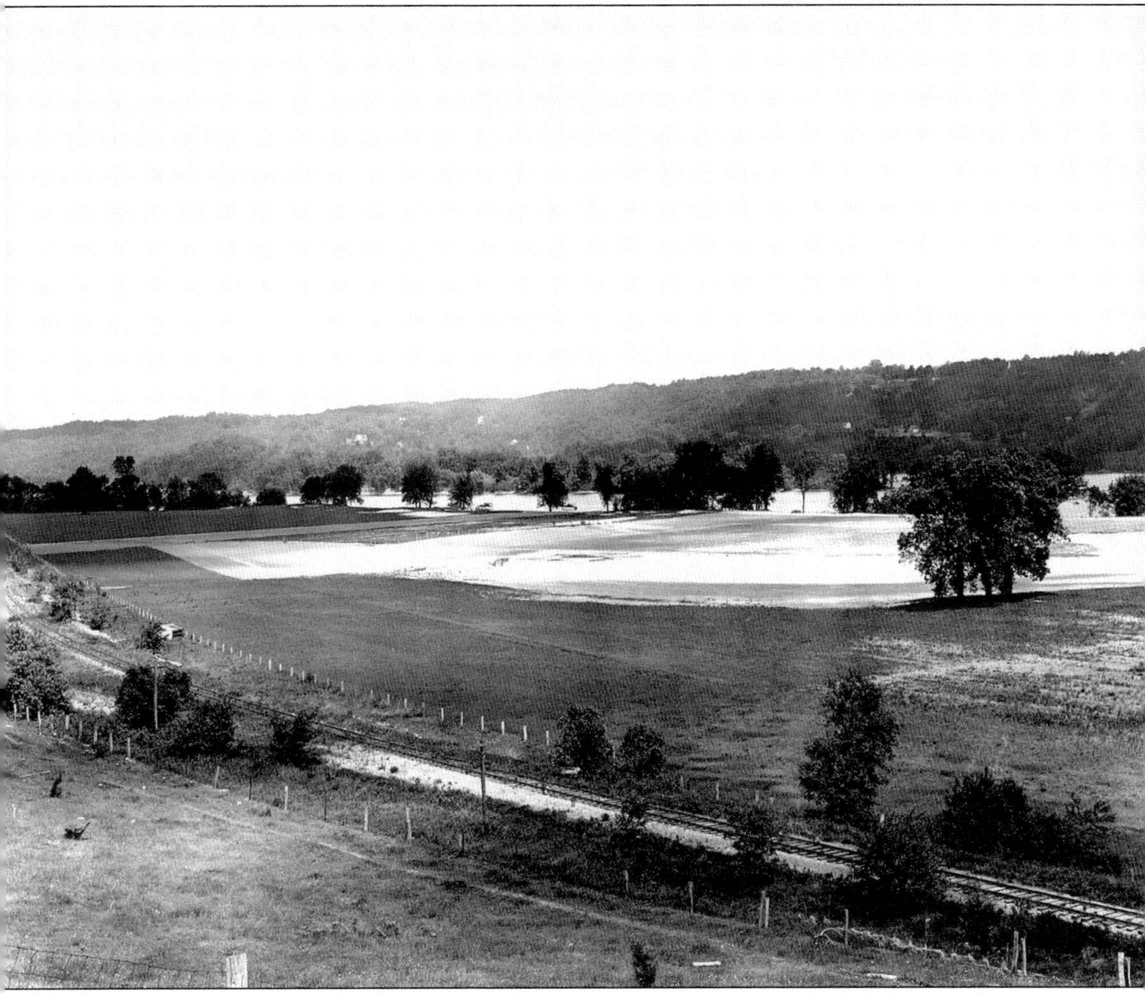

The Hazen Farm represents farming on another scale. Between 1913 and 1915, Edward Hazen purchased several farms along the river to create a 500-acre agricultural enterprise of pasture, orchards, and woodland that he called Hazenhurst. After Hazen's death in January 1929, the property was divided and sold. Part of the original farm became Haddam Meadows State Park, with additions made by eminent domain.

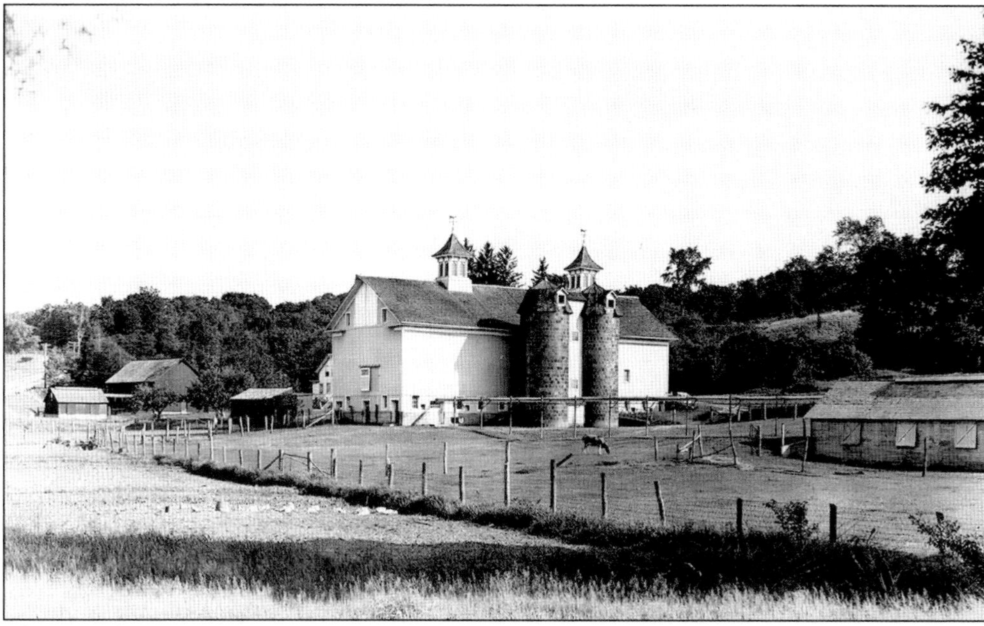

The two-silo main dairy barn was distinguished by a pair of cupolas with weather vanes, each topped with a cow. A horse barn and other buildings are to the left. At the right is the manure shed, which is connected by a conveyor belt to the dairy barn, the home of the milk cattle.

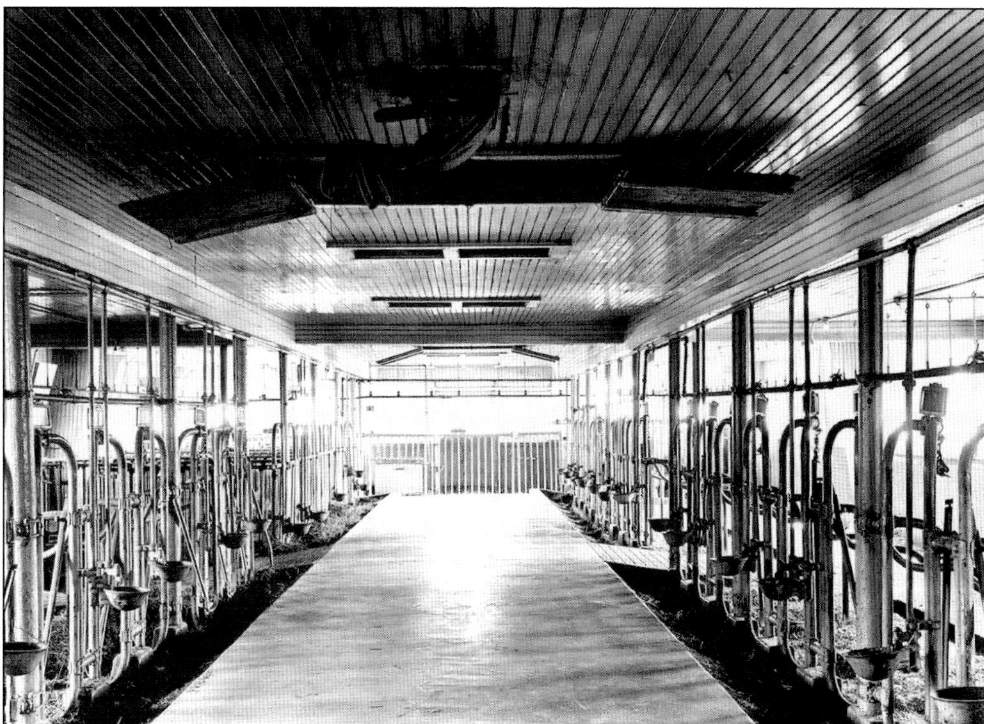

The farm was primarily a dairy operation, with room for a maximum of 45 cows and a bull or "sire." The latest equipment included milking machines, refrigerators for storing milk, and sterilization equipment. This view shows the interior of the main dairy barn.

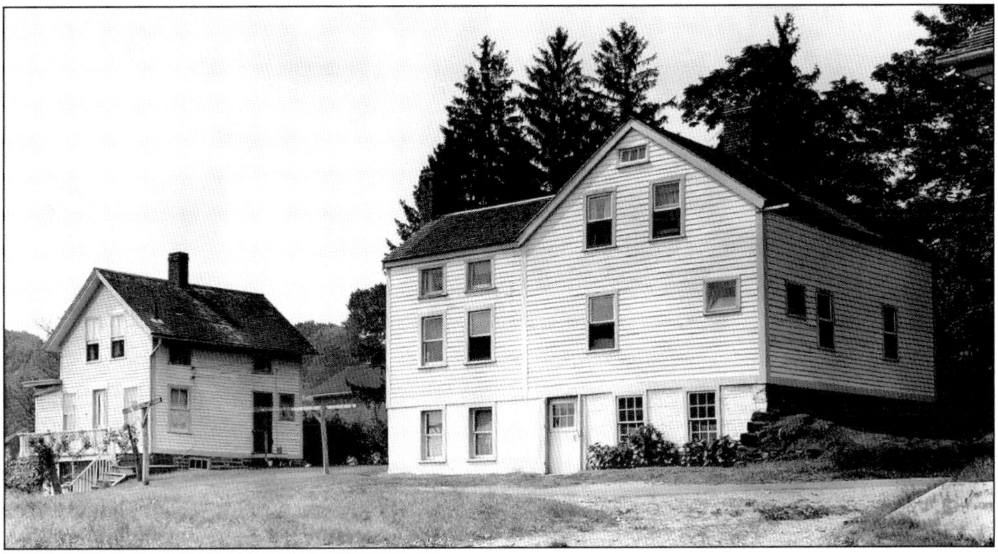

Edward Hazen was a gentleman farmer. The business was directed by a superintendent and employed several workers who occupied some of the eight dwellings on the property, two of which are shown here.

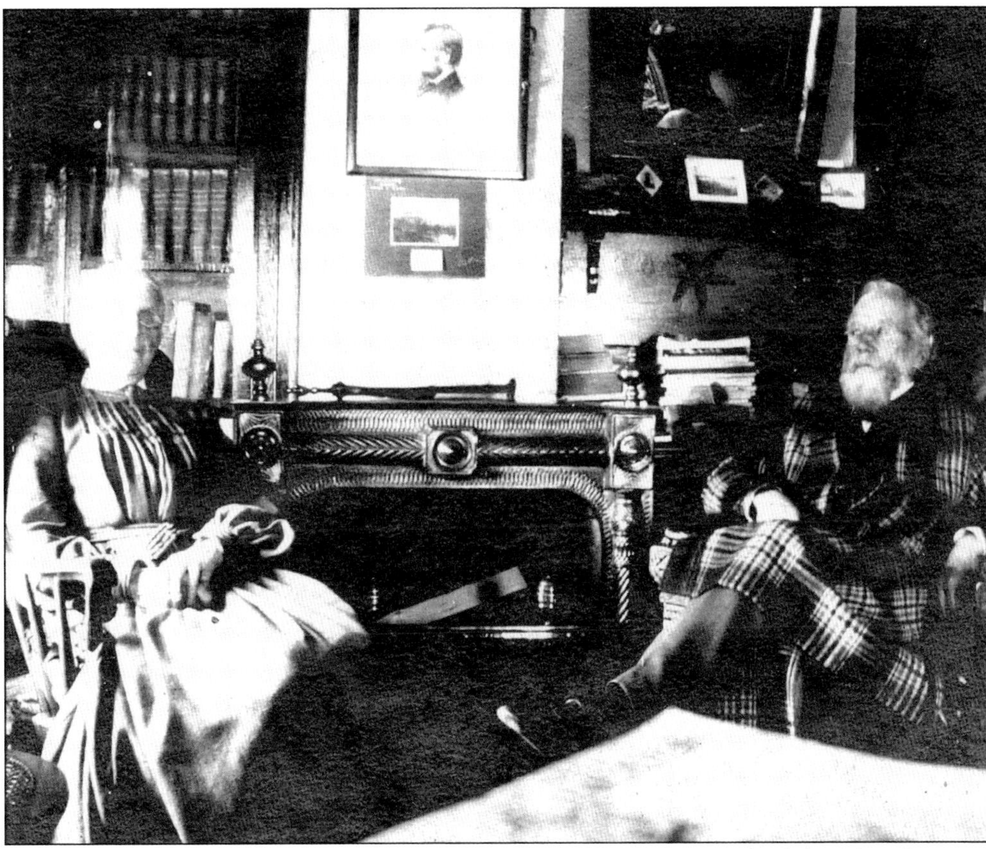

Hazen and his wife are pictured at home in the Miner C. Hazen House, built by Edward Hazen's parents in 1869. (Courtesy Parmelee family.)

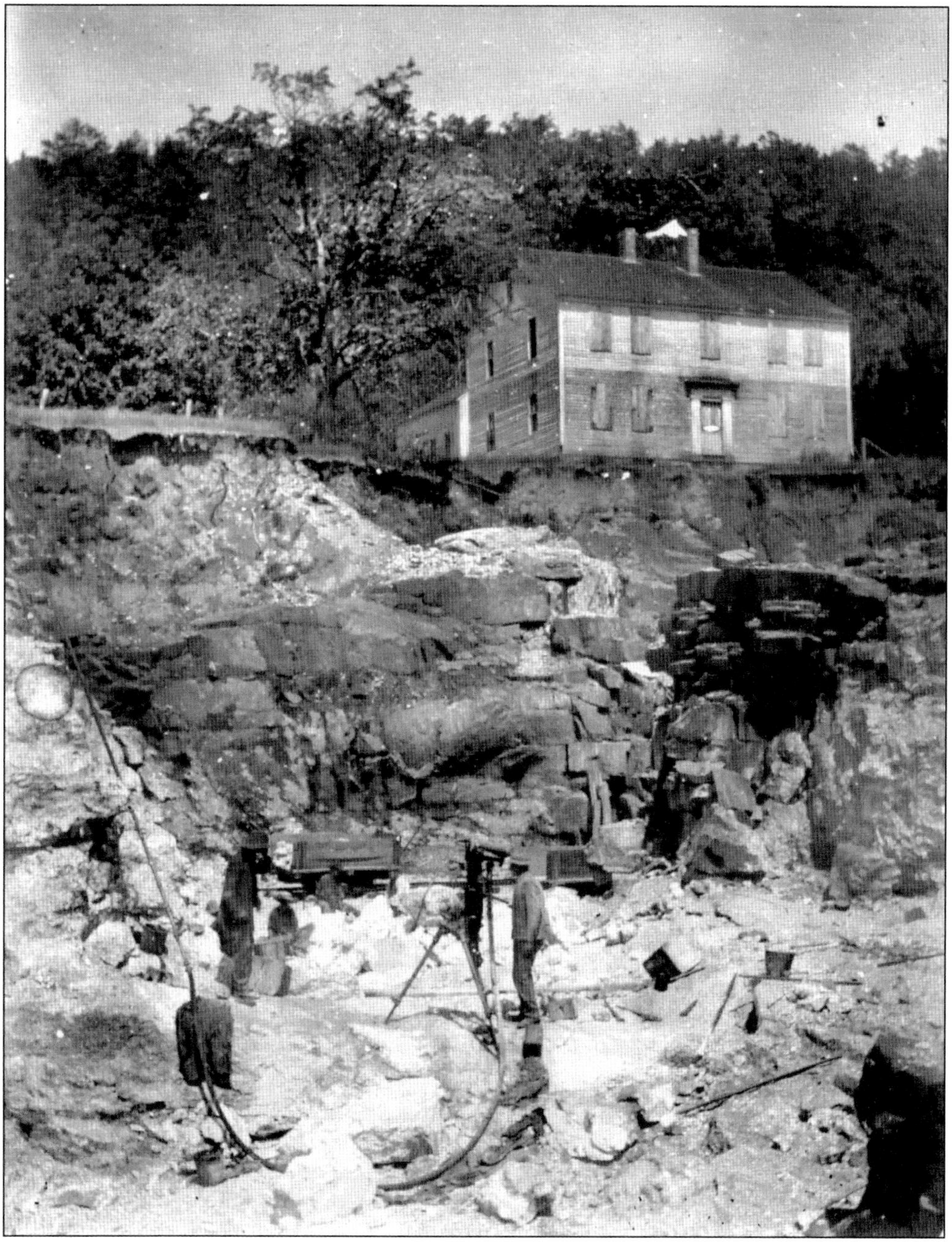

The men shown here are mining granite in Gillette's Quarry on Injun Hollow Road. Capitalizing on the area's extensive rocky outcroppings, Deacon Ezra Brainerd opened the first quarry in Haddam Neck in 1762. Gneiss (or "Haddam granite") and feldspar were shipped downriver to New York and as far away as England. Mica, trap rock, and graphite were also mined in the 19th century. The quarries stimulated boatbuilding, a second major industry in the "Neck." (Connecticut Historical Society, Hartford, CT.)

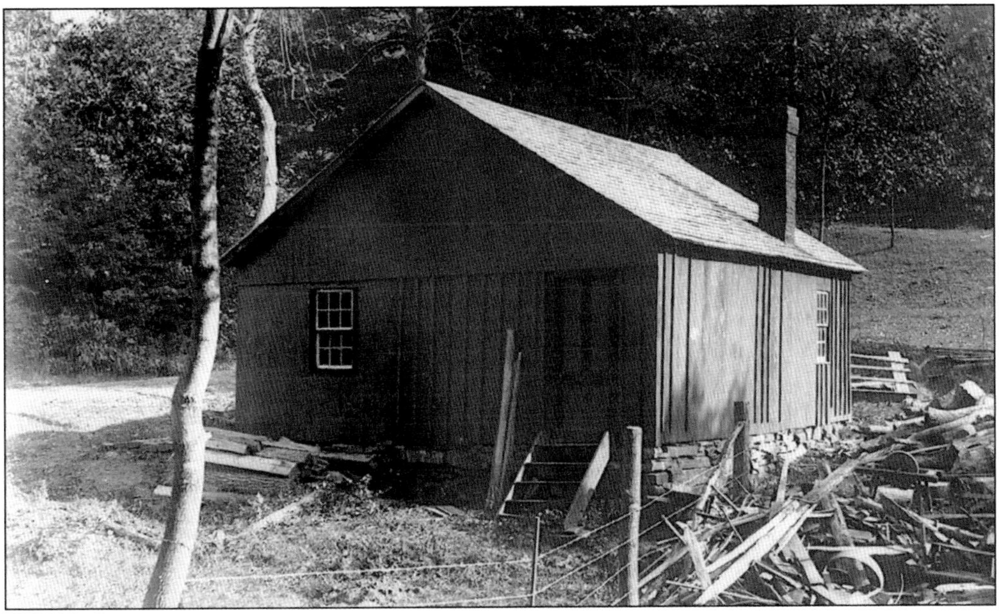

Pictured here is the Gillette basket shop. Ezra Gillette operated a basket-making manufactory on Basketshop Road in Haddam Neck beginning in 1852. By the 1880s, he and his sons, Charles O. and Merritt P. Gillette, operated two factories and produced 14,400 baskets annually. There were also several smaller basket-making operations in Haddam Neck around this time. (Courtesy Middle Haddam Library, Olsen Collection.)

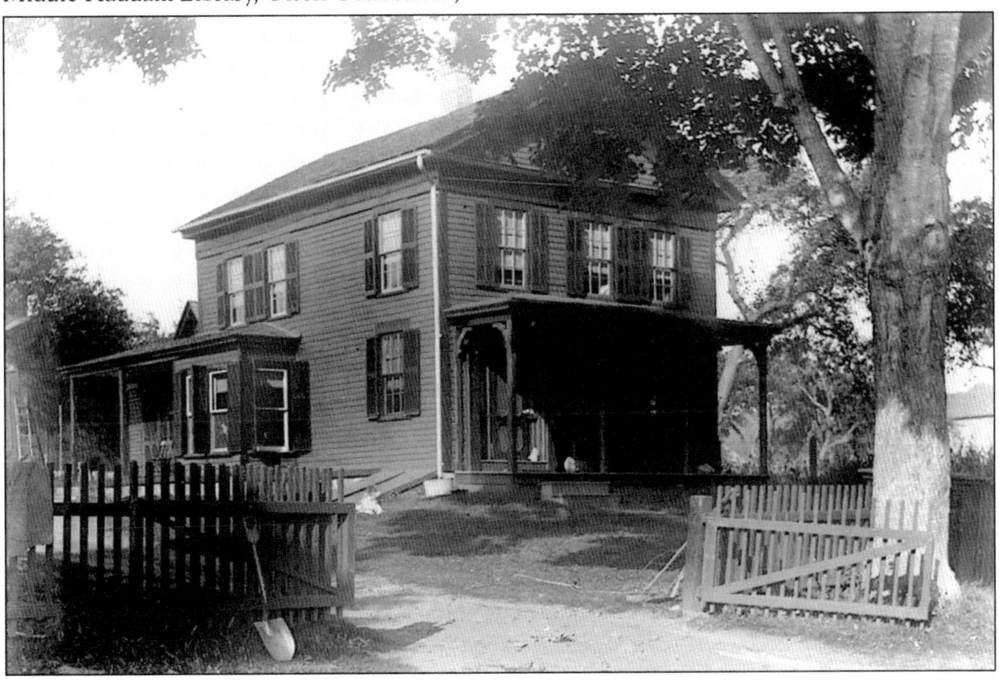

Merritt Gillette's house stood on Rock Landing Road, opposite the basket shop. Backyard industries were prevalent in Haddam and were typical of the early industrial revolution. Farmers combined manufacturing with agriculture to eke out a living. (Courtesy Middle Haddam Library, Olsen Collection.)

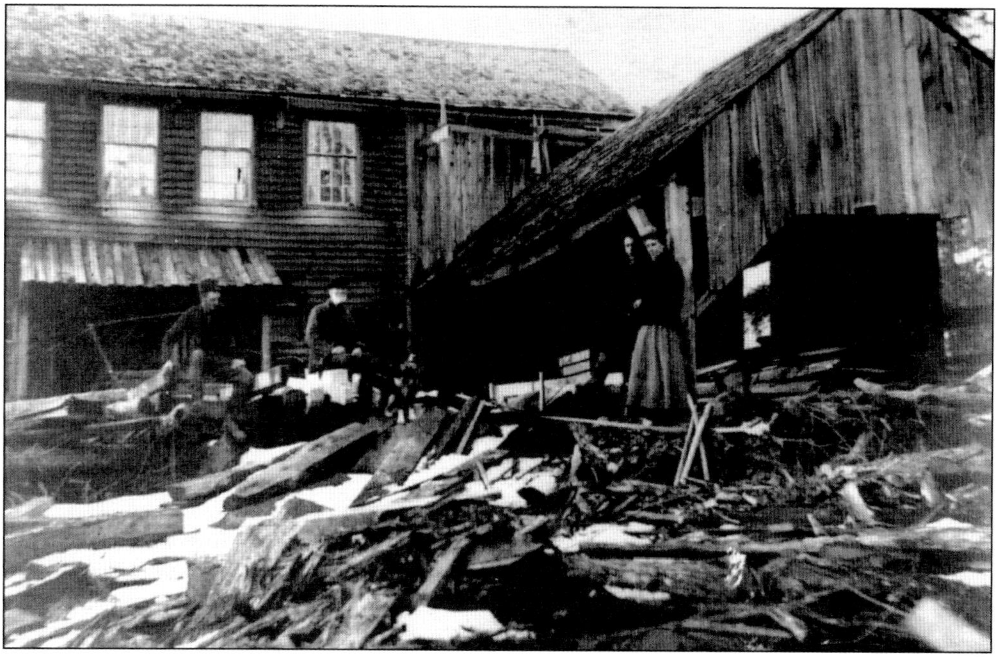

Numerous streams in town provided waterpower to factories. Pine Brook in Haddam Neck powered a number of them, including this paper mill, owned by House and Brothers, as well as a sawmill and a gristmill operated by Lt. Simon Brainerd. (Courtesy Kruger family.)

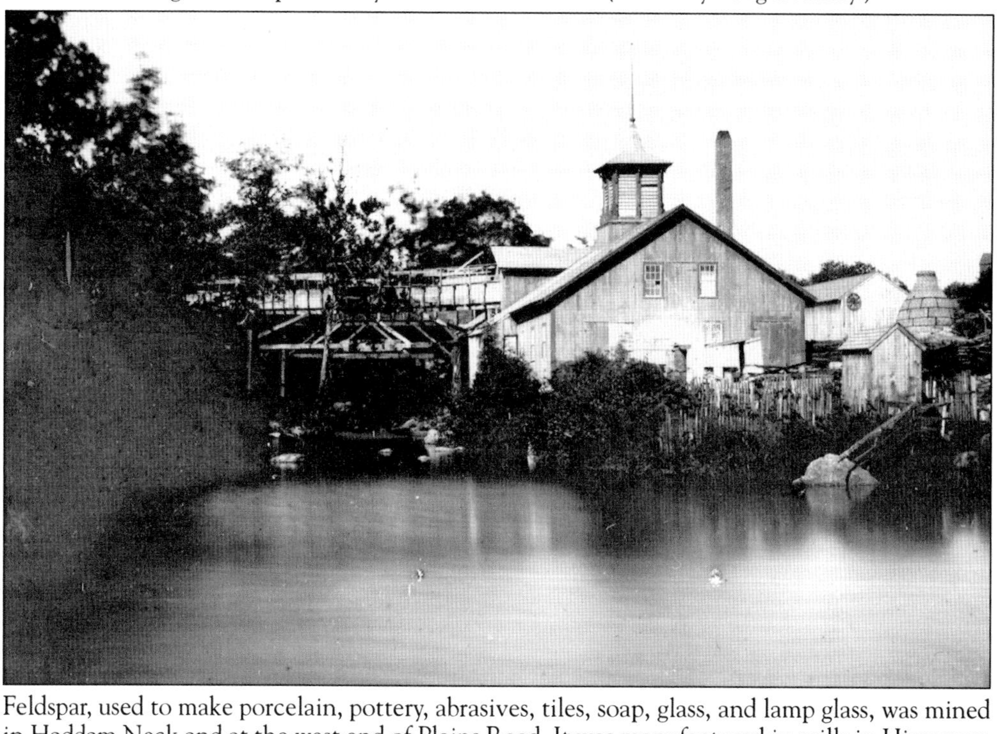

Feldspar, used to make porcelain, pottery, abrasives, tiles, soap, glass, and lamp glass, was mined in Haddam Neck and at the west end of Plains Road. It was manufactured in mills in Higganum and Haddam Neck. This photograph shows the Higganum mill in 1877. (George Bradford Brainerd photograph, courtesy Brainerd Library.)

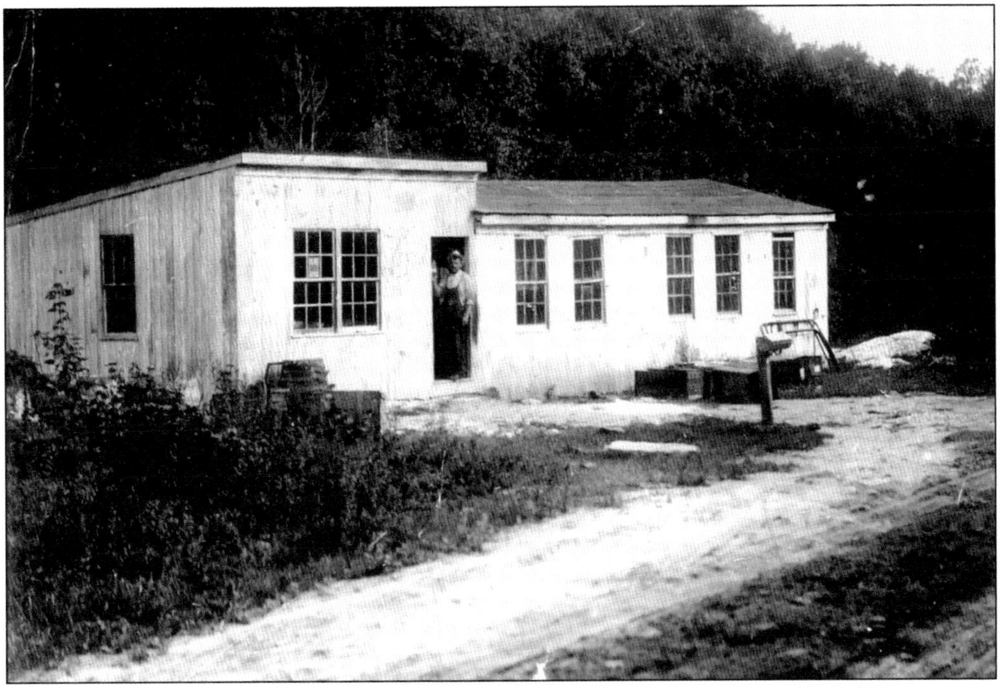

The owner of Joseph Prchal's button shop on Hubbard Road poses in 1918. Beginning in 1835, numerous "backyard" button shops employed two to five people. Haddam buttons were manufactured from mother-of-pearl from native clam and oyster shells, abalone shells from Australia, or "vegetable ivory," the kernel of the corozo or taqua nut from South America and Africa. The buttons were sold in New York City.

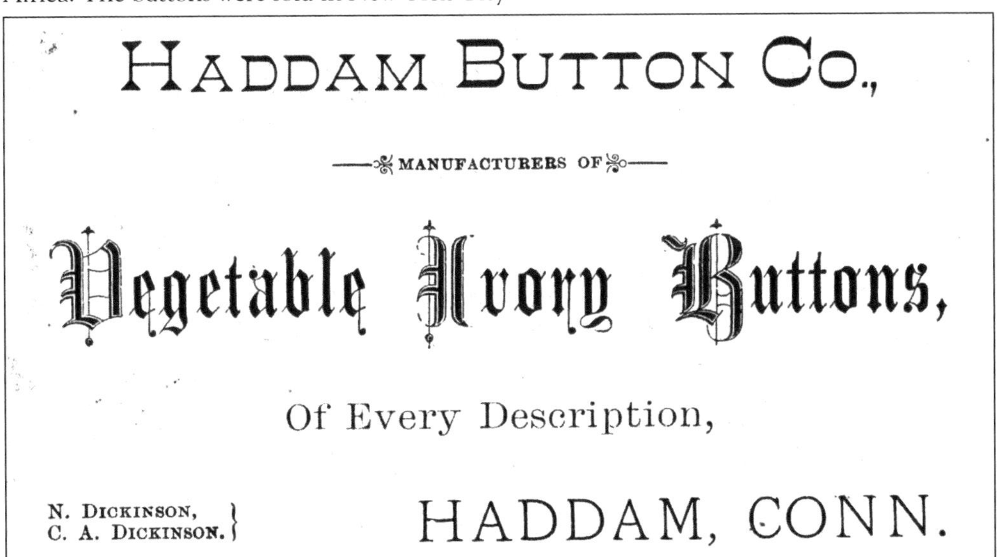

Mary Soobitsky remembered, "A cutter took the large Abalone or Nacre shells . . . and with the rotating hollow drill cut out a long circular strip. This strip was then cut down to individual sized circles . . . Each type of button had a special chuck and drill to form the necessary design that was desired. They were placed into mixtures of chemicals to bleach them . . . and finally polished in a rotating barrel of sawdust. Lastly they were . . . sorted into grades."

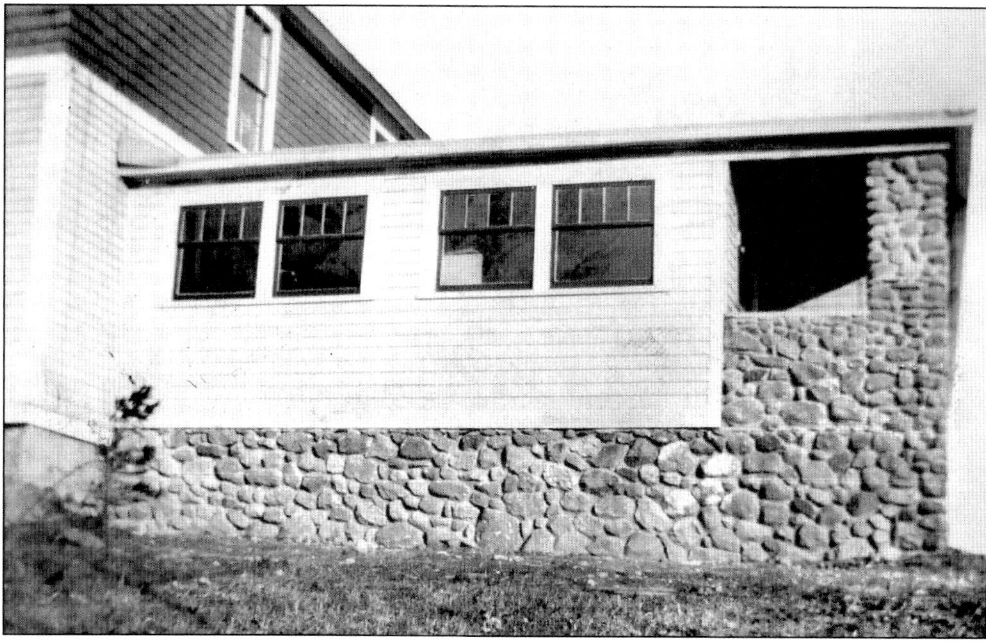

Granite Rock Spring Bottling Works, later Undina Company, was founded by Swedish immigrant Otto Carlson in 1872. He was inspired by a desire to reproduce the soft drink he remembered from his childhood in Sweden. By 1903, sons Charles and Edward had expanded the business to sell all kinds of carbonated beverages. The company passed through the hands of different owners and remained in operation until the late 20th century. (Courtesy Alan Webb.)

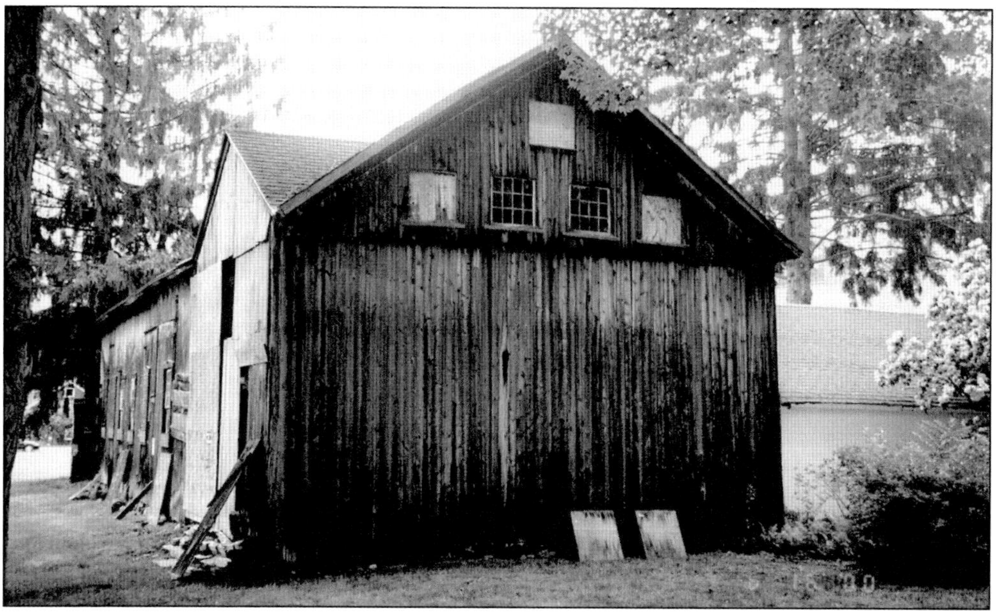

Beginning in the late 19th century, the Shailer and Knowles factory made stamped and pressed metal products that were sold through an office in New York City. The Shailer and Knowles factory was typical of numerous small hardware producers in the lower Connecticut Valley at this time, except it was powered by steam rather than water. The factory ceased operations in 1914, but one of its buildings survives on Saybrook Road.

The Shailer factory manufactured a variety of products using tin-plated iron and steel sheets. These included canning jar lids, sheet metal holders for lamp oil bottles, and a variety of decorative hardware. The products were sold to retailers and other distributors. The dies shown here were used to form the products.

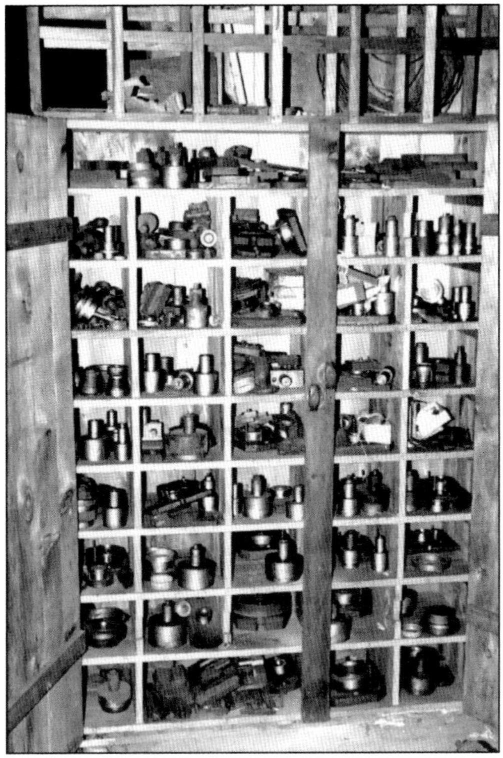

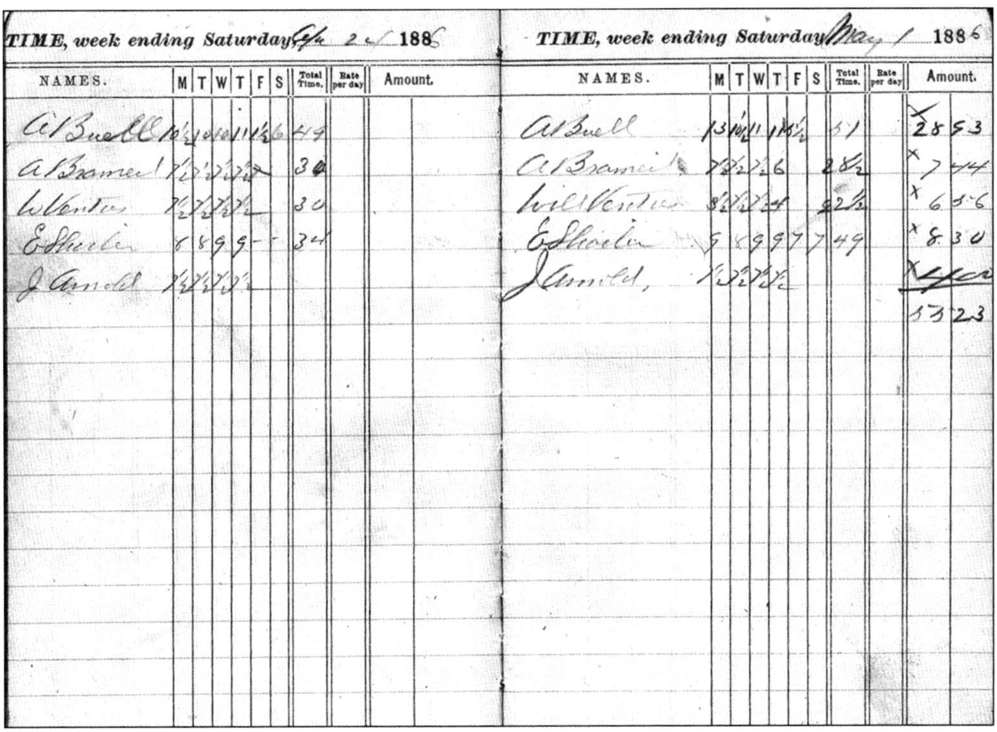

TIME, week ending Saturday 188

NAMES.	M	T	W	T	F	S	Total Time.	Rate per day	Amount.

TIME, week ending Saturday 188

NAMES.	M	T	W	T	F	S	Total Time.	Rate per day	Amount.

About 17 men and women worked at the Shailer and Knowles factory. In 1886, they earned between 37.5¢ and 66.5¢ per day. Full-time employees regularly worked up to 12 hours a day.

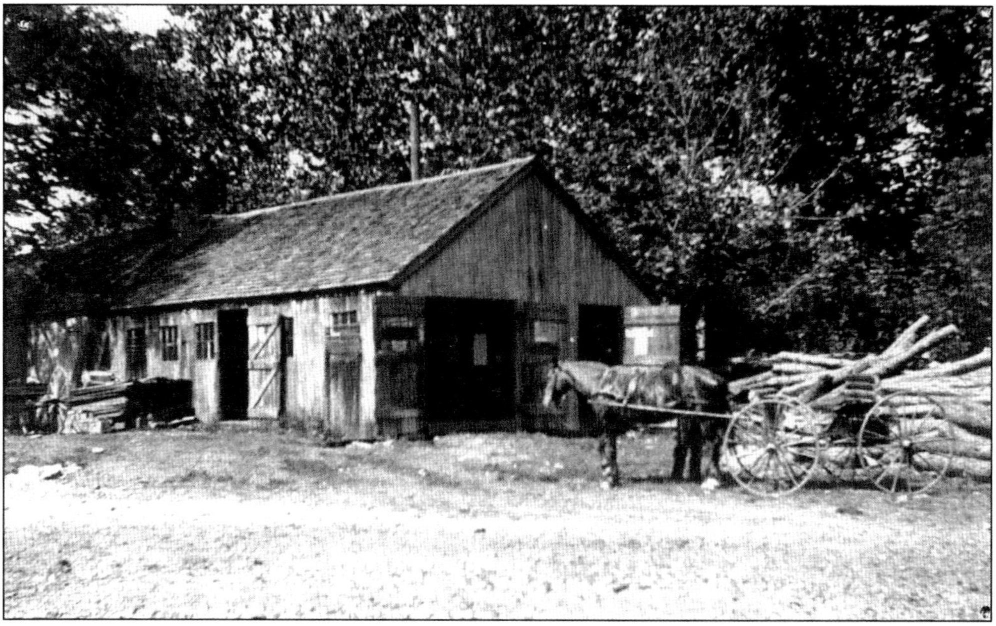

This blacksmith shop on Candlewood Hill Road produced hardware and horseshoes. Blacksmith shops were more than artifacts of agricultural life: they were the bridge between the rural past and the industrial age. For example, Hezekiah Scovil expanded his blacksmithing business on Candlewood Hill to make gun barrels for Eli Whitney. Scovil's sons Hezekiah and Daniel founded the Scovil Hoe Company, one of the largest factories in Higganum.

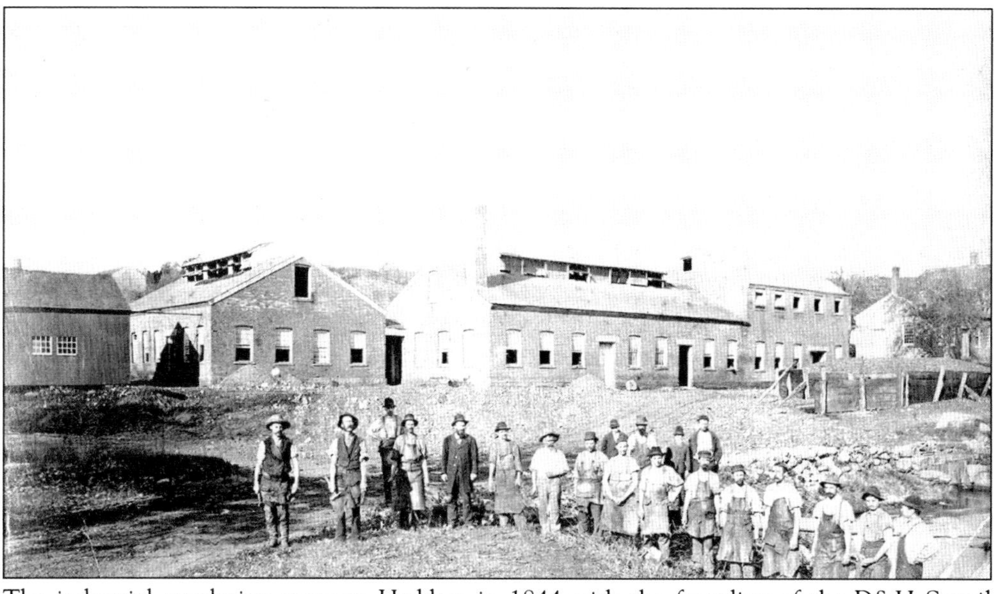

The industrial revolution came to Haddam in 1844 with the founding of the D&H Scovil Hoe Company in Higganum. The factory was still part of the everyday landscape of the village at the beginning of the 20th century. The men posing here in front of the factory building manufactured the self-sharpening Scovil Hoe, invented by Daniel Scovil after he observed slaves cultivating cotton with an inferior model.

Local history relates that Hezekiah Scovil Jr. ruthlessly pursued water rights along Candlewood Brook, even to the extent of pressuring (unsuccessfully) widow Hannah Knowles to sell him her property on Candlewood Hill. Beginning in 1861, the D&H Scovil Hoe Company built a number of shops along the brook to manufacture hoes. These factories used improved waterpower technology and replaced artisan labor with the techniques of mechanized mass production.

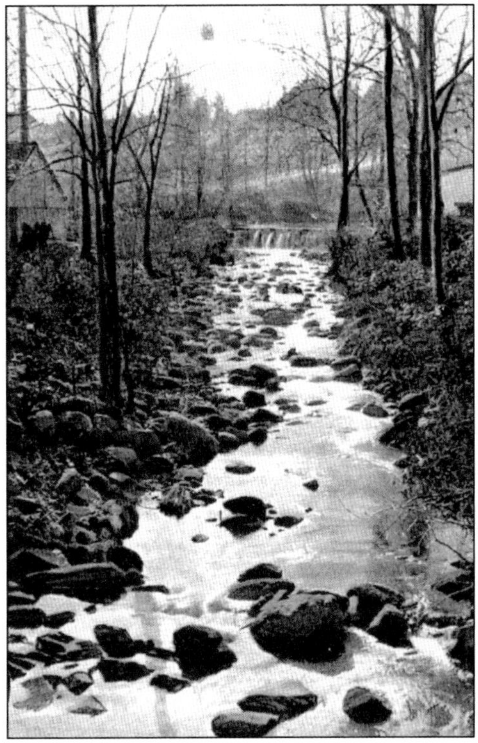

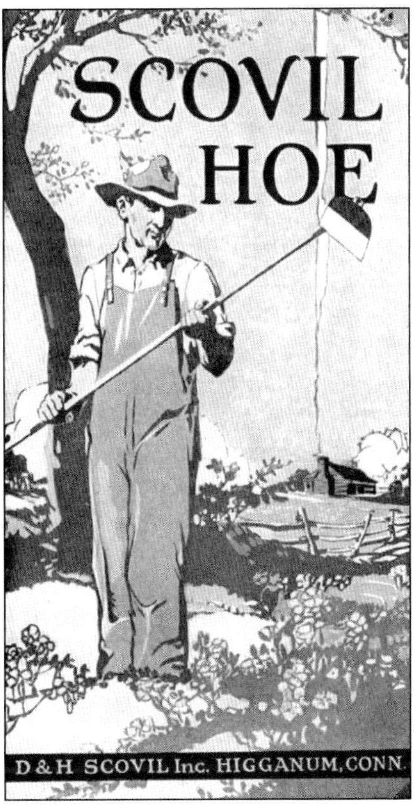

Both Scovil sons were trained in the metal trades by their father. Hezekiah Jr. provided business acumen, and Daniel was the inventive genius. Having observed slaves in the American south using traditional hoes, Daniel realized that by encasing the harder metal with softer material, hoes would effectively sharpen themselves as they were used. This more efficient implement replaced British models and was manufactured and sold by the company for over 60 years.

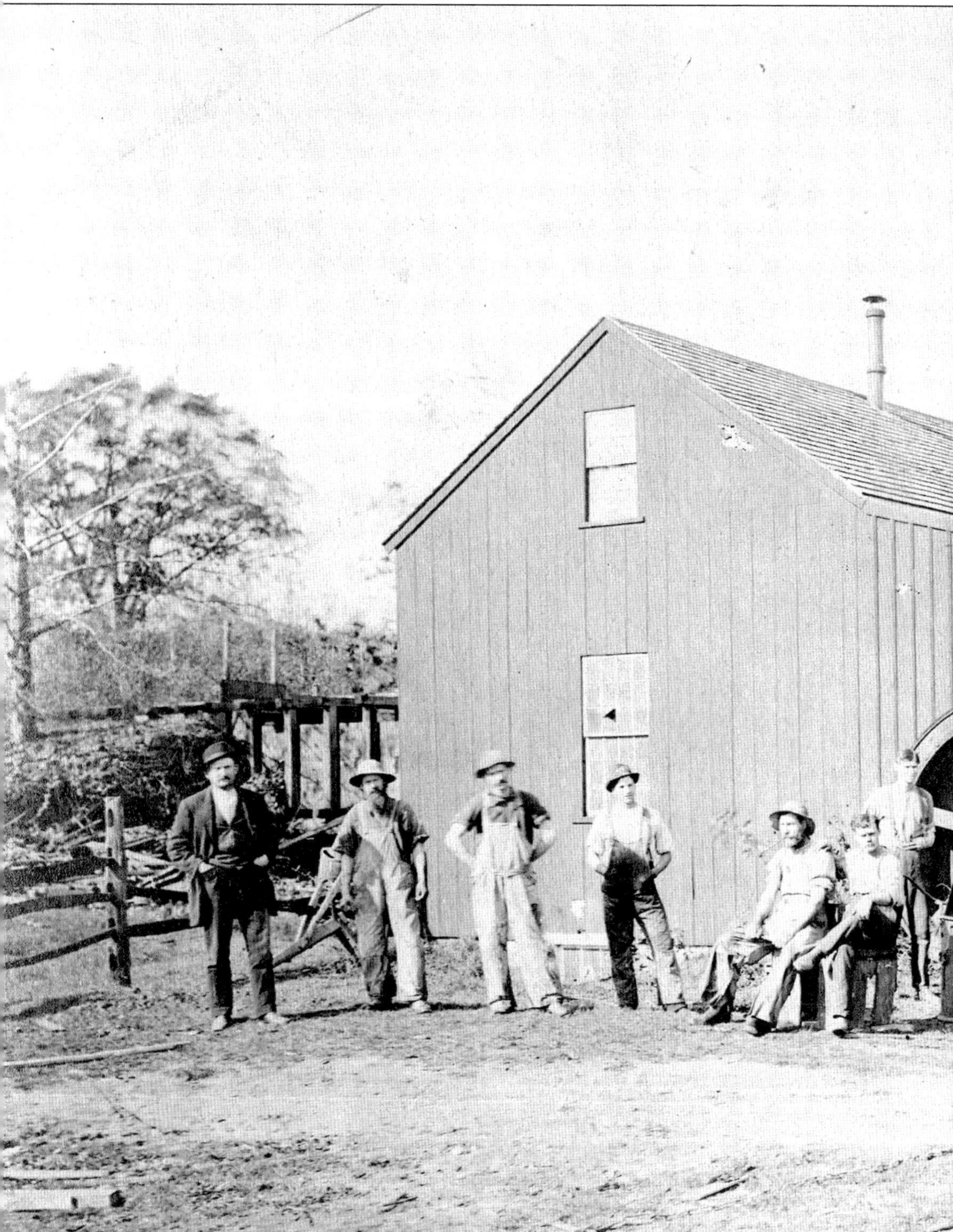

Workers at the Scovil grinding shop included Charlie Barker (fifth from the left), Brad Treadwell (eighth from the left, wearing an apron), Orlando Burr, and a Mr. Spencer. Owners Hezekiah

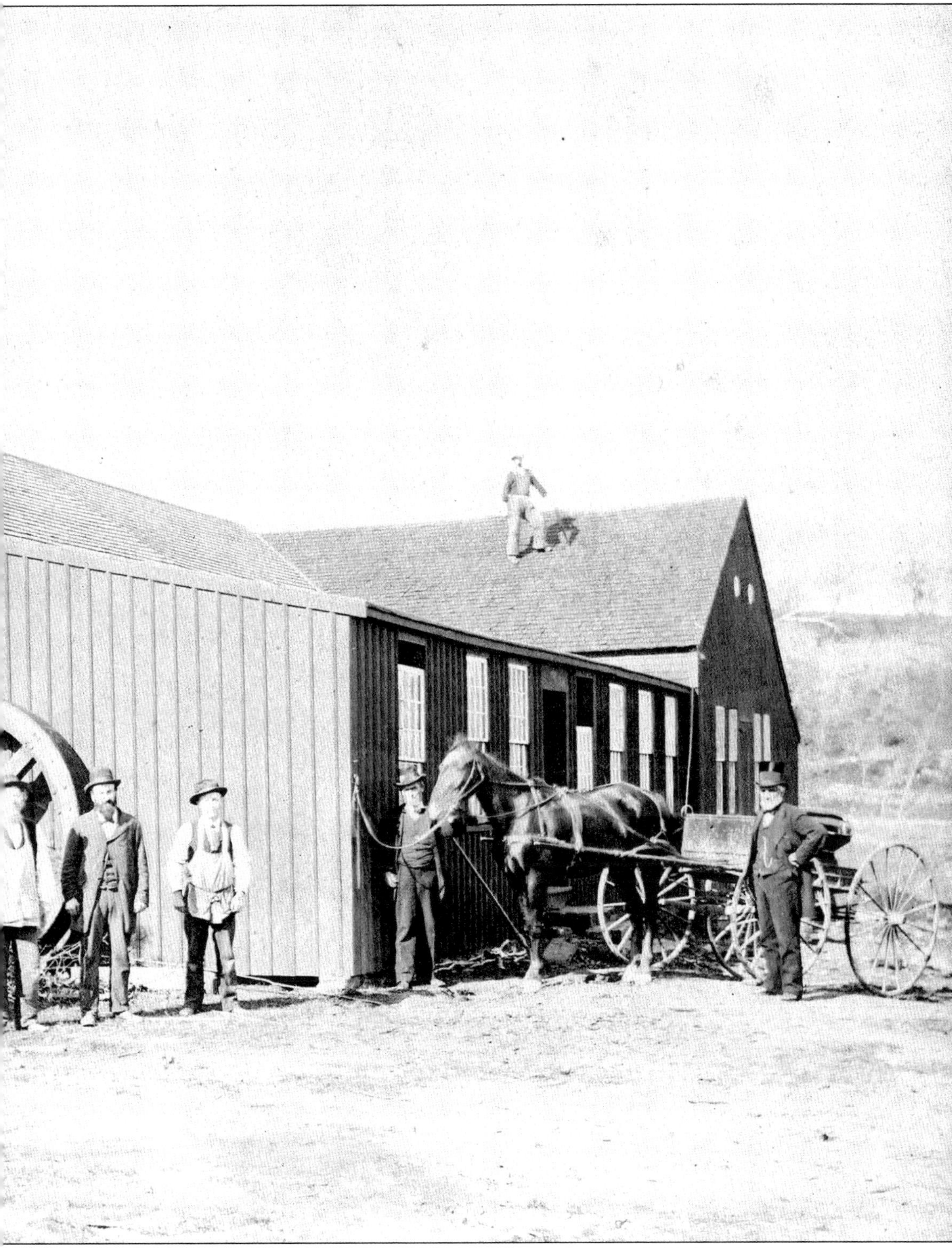

and Daniel Scovil stand on either side of the horse and wagon. As a child, Charlie Barker was a drummer in the Civil War. He later established the Haddam Fife and Drum Corps.

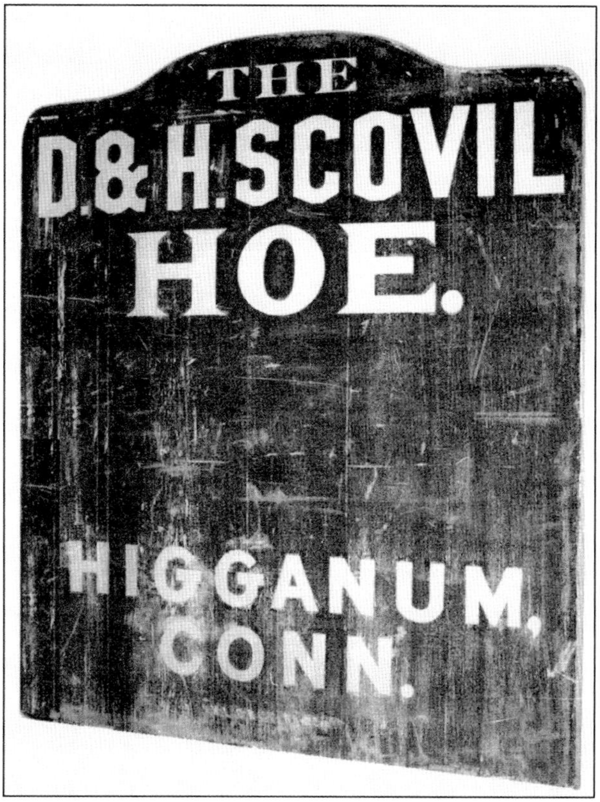

This sign hung for many years outside the company office. (Courtesy Dave Lenzi.)

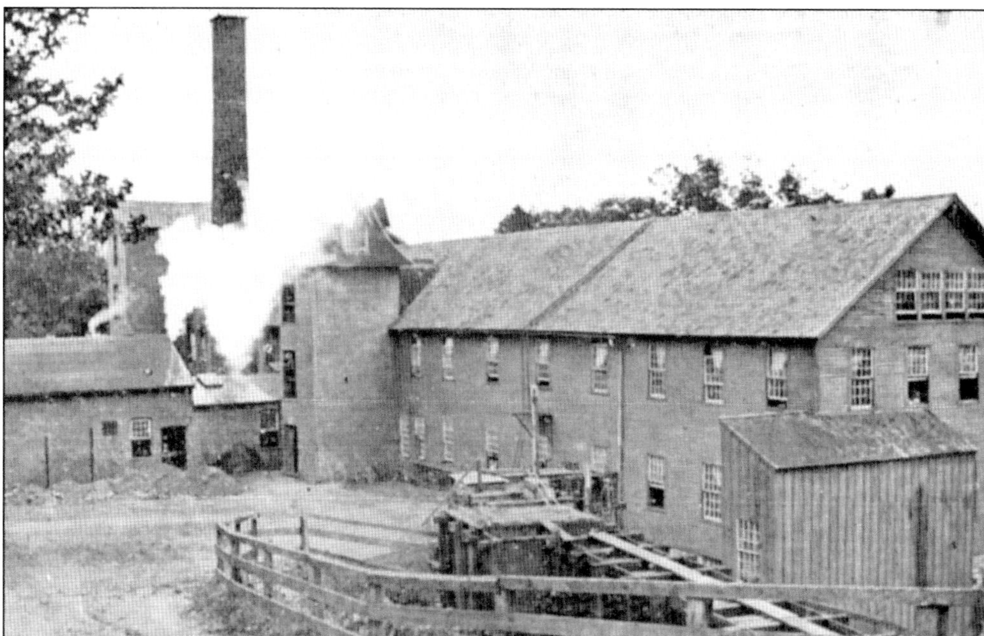

Textile manufacturing was the first industry to be mechanized. Here, steam escapes from the cotton mill on Higganum Creek. (Courtesy Don Sampson.)

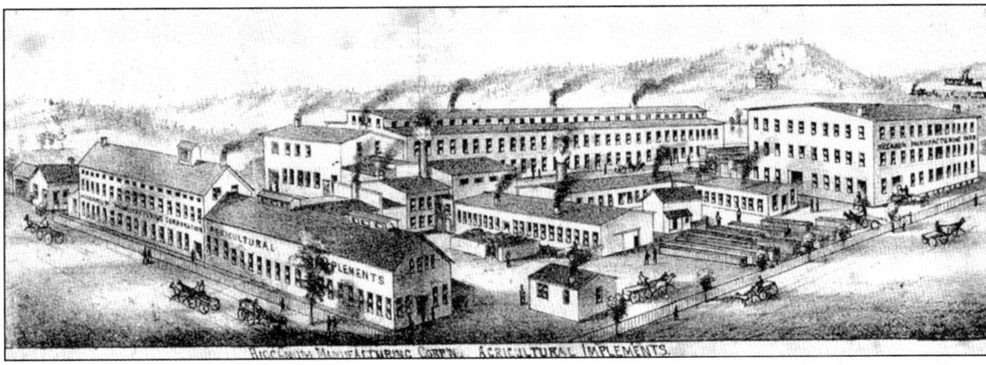

The Clark Cutaway Harrow Company sold its unique design of harrow and other agricultural implements to customers throughout the country. The business was founded by brothers Thomas Clark and George W. Clark as the Higganum Manufacturing Company in 1867. In 1891 it was renamed Clark Cutaway Harrow after its signature product. The company's factory building, shown here in 1914, was constructed in 1867. At its height, the business employed 150 men.

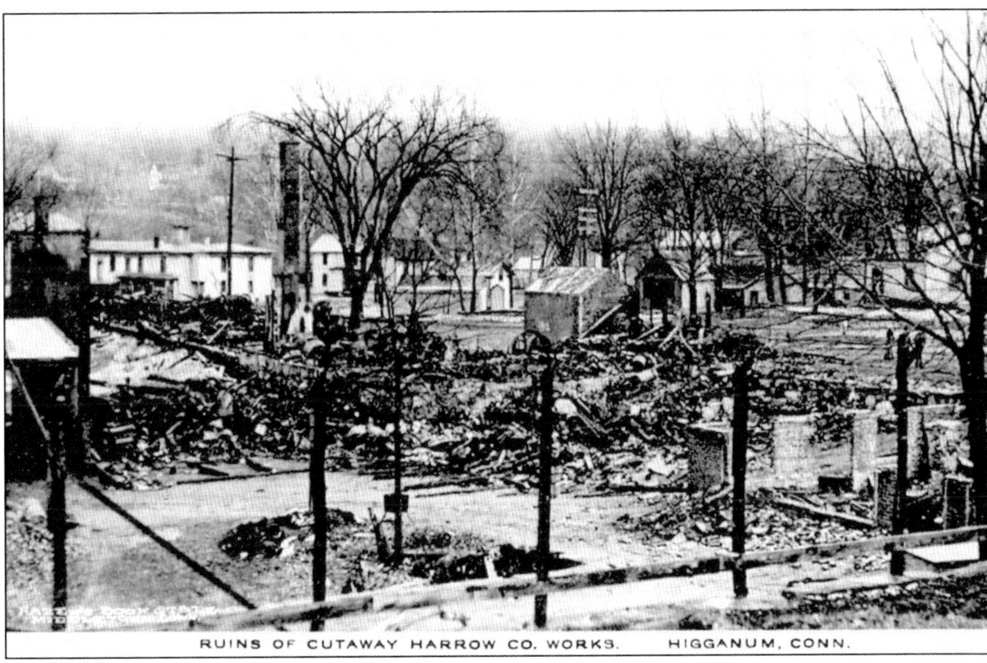

On the night of December 6, 1914, a fire that began in Cutaway Harrow's blacksmith shop destroyed it and the machine shop, the grinding room, and the company office, throwing 100 men out of work. The buildings were never replaced, although the company continued to operate. The remaining factory building, reservoir, and dam were sold to Orkil Company in 1942.

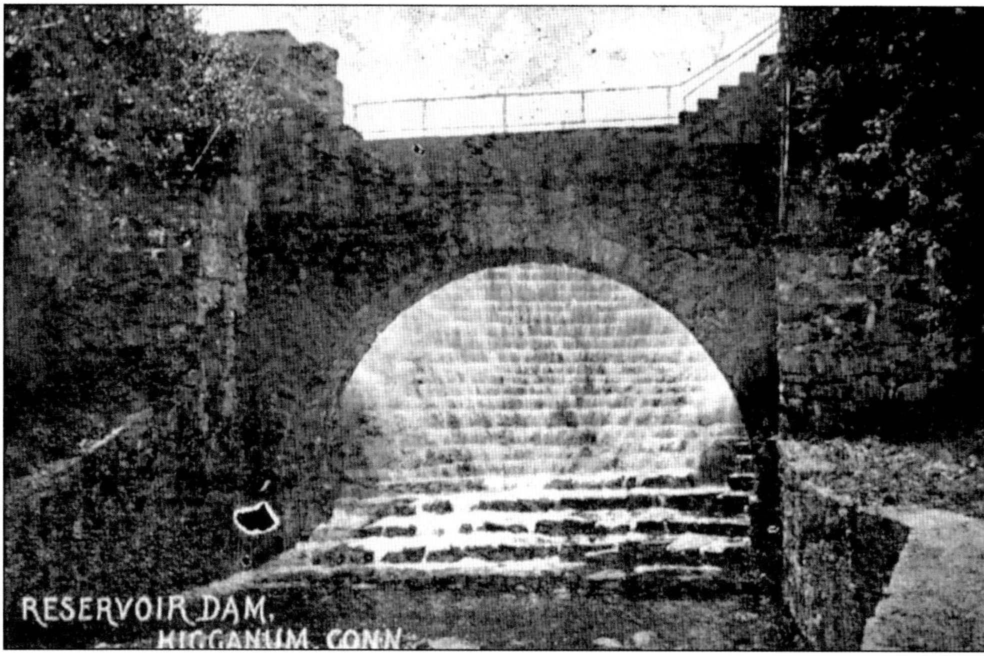

These picturesque falls at the Higganum reservoir dam provided the water that was diverted through an underground flume pipe to the factory. This provided the power that enabled Cutaway Harrow to produce 400 sizes and types of plows, two-thirds of which were sold outside of the United States.

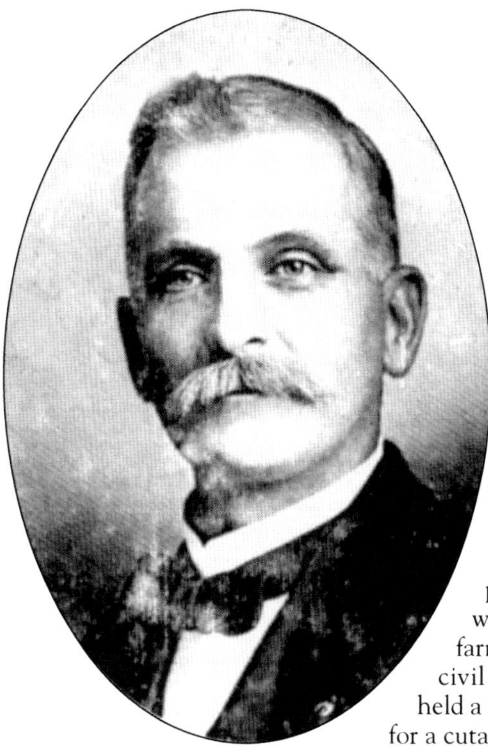

The dam and other waterpower facilities were designed by George M. Clark. The company's competitive edge came in part from its reliance on waterpower, which was cheaper than steam power. Like Hezekiah Scovil, Thomas Clark was familiar with the problems of Southern farmers, since he had worked in the South as a civil engineer when he was a young man. Clark also held a number of patents; the most important was one for a cutaway harrow.

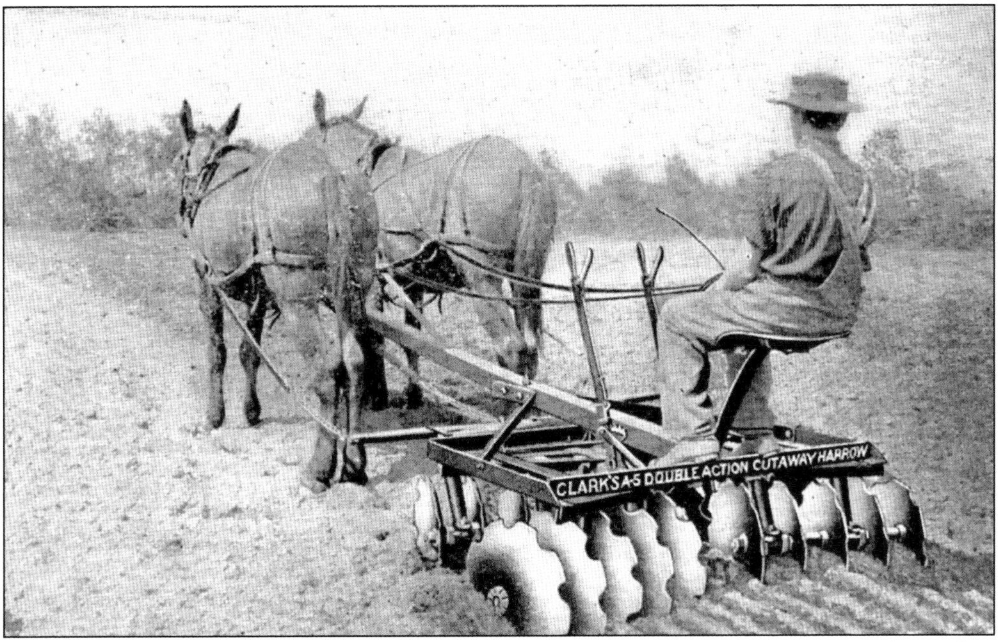

A Clark double-action cutaway harrow makes light work for mules Prince and Charlie as they plow Rob Priest's field on Candlewood Hill Road on a spring day sometime before 1920. This harrow improved on previous designs: its forged (rather than ground) steel discs, with their scalloped design, were capable of severing thick tree roots. (Courtesy Augusta Priest Chadsey.)

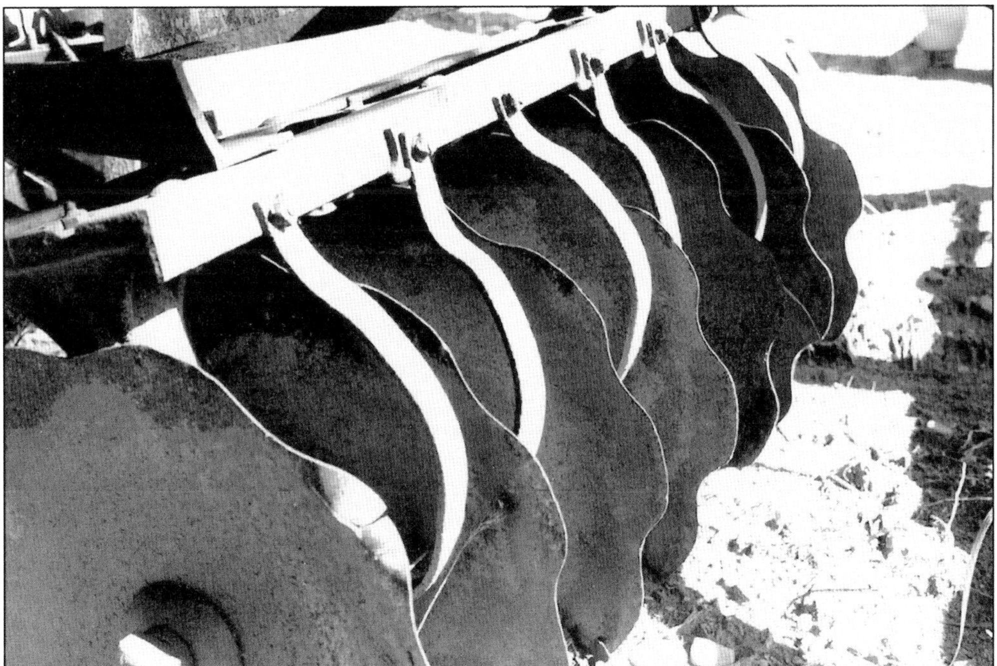

Other agricultural tools invented by Clark and produced by Cutaway Harrow were a potato digger, a cultivator, a disc harrow, a smoothing harrow, and a reversible sulky plow. This harrow, made in the 1920s, was still in use in 1997. Note the scalloped design.

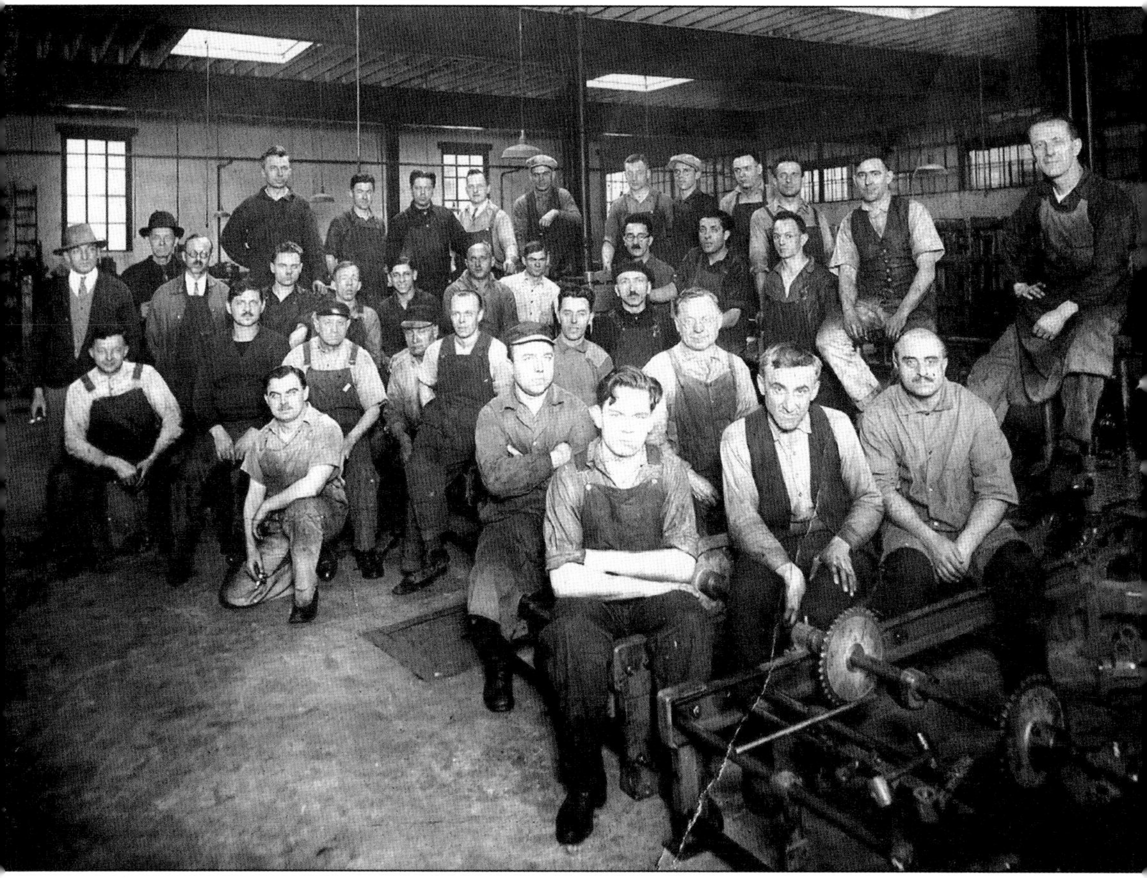

These Cutaway Harrow employees stop work for a rare interior photograph. As factories flourished along the streams of Higganum, immigrants from Ireland, and later, Germany, Sweden, Czechoslovakia, and Poland arrived to provide labor. Like the shipyards that preceded them, Higganum factories connected Haddam to the wider world.

Five

AT HOME IN HADDAM

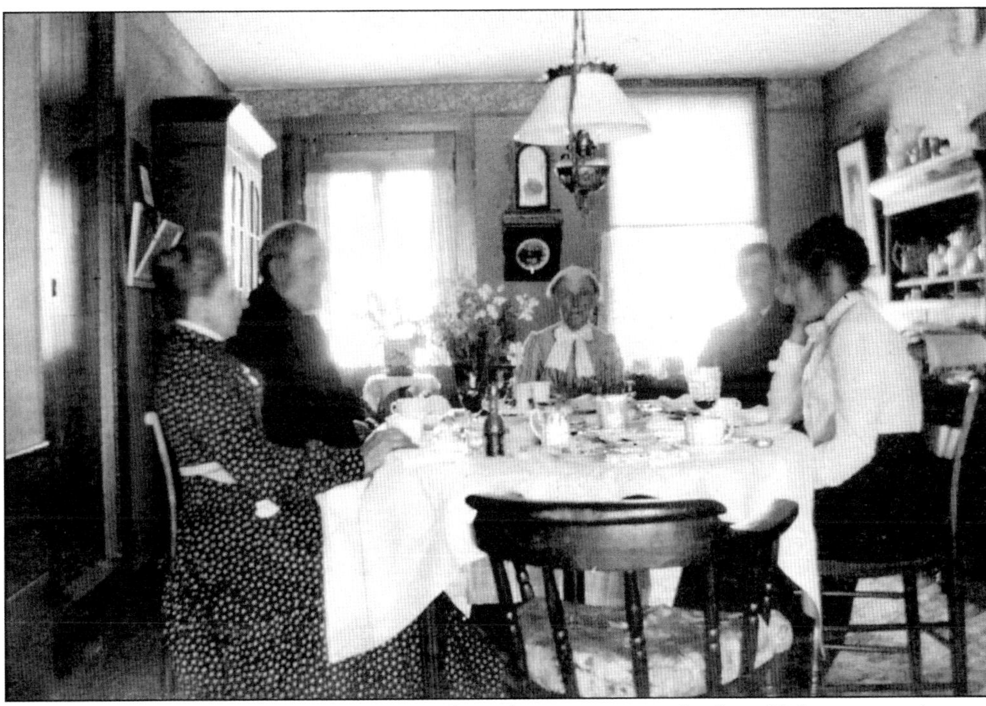

Carlson family members are gathered in their dining room in the late 19th century. Around this time, many wealthy businessmen built elaborate Victorian-style houses and mill owners constructed factory housing, but Haddam's older structures remained. According to Wallace Nutting, "If we were restricted to one town in Connecticut to stand for quaintness, beauty and variety, we should name Haddam. It combines in a delightful way the cottage and the mansion . . . (it is) the epitome of early Connecticut." This romantic view ignored the lack of conveniences in older houses.

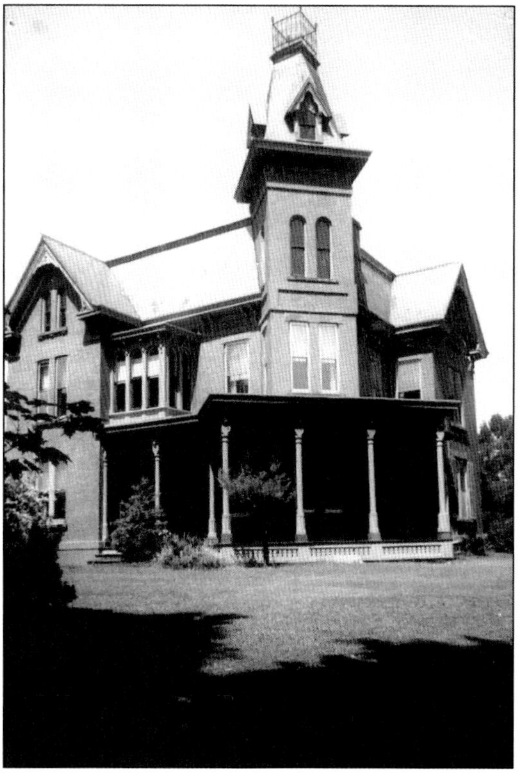

Hezekiah Scovil Jr. included brownstone windowsills in this brick Queen Anne–style house, which he built on Maple Avenue in Higganum in 1875. The house has unusual details, such as the polygonal tower and second-story sunroom, as well as elements of Victorian–Gothic Revival style, all of which displayed the owner's prominence. According to a contemporary account, it was a "large and handsome brick structure commanding extensive views on all sides and surrounded by pleasing, well-kept grounds."

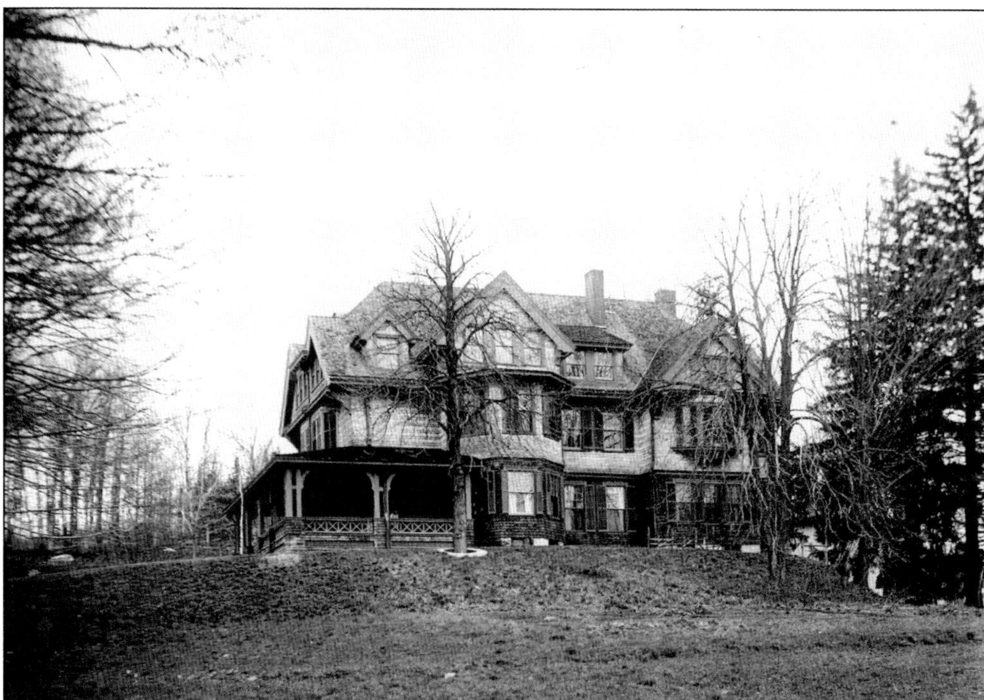

Hezekiah's brother and business partner, Daniel, built this 26-room American Shingle-style house on Christian Hill. It burned in February 1925.

This Victorian Italianate house, constructed by Thomas J. Clark on Saybrook Road in 1885, is an ornate expression of his status as a successful business owner. The property included a carriage house in the rear. Today it is a commercial building that houses several small businesses. (Courtesy Dave Lenzi.)

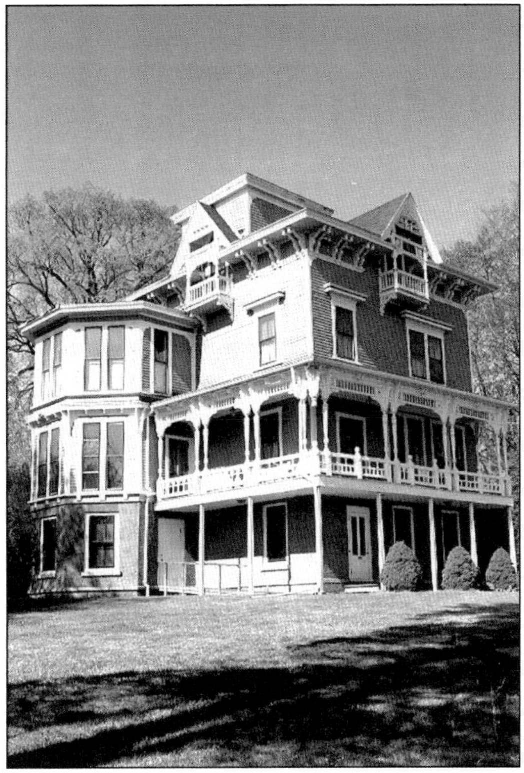

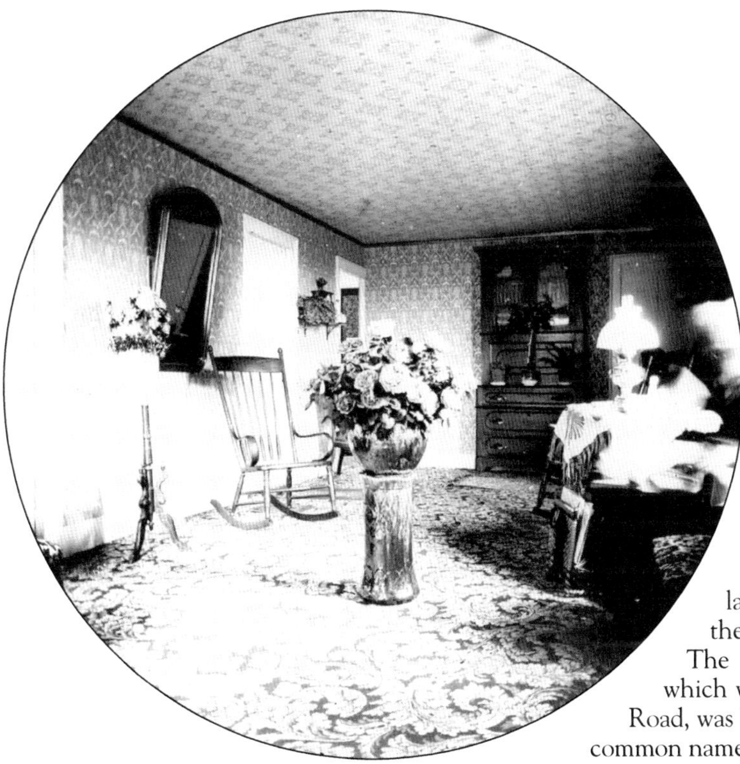

This Victorian parlor displays an abundant use of textiles and wallpaper, even on the ceiling. Kerosene lamps provided light in the days before electricity. The owner of this dwelling, which was located on Saybrook Road, was Noah Clark. Clark was a common name at the time.

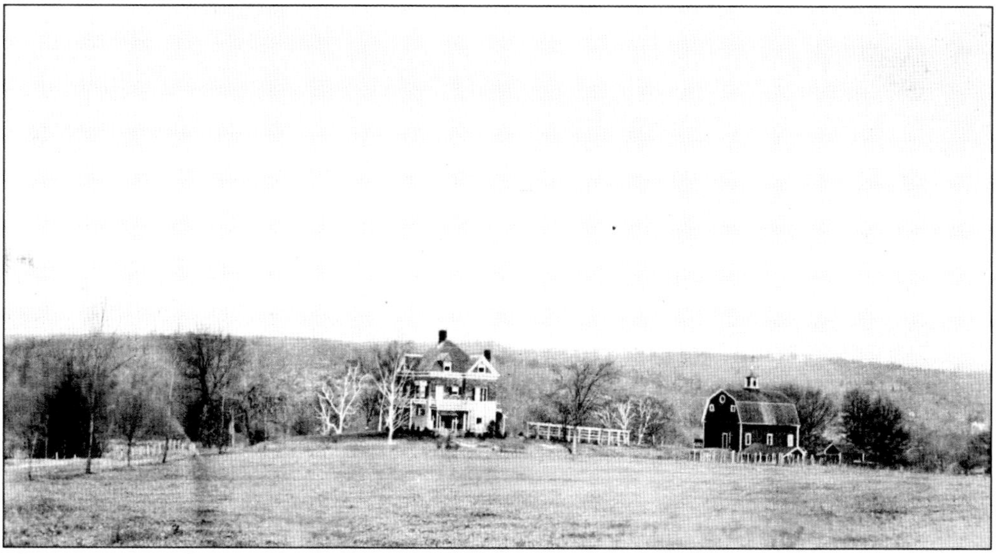

The J. H. Aristarchus Huntington House in Higganum, shown here in 1914, is also on Saybrook Road. It is an example of Queen Anne–style architecture and was built between 1885 and 1895. Huntington was a gentleman farmer and the son of a local shipbuilder.

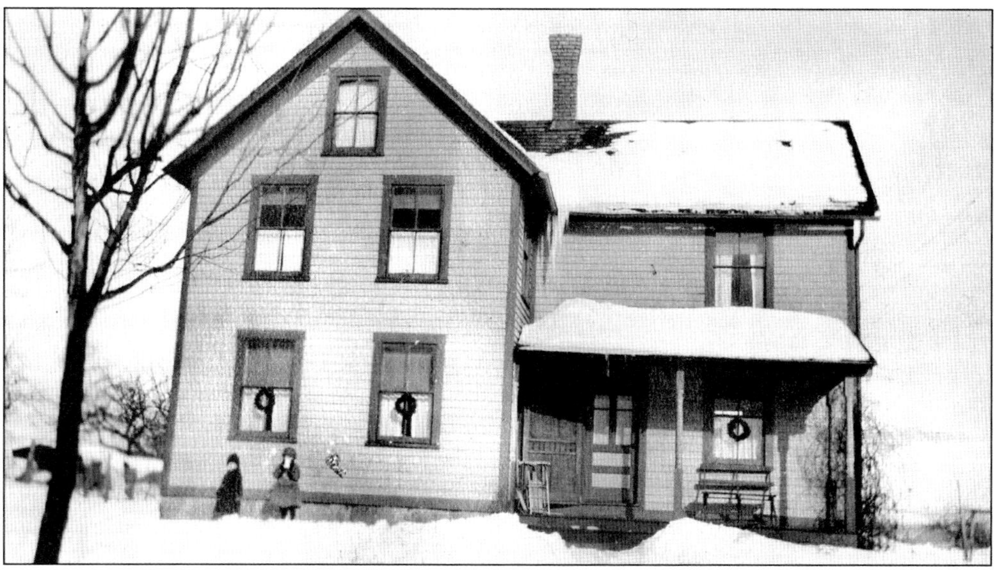

Between 1893 and 1903, the D&H Scovil Company hired Charles H. Bailey, a local dairy farmer, to construct four houses on Thayer Road for its workers, who rented them from the company. The Webb family home is decorated for Christmas in this 1923 photograph. (Courtesy Alan Webb.)

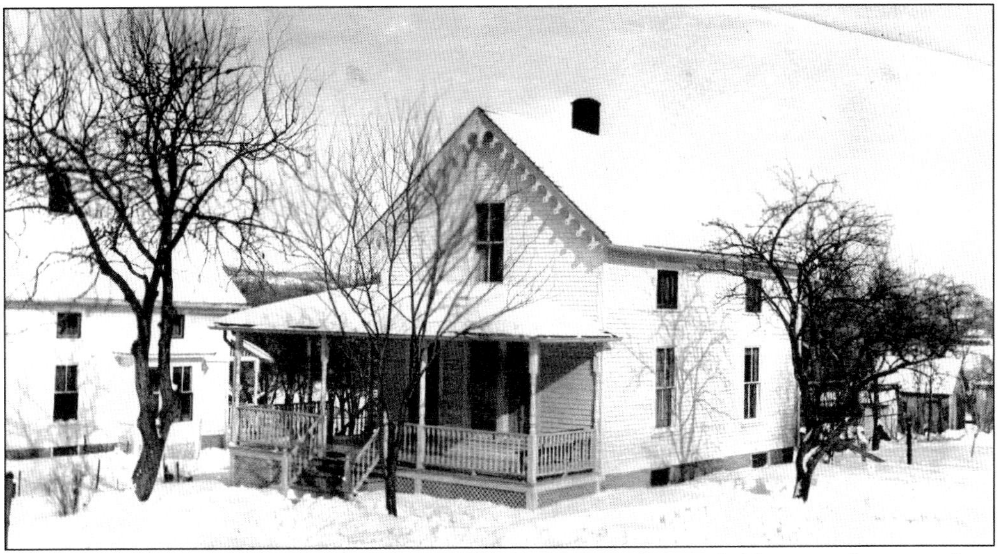

The Higganum Manufacturing Company (Cutaway Harrow) provided housing for its workers on Lake Avenue. The four houses, built between 1887 and 1888, were sold to factory employees for $772.50 each. One is shown here as it looked in 1914. Workers needing houses might have been immigrants; factory workers from local families, such as Charles Bailey, who worked until 1892 as a molder for Cutaway Harrow, might have had their own farms.

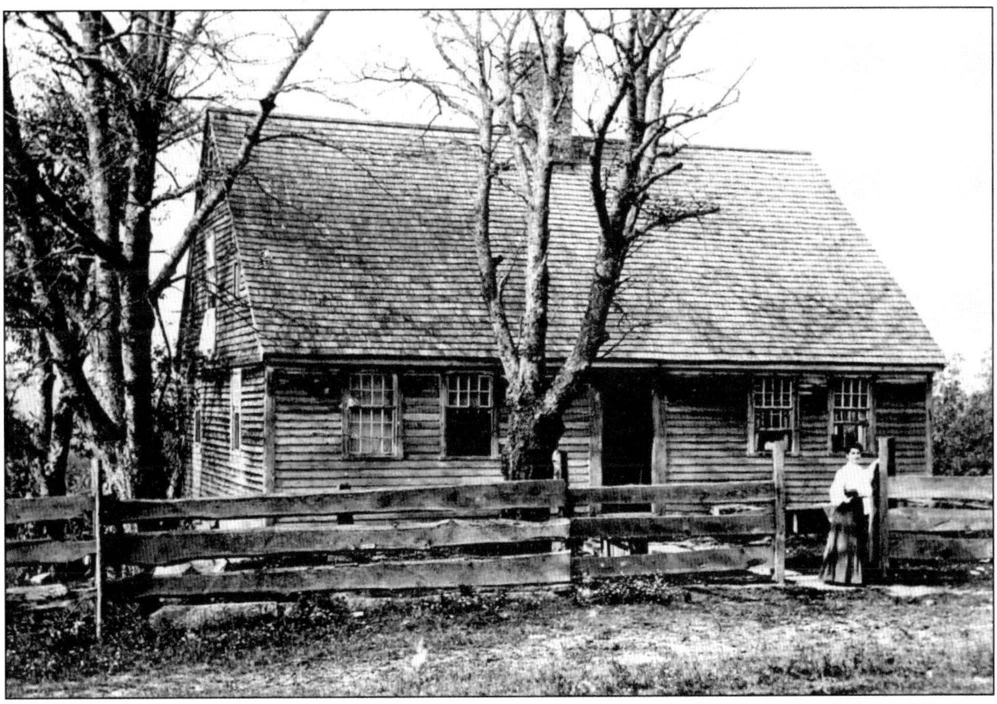

This post-and-beam, Cape Cod–style house was built by Capt. Gideon Brainerd about 1740 on what is now Filley Road. This style of house was popular in Haddam during the latter half of the 18th century, chiefly because it was economical for subsistence farmers to build. About 64 of these houses still remain, most in the outlying areas of town. Brainerd supplemented farming in Haddam Center with work across the river in a Haddam Neck quarry.

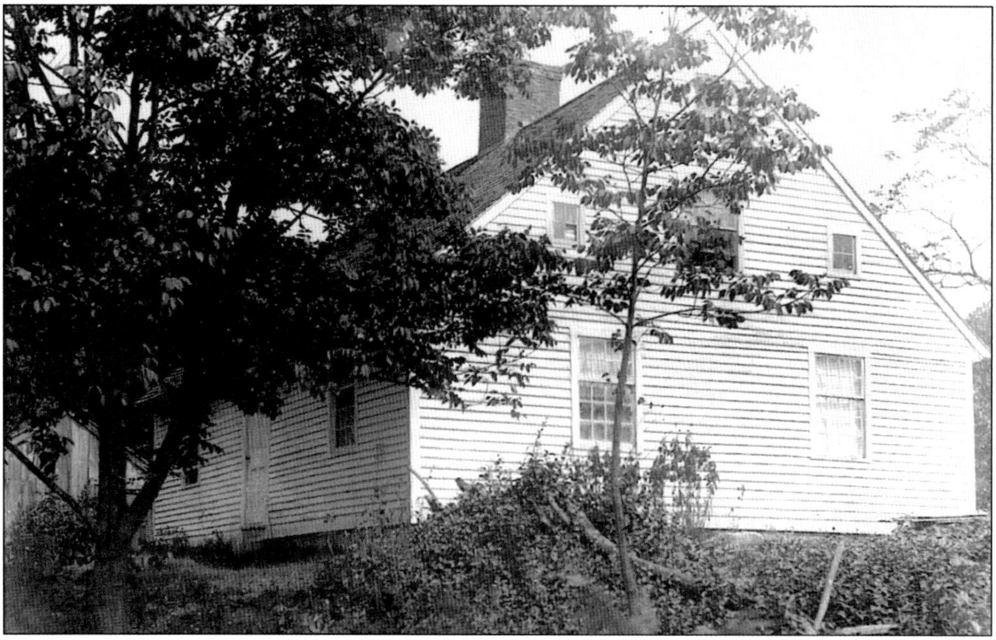

The Gideon Arnold House, built about 1740 on Rock Landing Road, is the oldest house still standing in Haddam Neck. This photograph of the structure's gable allows a view of its "Haddam windows," three small windows in the upper story that could be removed for ventilation. In keeping with the economical building technique of this style of house, Haddam windows saved on the expense of additional double-hung windows.

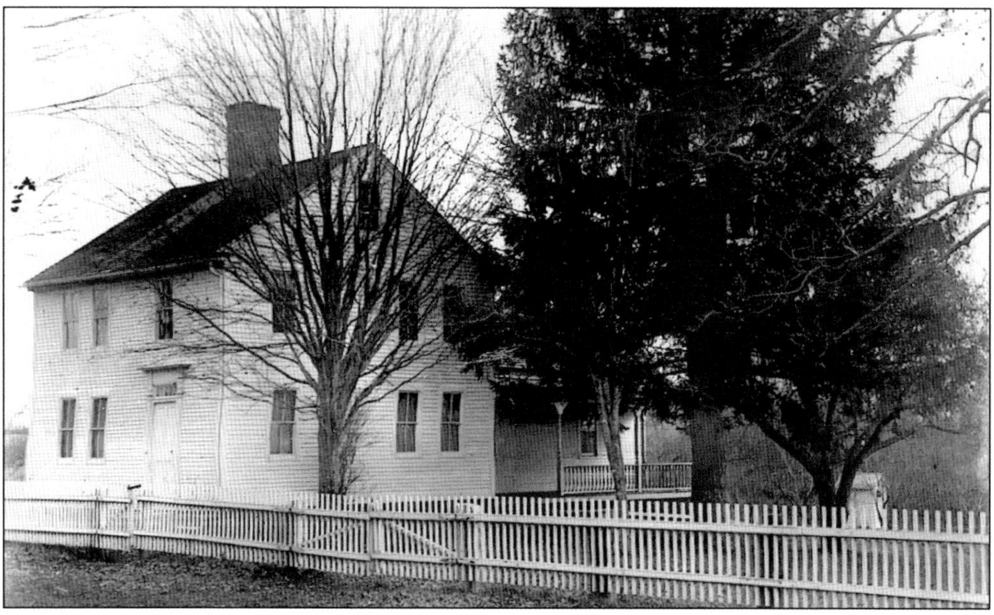

A more expensive but typical style of housing in Haddam was the five-bay, center-chimney dwelling, with the ridge facing the street. The term "five bay" indicates that the house has five windows on the second story. Some residents economized by building fewer than five bays. Pictured here is a Brainerd family house built about 1820. Designed with three bays, it is known as a half house. (Courtesy Middle Haddam Library, Olsen Collection.)

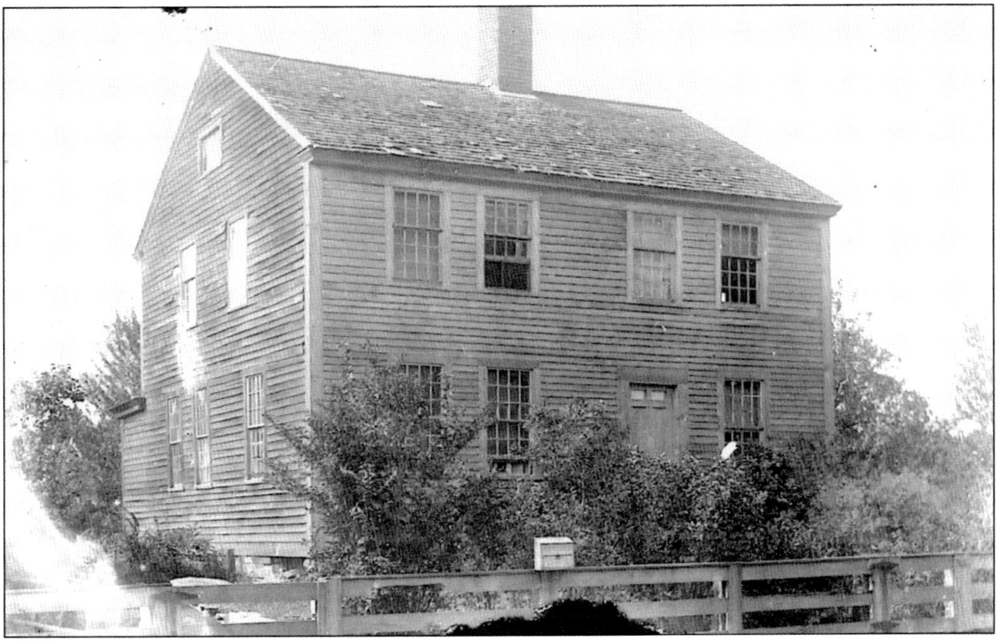

The Oliver B. Arnold House on Quarry Hill Road in Haddam Neck is an example of a three-quarter house. Note the four windows on the second story. Arnold was a carpenter by trade and was also associated with the Abolitionist Party. He built this house in 1822. (Courtesy Middle Haddam Library, Olsen Collection.)

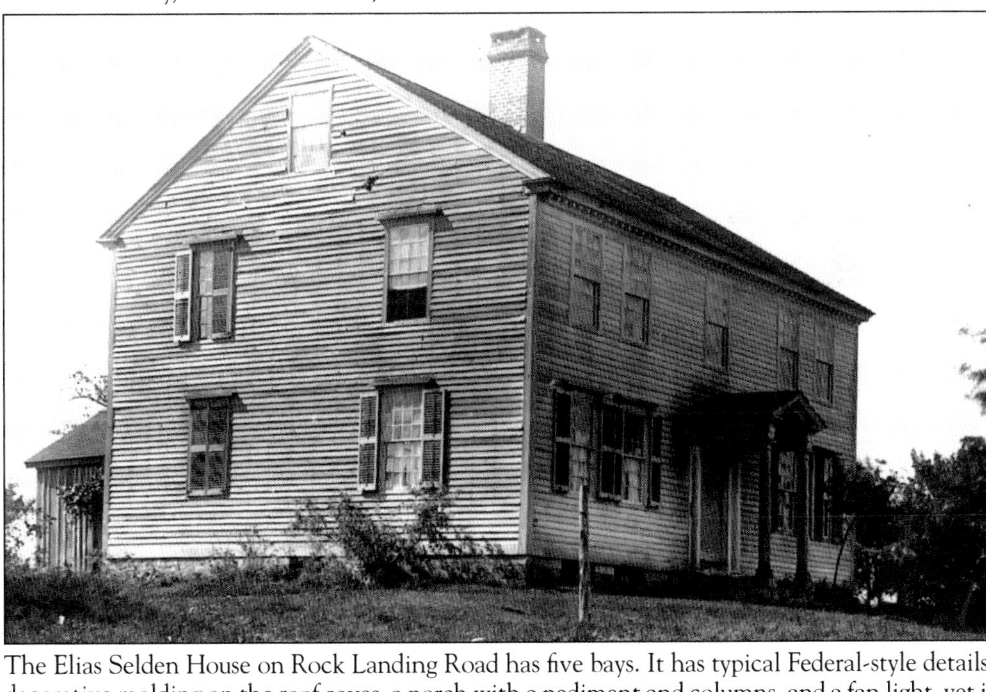

The Elias Selden House on Rock Landing Road has five bays. It has typical Federal-style details: decorative molding on the roof eaves, a porch with a pediment and columns, and a fan light, yet it retains the traditional Colonial center-chimney floor plan. One feature it has in common with at least three other Haddam dwellings is a second-floor ballroom. The Haddam Neck Post Office was located here between 1860 and 1908. (Courtesy Middle Haddam Library, Olsen Collection.)

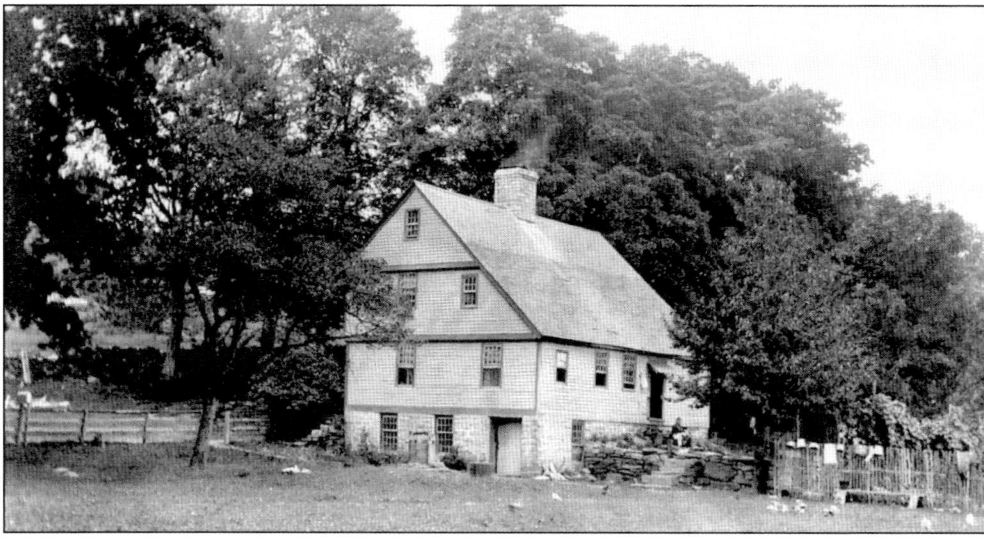

The addition to the rear of the Selden House is one of the many smaller buildings in Haddam that were moved to form an addition when a house was built. It was originally the home of Selden's father. A center-chimney house might also be expanded by adding a "lean-to" room in the rear, producing a saltbox. A fine example is the 1780 Hubbard farmhouse on Candlewood Hill Road. (Courtesy Linda Rigono.)

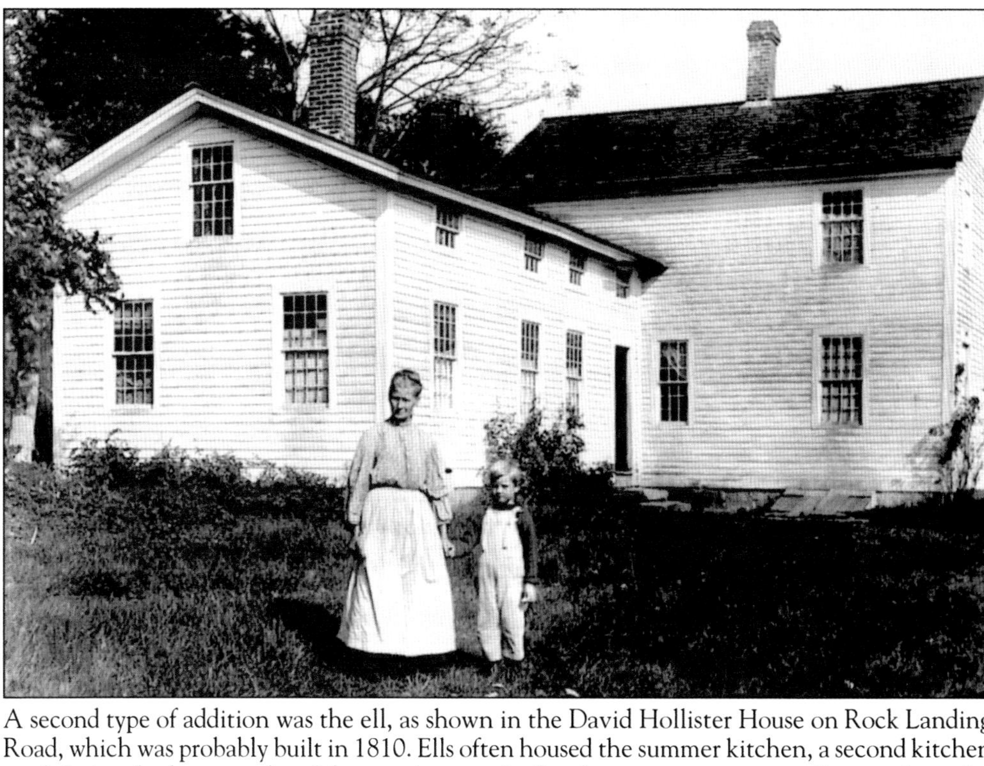

A second type of addition was the ell, as shown in the David Hollister House on Rock Landing Road, which was probably built in 1810. Ells often housed the summer kitchen, a second kitchen used during the hot months of the year because its fireplace or stove was at a distance from the main rooms of the house. (Courtesy Middle Haddam Library, Olsen Collection.)

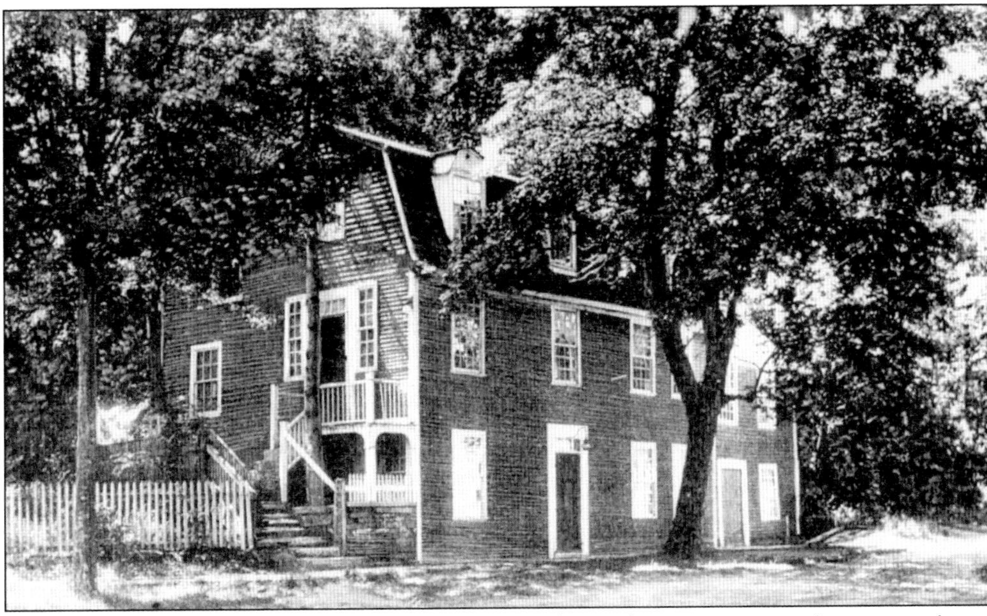

The Thankful Arnold House is an example of a residence that was extensively renovated over time. Built in 1794 as a two-room dwelling over a store, it was expanded to 12 rooms by the mid-19th century. The house was occupied by the Arnold family until 1962, when it was donated to the Haddam Historical Society as a museum.

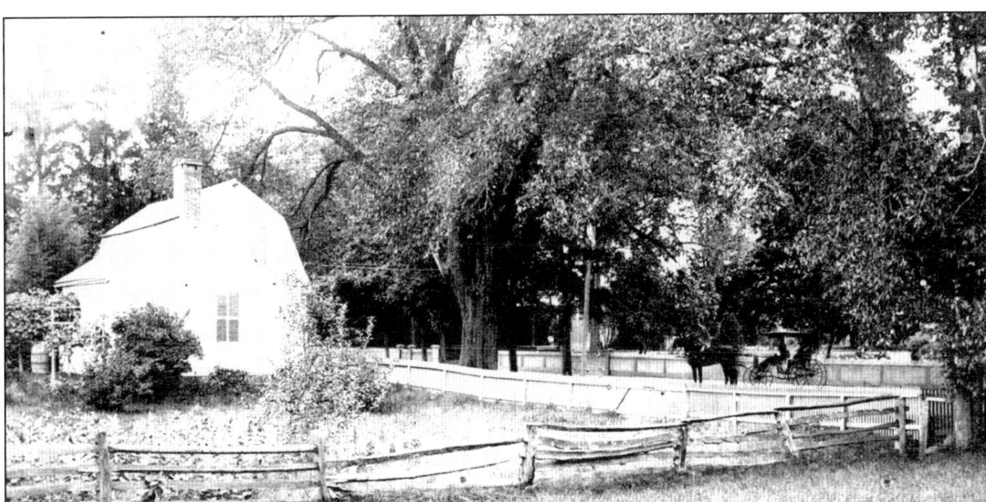

This picturesque house still stands on Camp Bethel Road. It is an example of a gambrel roof house, a style which became common at the end of the 18th century. Unlike a traditional gable roof, a gambrel roof has two angles, allowing for more space on the top floor. The Thankful Arnold House, in the previous photograph, also has a gambrel roof. (Courtesy Parmelee family.)

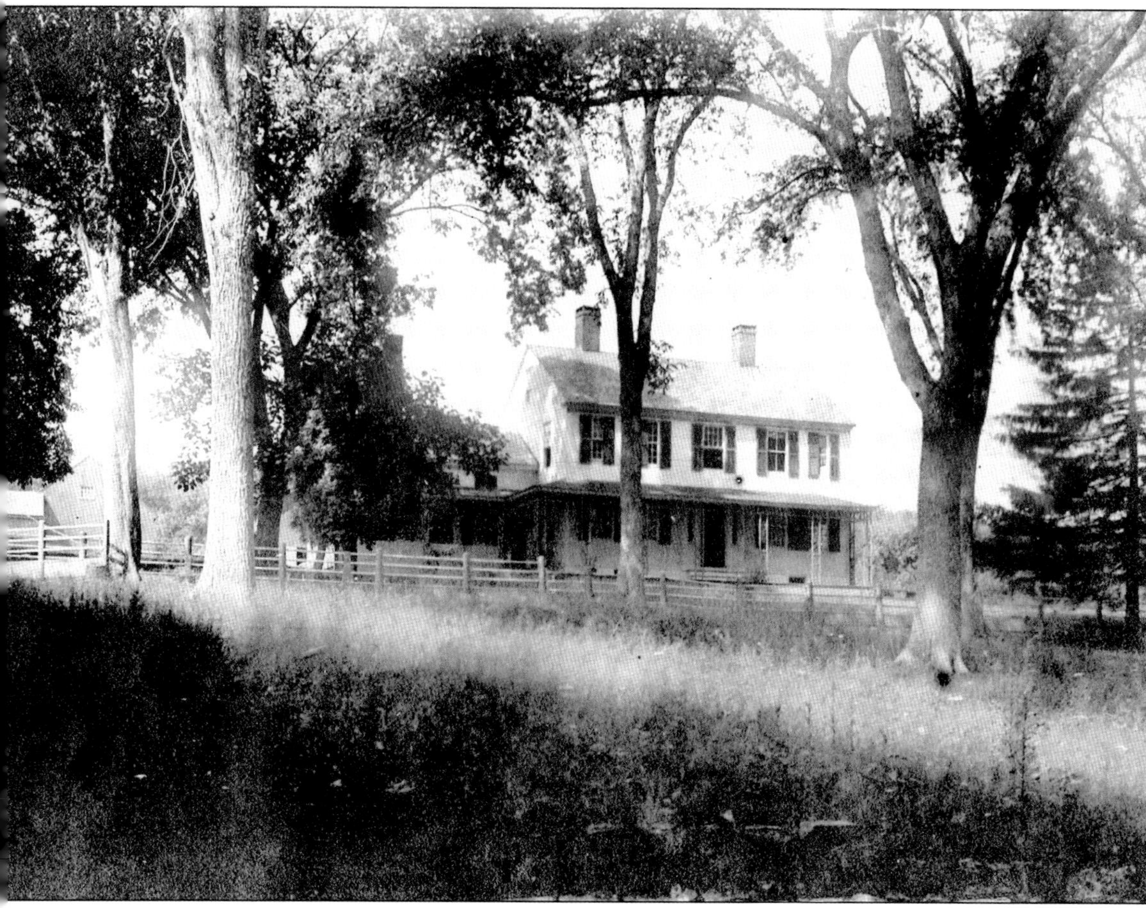

The grander Georgian style of housing was not common in Haddam. The Reverend John Marsh parsonage on Walkley Hill Road, known as Cold Water Raisin, is one example. Pictured here in 1880, it dates from 1818 and was the home of the Congregational minister, who, according to legend, was a teetotaler and rewarded the house builders with only water. The ell is said to have originally been the third Congregational meetinghouse, which was moved here when a larger church building was constructed on Saybrook Road in 1846.

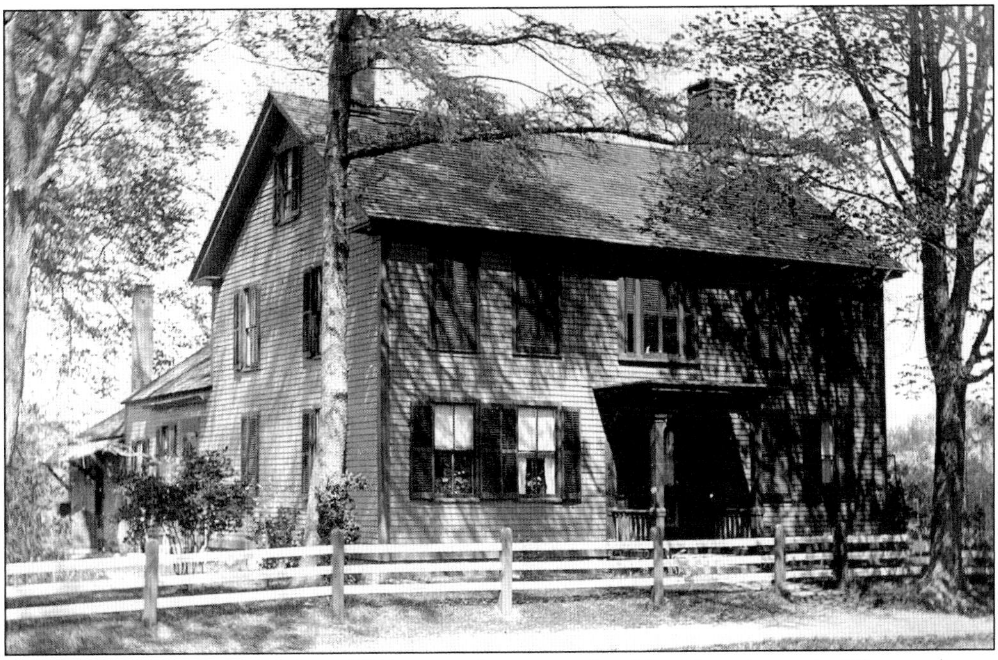

The Noah Clark tavern, built in 1791, is another example of the Georgian style. The porch was added at a later date. This establishment was a familiar sight on Saybrook Road throughout the 19th century and was one of six taverns in the neighborhood.

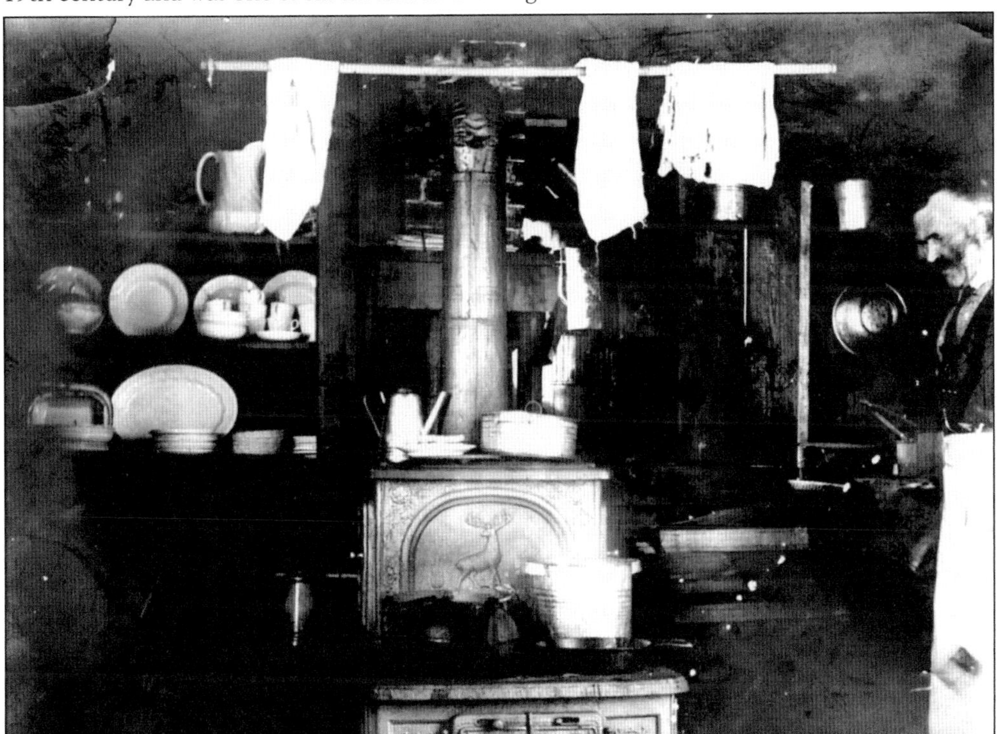

The kitchen of the Noah Clark tavern had a stove. An innovation at the beginning of the 19th century, stoves were commonplace by 1870.

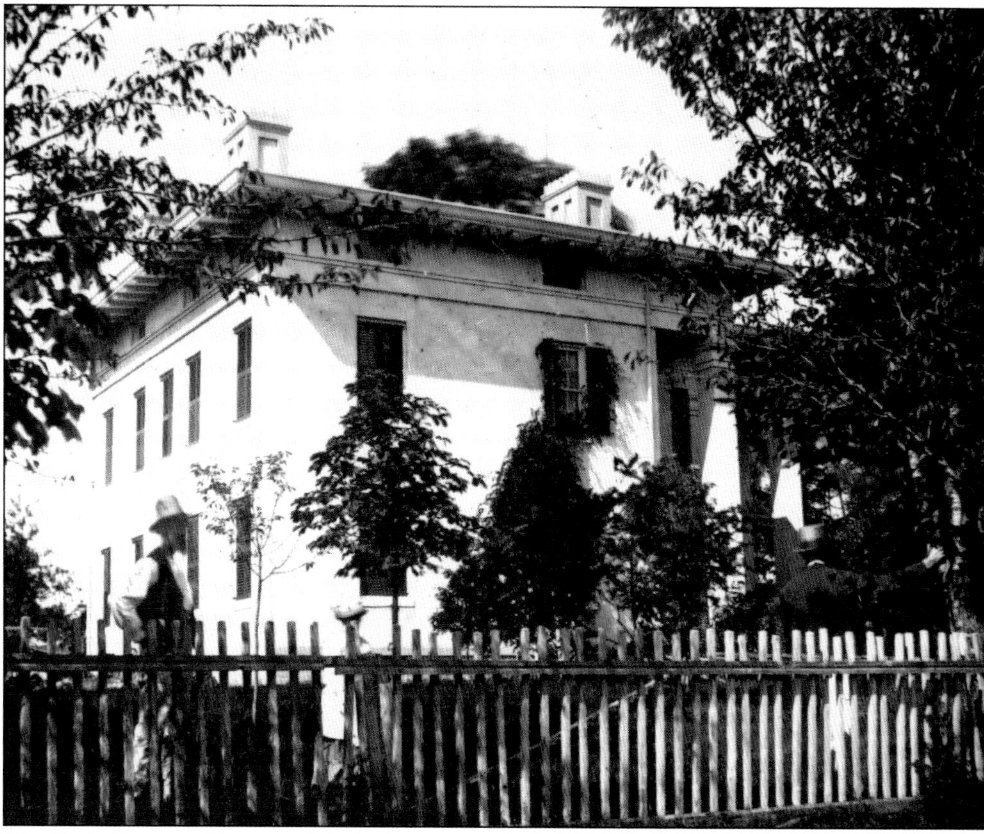

The Orrin Freeman House on Maple Avenue in Higganum was built in 1841 and is representative of the Italianate style of architecture. Freeman owned a number of businesses in town, including the second-largest lumberyard in Middlesex County and a brickyard, which manufactured the bricks used to construct his house. (George Bradford Brainerd photograph, courtesy Brainerd Library.)

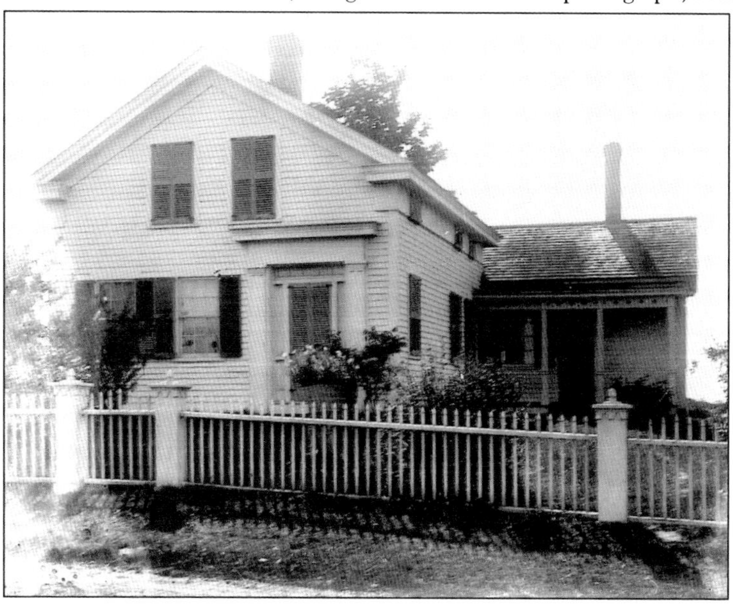

This architecturally eclectic house on Schoolhouse Hill in Haddam Neck contains elements of the Greek Revival style in the doorway and the roofline. (Courtesy Middle Haddam Library, Olsen Collection.)

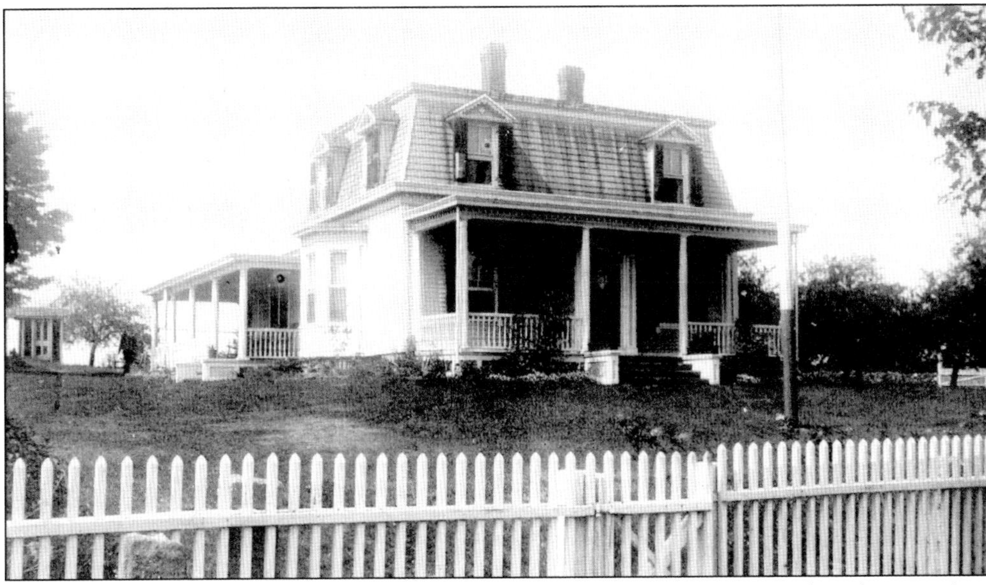

The Second Empire style arrived in Haddam Neck by 1875, as shown by this photograph of the Julius Burham House on Quarry Hill Road in Haddam Neck. This style is characterized by a mansard roof, which is sloped on all sides. The steeply pitched lower slope is topped by an almost flat roof. (Courtesy Lisa and David Malloy.)

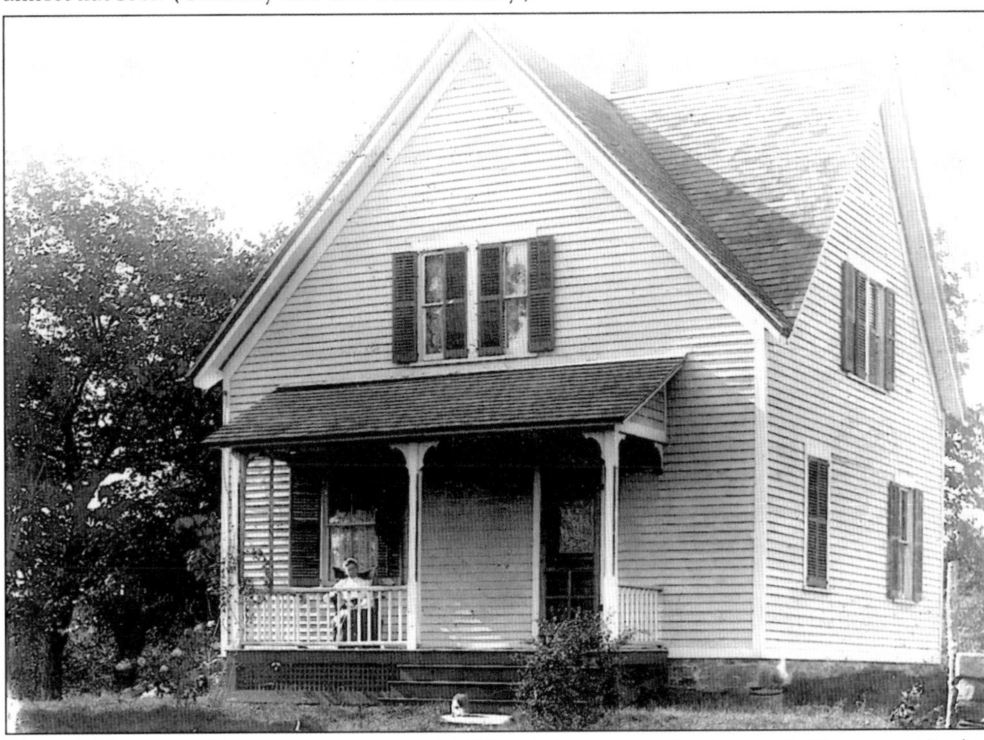

The John Swanson House, also on Quarry Hill Road, is an example of a simple Carpenter Gothic dwelling. It was built *c.* 1900 as a modern improvement over the Colonial-era gambrel-roof house originally located here, which the owner tore down to make way for the new dwelling. (Courtesy Middle Haddam Library, Olsen Collection.)

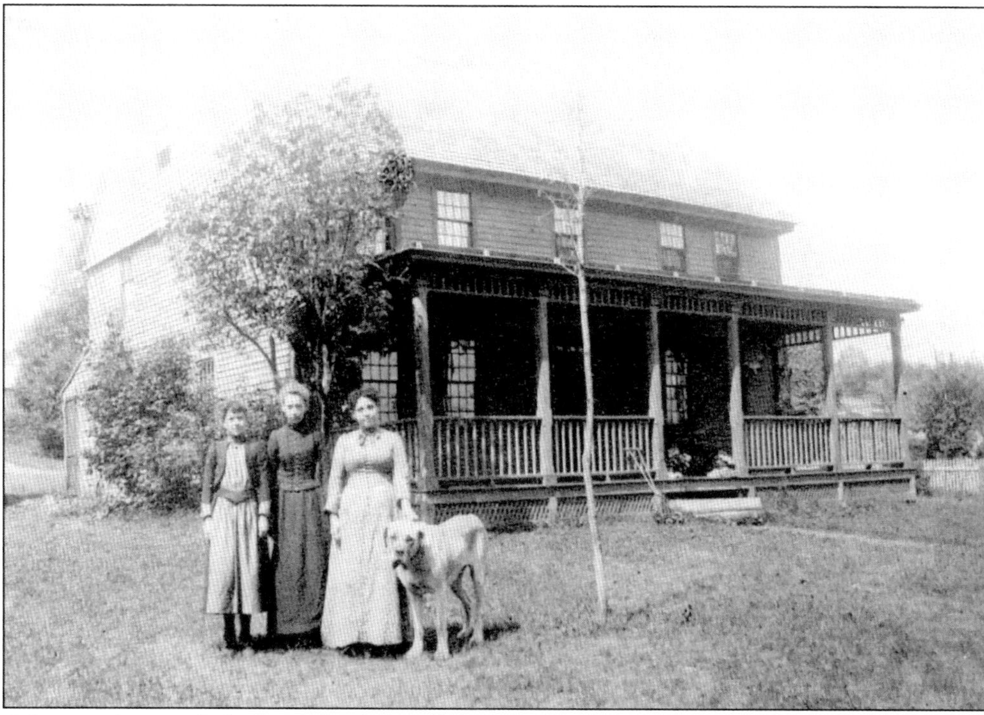

Other residents took the less radical step of modernizing existing buildings. The Jeremiah Hobart House, one of three that are claimed to be the oldest in Haddam, was altered in the late 19th century by the addition of a front porch, a typical embellishment in the Victorian period.

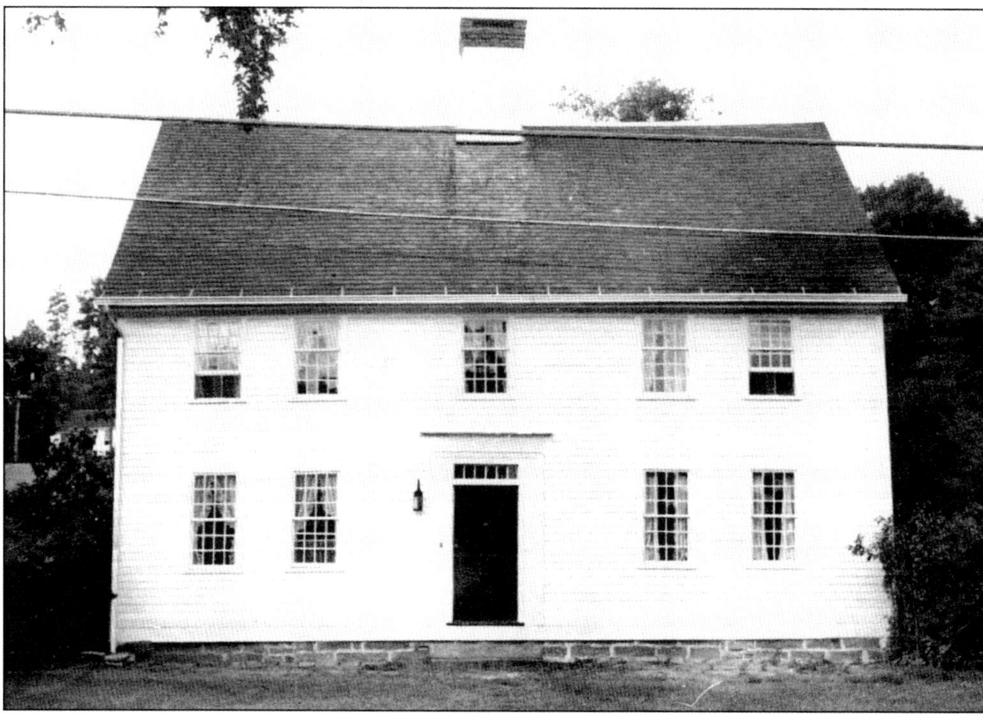

In the 20th century, the Jeremiah Hobart House was restored to its late-18th-century appearance.

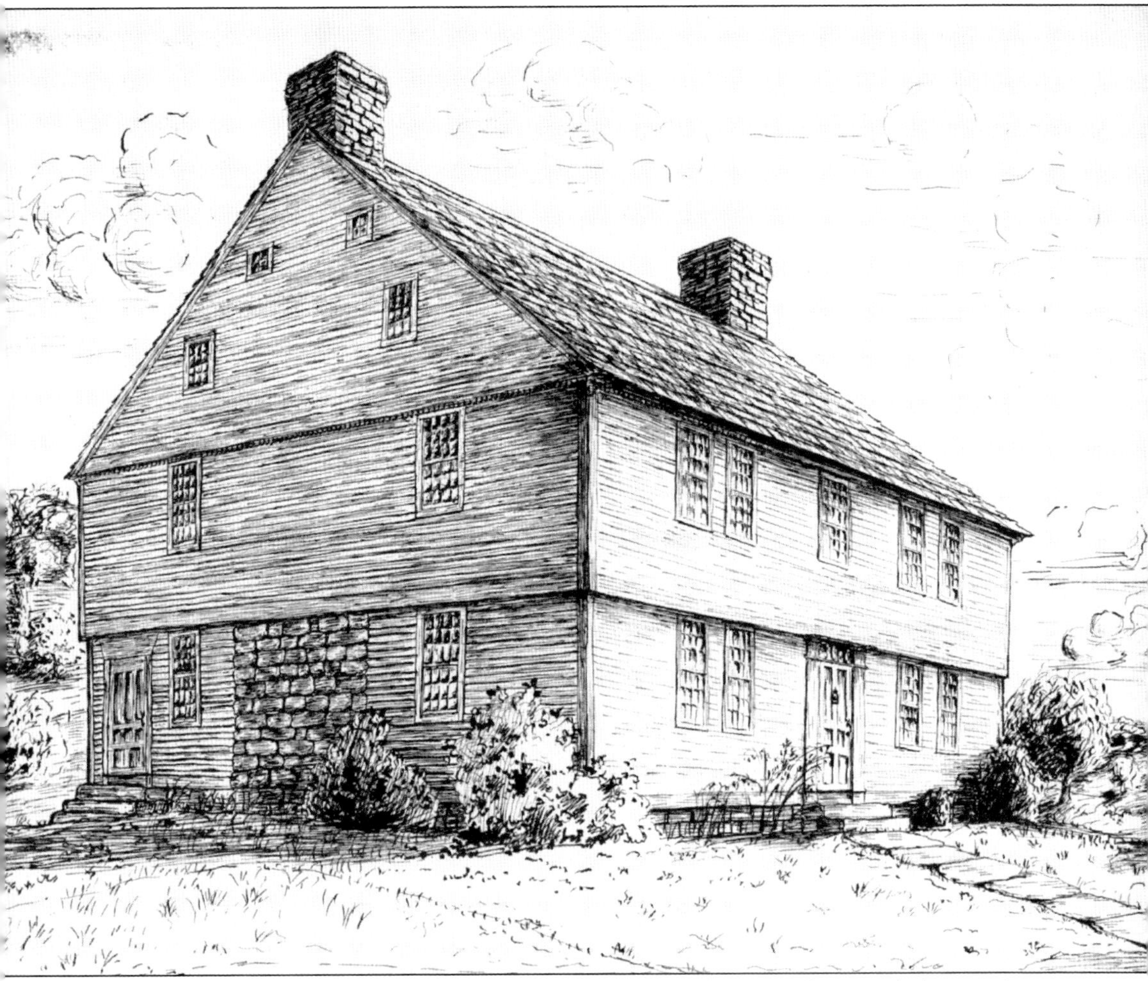

This c. 1740 dwelling was torn down in 1930. The double overhangs and exposed chimney bay are indicative of a very early style of building. It stood on Old Turnpike Road in Shailerville and was owned by a member of the Shailer family.

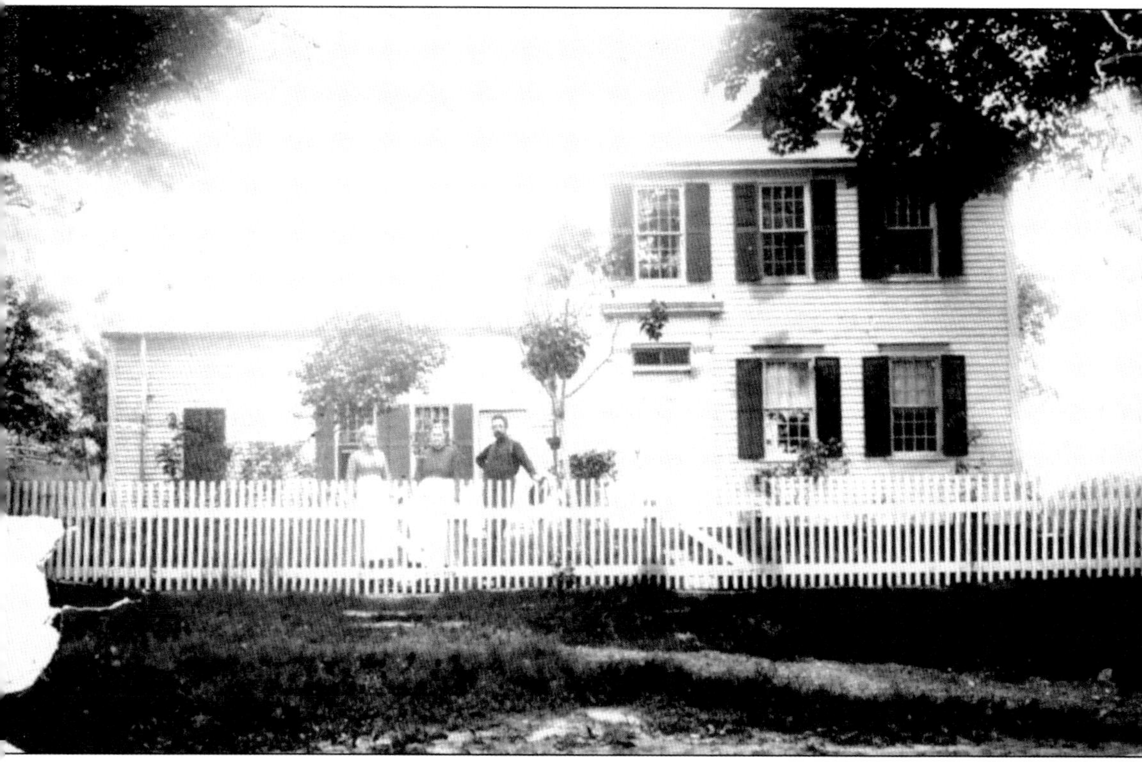

This Greek Revival structure on Christian Hill stood in the path of Route 9, which was constructed in the 1960s.

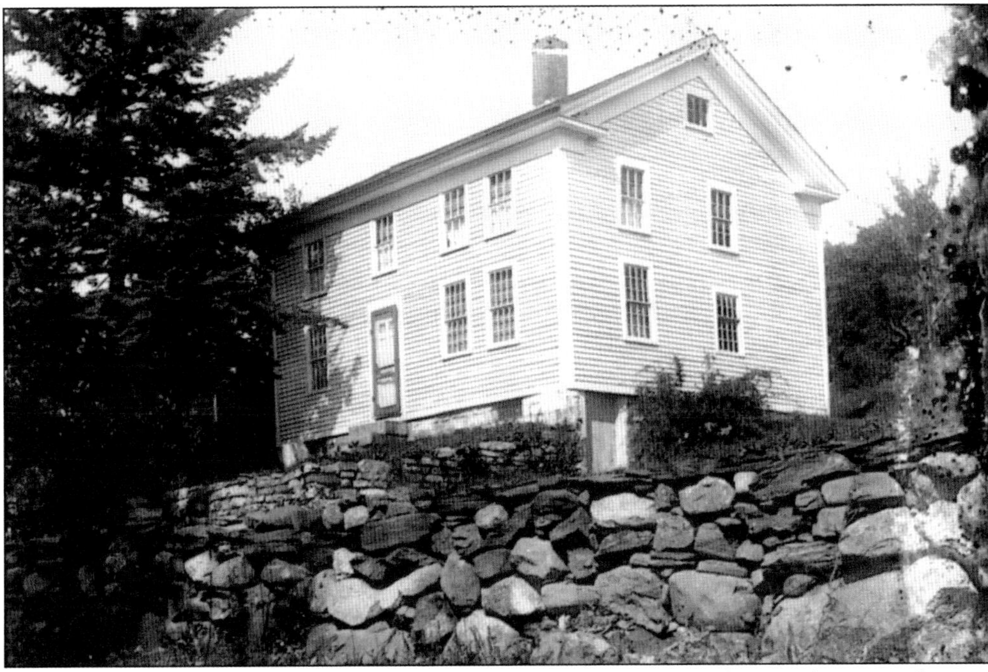

Although in good repair when this photograph was taken in 1890, the Smith-Brainerd House near Ben Clark Hill Road in Haddam Neck was later abandoned, and it was finally torn down in the 1970s. (Courtesy Middle Haddam Library, Olsen Collection.)

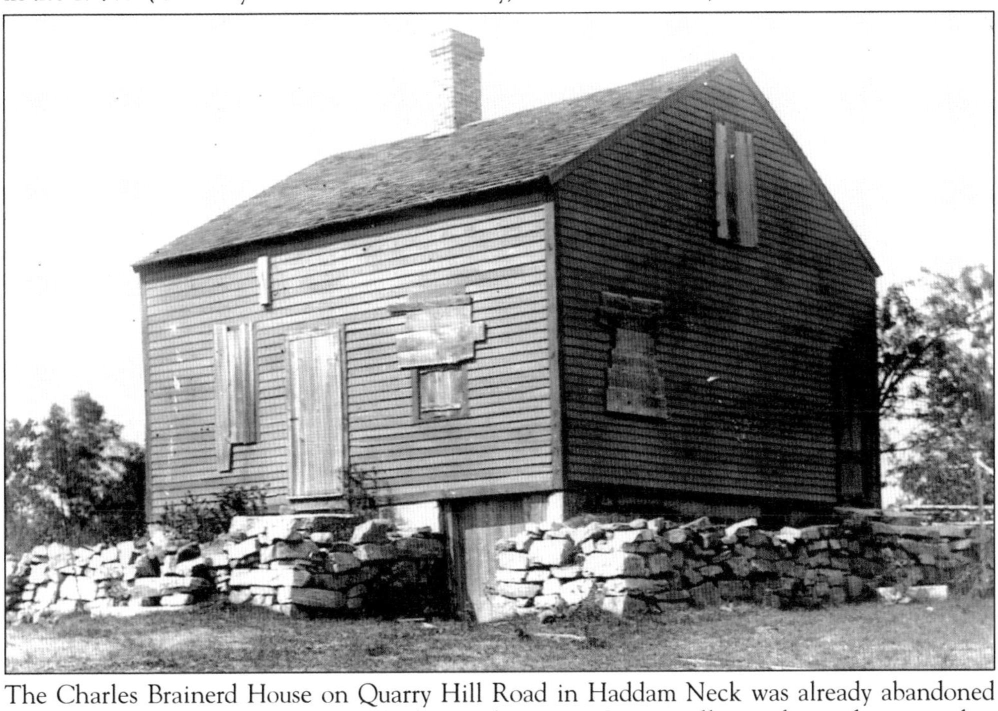

The Charles Brainerd House on Quarry Hill Road in Haddam Neck was already abandoned when this photograph was taken in the late 19th century. It originally stood near the quarry, but it was moved back when a stone flew through the window, narrowly missing the family's baby. (Courtesy Middle Haddam Library, Olsen Collection.)

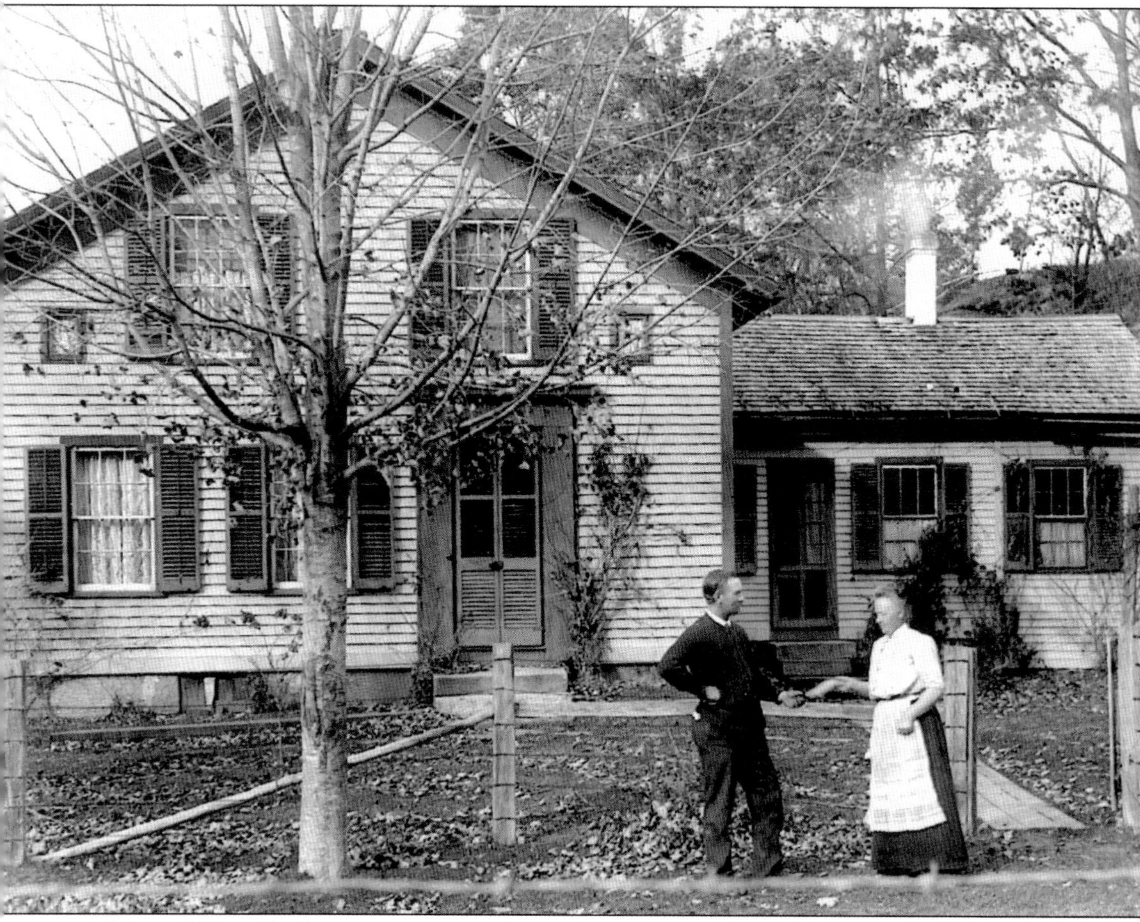

Mr. and Mrs. Charles Larson pose in front of their house at the bottom of Clarkhurst Road in Haddam Neck. This house later burned. (Courtesy Middle Haddam Library, Olsen Collection.)

Six

CHANGING TIMES

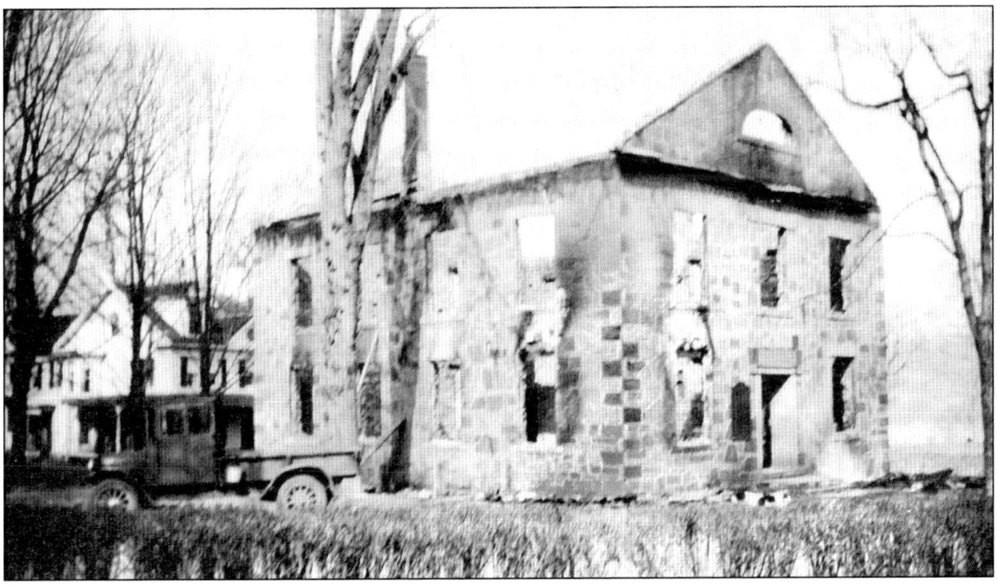

The loss of the town hall in 1929 resulted in the establishment of the first fire department. The 1920s brought changes to Haddam, but some things remained the same. Steamboat service from Rock Landing ended in 1931, but the Connecticut Valley Railroad still ran. Women held political office, but the town meeting form of government was maintained. Schools were consolidated and new families moved in, but the population of Haddam expanded only slightly. The mix of rural pursuits with manufacturing also persisted. (Courtesy Richard Williamson Jr.)

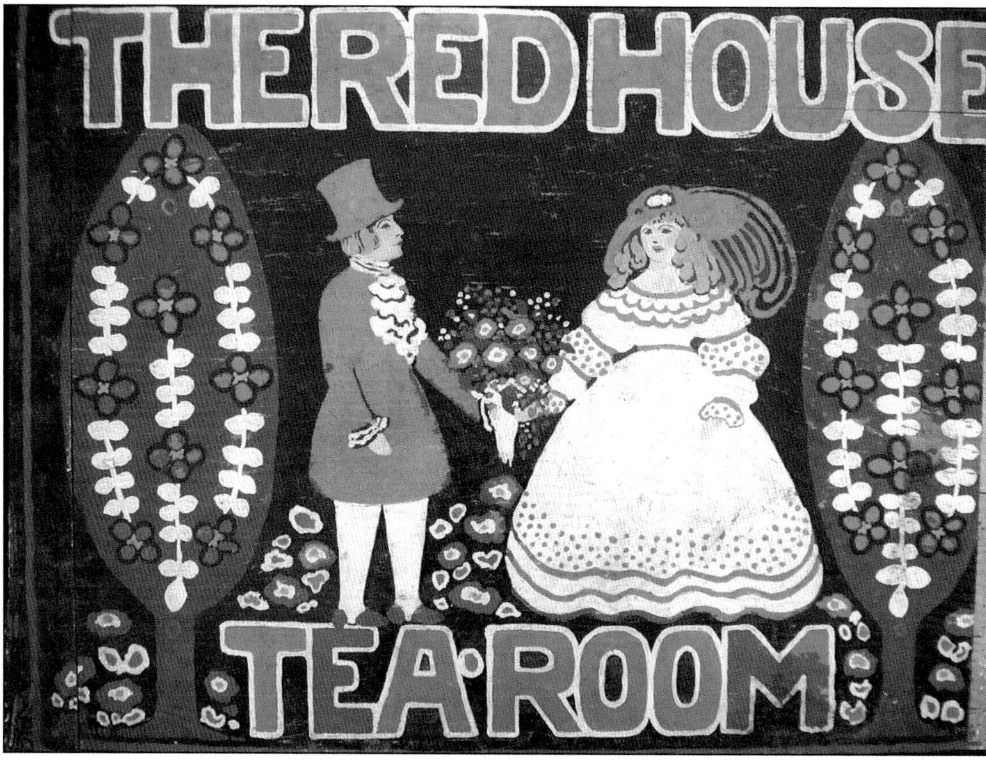

The automobile and prohibition were two developments that may have encouraged Charlie and Nell Ingersoll, owners of the present-day Thankful Arnold House, to open a tearoom about 1927. Customers might have been travelers to the Connecticut shore driving through Haddam along Saybrook Road, which was first paved in 1929. (Courtesy Dave Lenzi.)

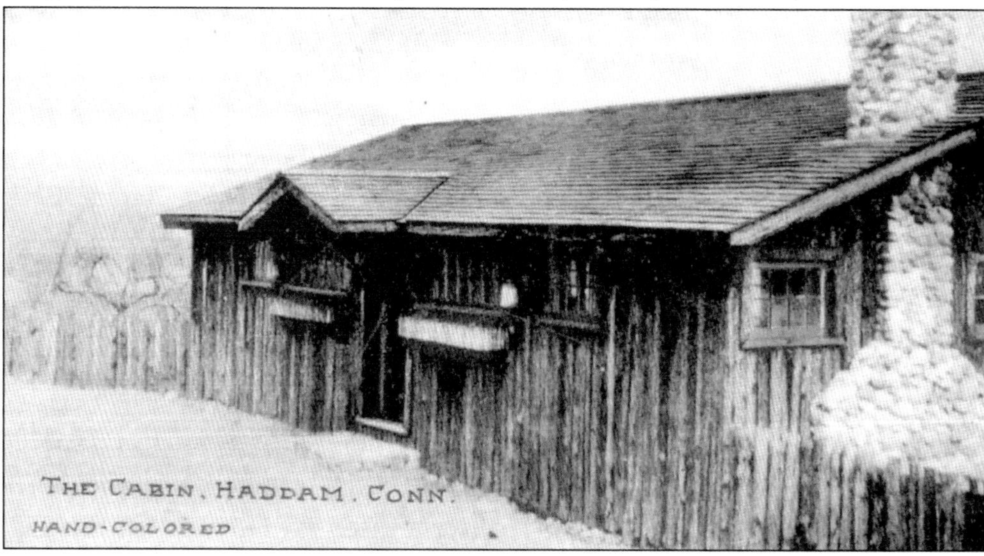

By 1930, thirty-nine eateries had been established in Haddam, creating work for the new public-health nurses, who were required to inspect the outhouses and to encourage owners to install screens. Here we see an establishment known as the Cabin, which was located on Walkley Hill. In the distance is a view of the Connecticut River.

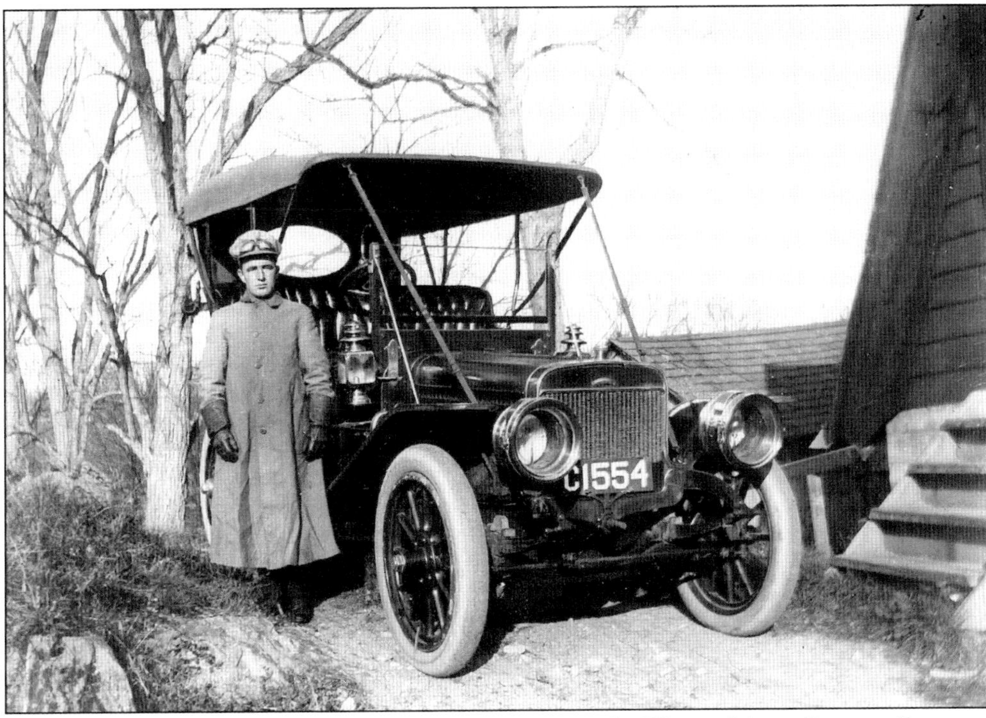

His chauffeur poses beside Edward Hazen's 1909 Winton. The Winton Motor Carriage Company of Cleveland, Ohio, was one of many automobile companies that were active in the early 20th century. Established by Scottish immigrant Alexander Winton, it had the distinction of selling the first commercial American-made automobile in 1898. Wealthy customers such as Reginald and Alfred Vanderbilt established the car's reputation as an automobile for the wealthy. The company ceased operations by 1920. (Charles Church photograph.)

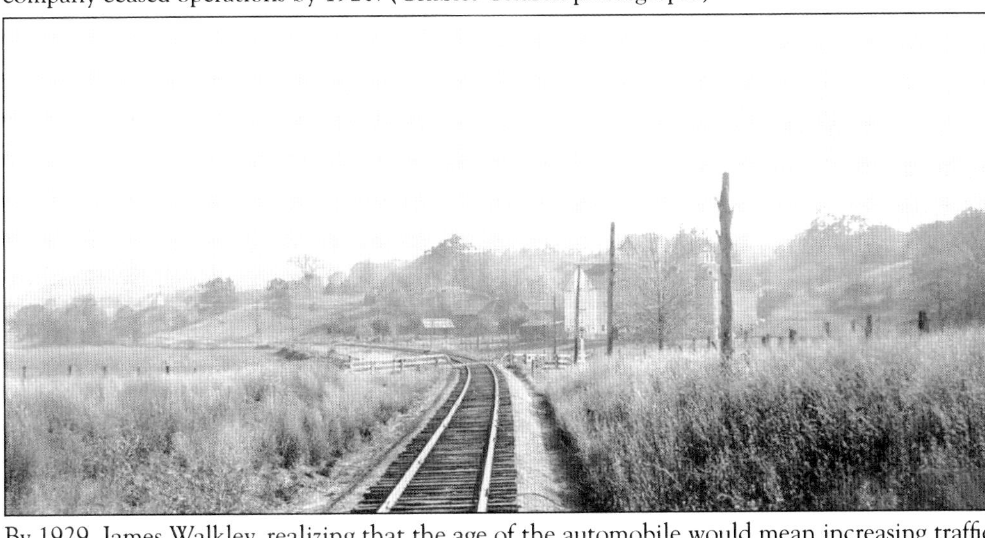

By 1929, James Walkley, realizing that the age of the automobile would mean increasing traffic over Walkley Hill, persuaded the state of Connecticut to reroute Saybrook Road closer to the river along land that he donated for this purpose. This meant that the Connecticut Valley Railroad lines also had to be shifted east. The road was first paved in concrete at this time. (Courtesy Max Miller.)

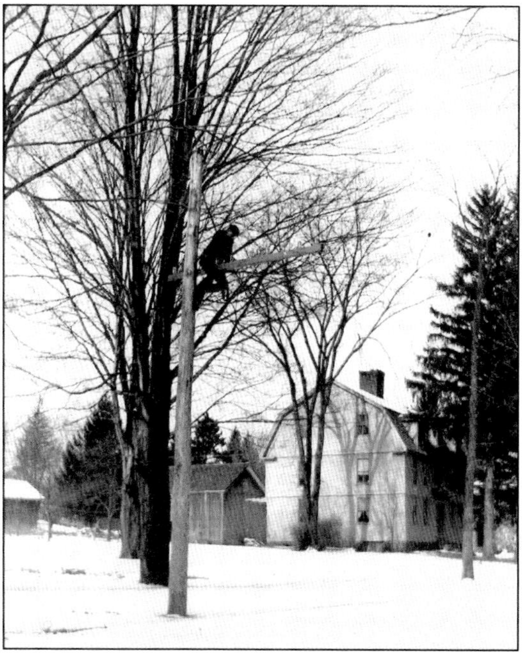

With snow on the ground in Haddam Center, a worker installs insulators for electrical lines connecting to Brainerd Hall. Katherine Sandin relates that Haddam Neck was electrified in 1925. Telephones also appeared in town about this time. One was first installed in the town clerk's office in 1926. (Charles Church photograph.)

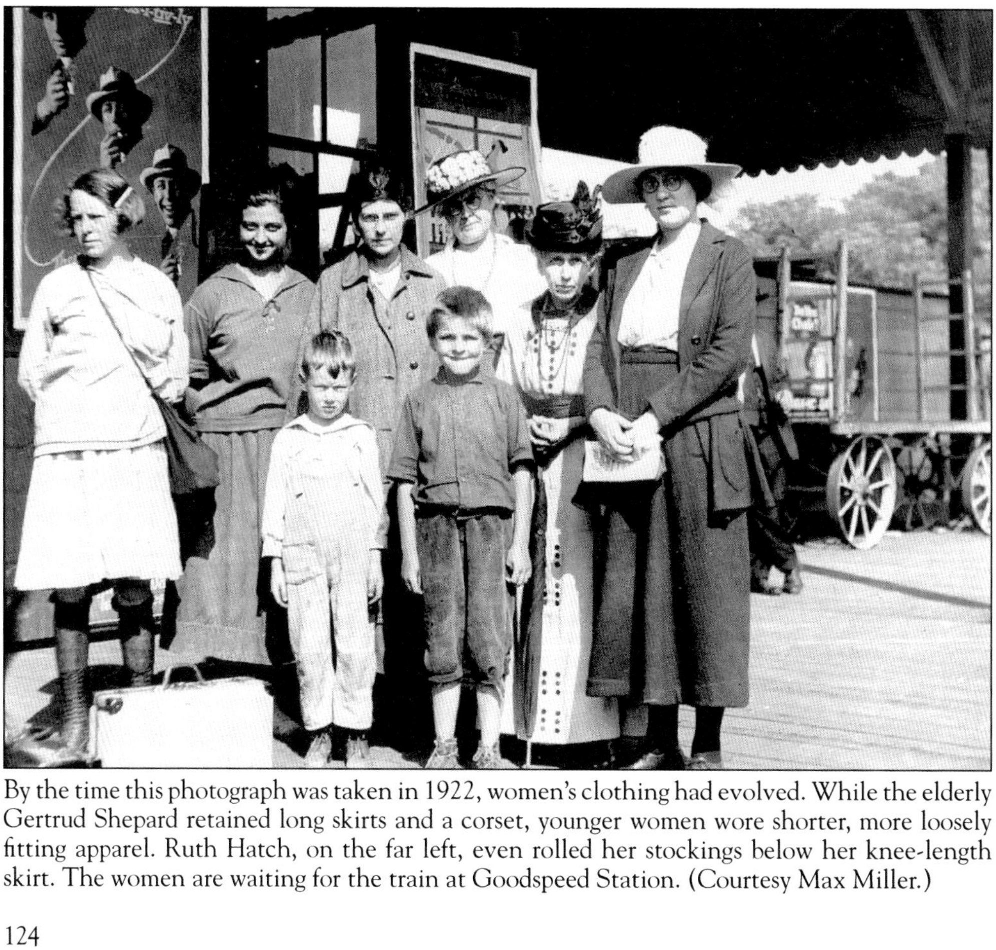

By the time this photograph was taken in 1922, women's clothing had evolved. While the elderly Gertrud Shepard retained long skirts and a corset, younger women wore shorter, more loosely fitting apparel. Ruth Hatch, on the far left, even rolled her stockings below her knee-length skirt. The women are waiting for the train at Goodspeed Station. (Courtesy Max Miller.)

Short skirts and silk stockings reveal that Dorothy Gesner Drake was also a modern young woman when she posed on the steps of the Tylerville School in the 1920s. Consolidation meant the end of this and other one-room schools in town. Out of a total of 15 one-room school buildings in Haddam, 10 have been preserved and are now used for other purposes.

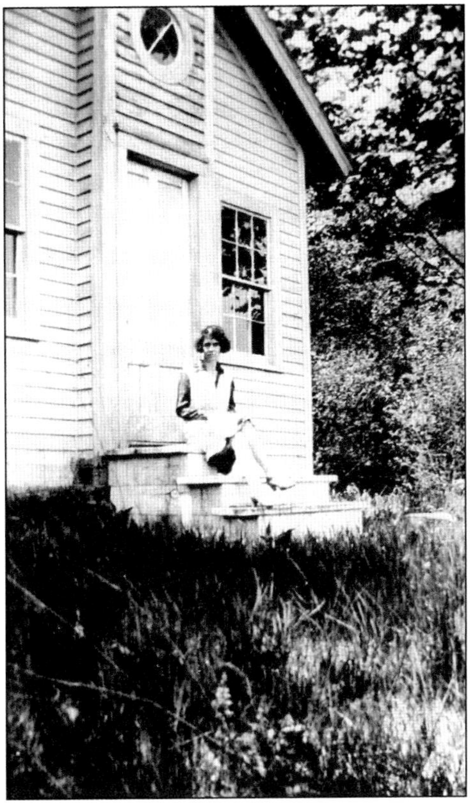

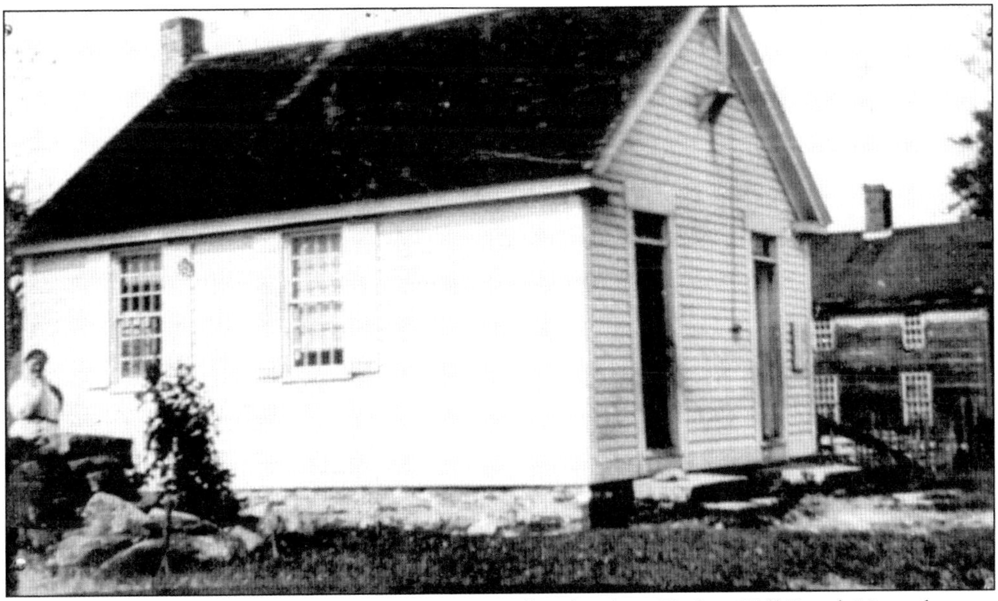

Teacher Grace Edict poses next to the Turkey Hill School on Turkey Hill Road. Note the two entrances, one for boys and the other for girls.

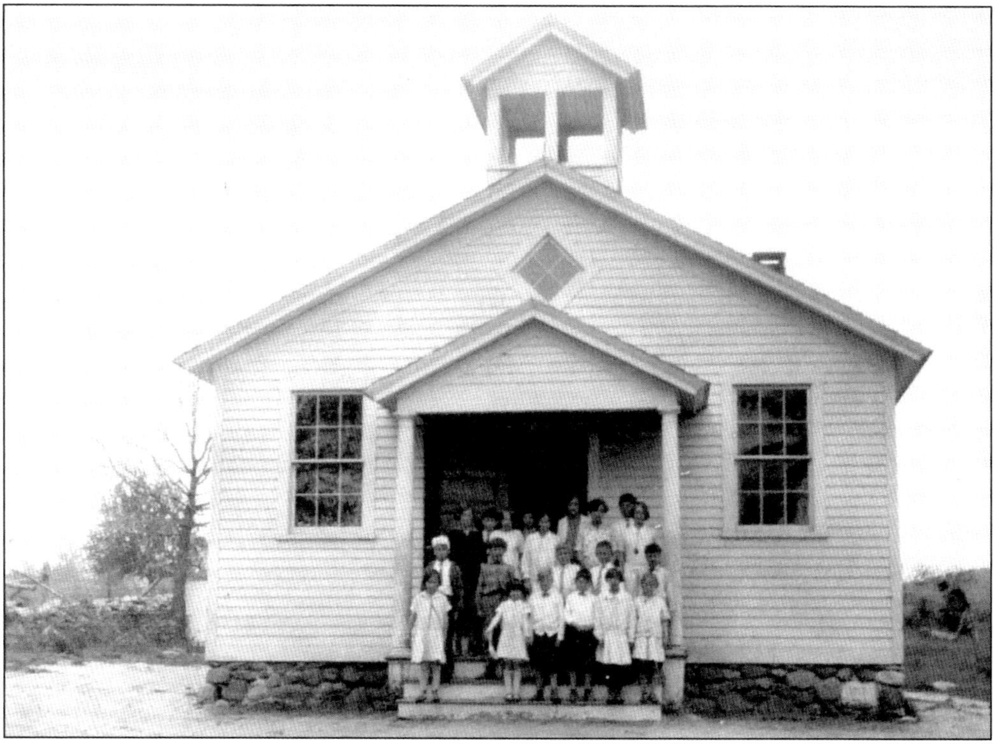

Students pose at Ponsett School in 1927, the last year that eight grades attended here. Constructed in 1916, this building is today the Episcopal church hall. The first Ponsett School was combined with Little City School in 1890. Pictured are, from left to right, the following: (first row) Mary Klas, Minnie Klein, Everett Ellins, George Klein, Helen Kazimir, and Mary Pokorny; (second row) Joseph Kazimir, Frank Planeta, Charles Ellis, Frank Pokorny, and Richard Washburn; (third row) Mary Beranek, Mary Nocar, Anna Klas, Elsie Kazimir, and Bertha Klas; (fourth row) Francis Washburn, Steven Pavco, teacher Helen Isenberg, and Stanley Planeta.

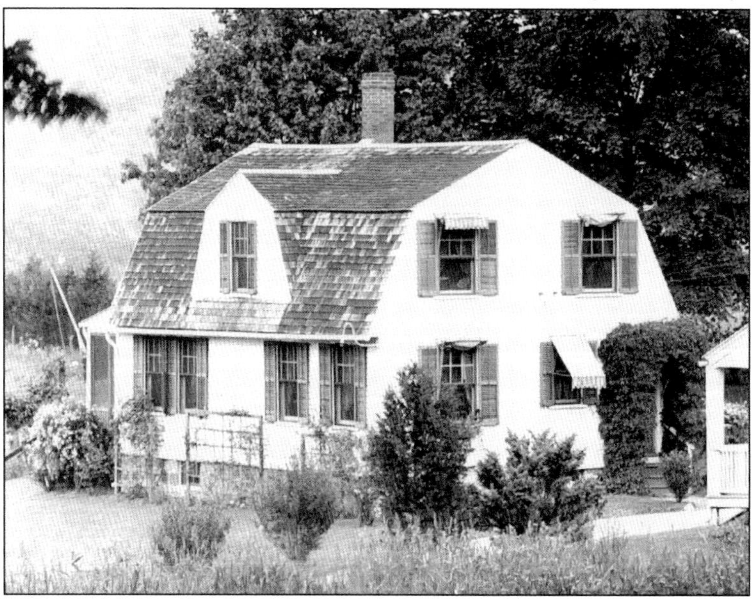

Miss Lewis' School, a private school for grades one through eight, has the distinction of being the last one-room school to operate in Haddam. It was also the home of Miss Lewis, who was the daughter of the Congregational minister. The school closed in the 1950s.

The Burr District School on Killingworth Road, shown here with an unidentified teacher, was converted to a private residence. The Tylerville, Shailerville, and Higganum Center schools also became residences.

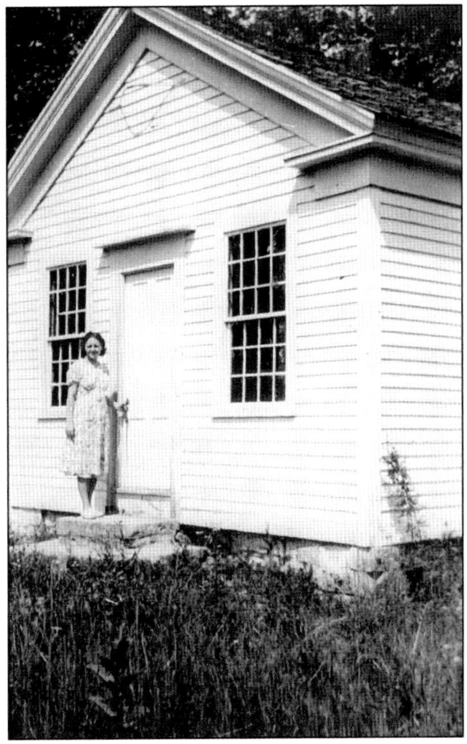

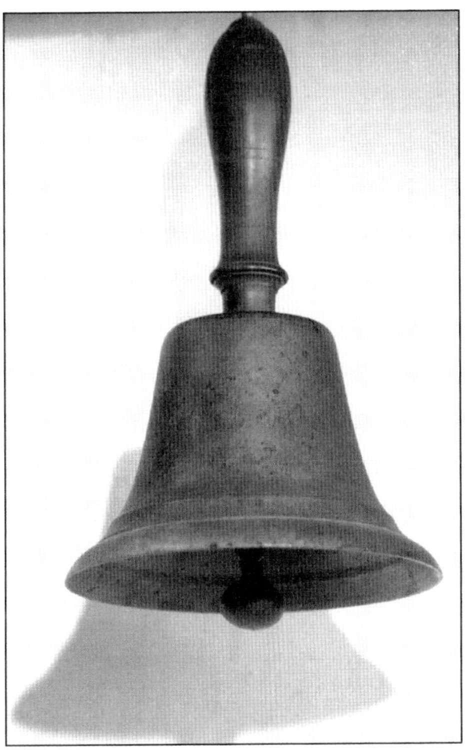

This bell from the historical society's collection was used in the Shailerville School. When automobile traffic increased, the schoolhouse was moved from Saybrook Road to Old Turnpike "in case a car should come by" and hit one of the children. (Courtesy Dave Lenzi.)

BIBLIOGRAPHY

Beers, J. B., ed. *History of Middlesex County, Connecticut*. New York: J. B. Beers and Company, 1884.

Beers, J. H., ed. *Biographical Record of Middlesex County, Connecticut*. Chicago: J. H. Beers and Company, 1903.

Brooks, Lillian Kruger. *"Life Flows along like a River": A History of Haddam Neck*. Haddam, CT: Haddam Neck Genealogical Group, 1972.

Burr, Nelson. *The Episcopal Church in Haddam*. Hartford: The Church Missions Publishing Company, 1942.

Cunningham, Jan, and Elizabeth Warren. *Portrait of a River Town: The History and Architecture of Haddam, Connecticut*. Middletown, CT: Greater Middletown Preservation Trust, 1984.

Douglas-Lithgow, R. A. *Native American Place Names of Connecticut*. 1909. Reprint, Bedford, MA: Applewood Books, 2000.

Guinness, Alison C. "Mining and Quarrying Along the Lower Connecticut River Valley." Master's thesis, Wesleyan University, 1993.

Nutting, Wallace. *Connecticut Beautiful*. New York: 1923.

Perkins, Julia, Bernadette Prue, and Claudette Kosinski. *Long Ago, Not Far Away: An Illustrated History of Six Middlesex County Towns*. Middletown, CT: Greater Middletown Preservation Trust, 1996.

Pokorny, Frank W. "Memories of Ponsett." Haddam, CT: Haddam Historical Society, 2004.

Sandin, Katharine G. *Country Church, Country People, 1740–1974*. Detroit: Harlo Press, 1976.

The Story of Clark "Cutaway" in Pictures. Higganum, CT: The Cutaway Harrow Company, n.d.

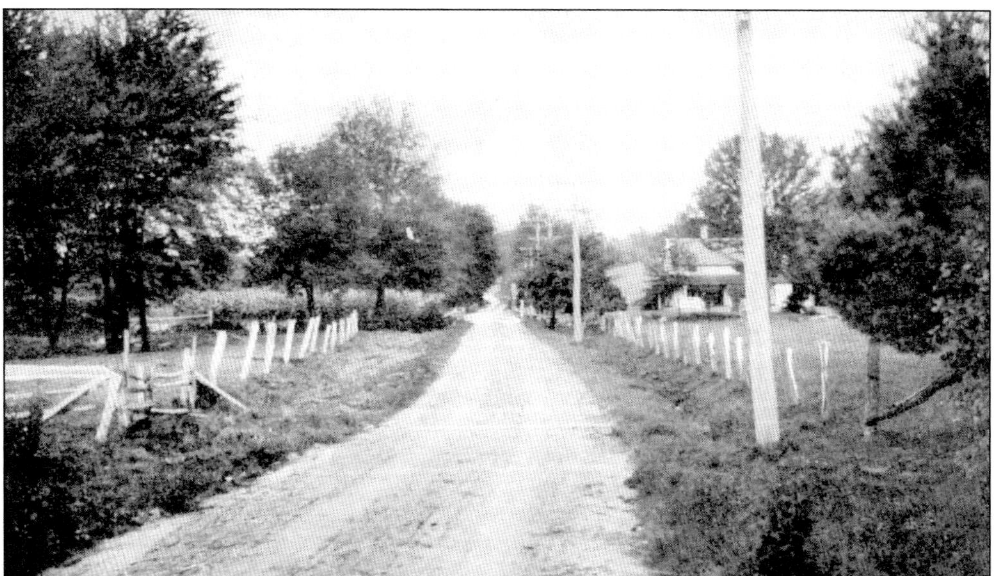

Change sometimes comes slowly to Haddam. This view of Candlewood Road is undated; part of this thoroughfare between Haddam and Durham was unpaved until the 1980s.